STORIES OF THE SELF

POSTMILLENNIAL POP
General Editors: Karen Tongson and Henry Jenkins

Stories of the Self

Life Writing after the Book

Anna Poletti

NEW YORK UNIVERSITY PRESS

New York

NEW YORK UNIVERSITY PRESS
New York
www.nyupress.org

References to Internet websites (URLs) were accurate at the time of writing. Neither the author nor New York University Press is responsible for URLs that may have expired or changed since the manuscript was prepared.

Library of Congress Cataloging-in-Publication Data
Names: Poletti, Anna, author.
Title: Stories of the self : life writing after the book / Anna Poletti.
Description: New York : New York University Press, 2020. | Series: Postmillennial pop |
Includes bibliographical references and index.
Identifiers: LCCN 2019043251 | ISBN 9781479863600 (cloth) |
ISBN 9781479836666 (paperback) | ISBN 9781479821495 (ebook) |
ISBN 9781479898961 (ebook)
Subjects: LCSH: Autobiography. | Identity (Psychology) and mass media. |
Digital media—Social aspects.
Classification: LCC CT25 .P64 2020 | DDC 808.06/692—dc23
LC record available at https://lccn.loc.gov/2019043251

New York University Press books are printed on acid-free paper, and their binding materials are chosen for strength and durability. We strive to use environmentally responsible suppliers and materials to the greatest extent possible in publishing our books.

Manufactured in the United States of America

10 9 8 7 6 5 4 3 2 1

Also available as an ebook

This book is dedicated to the memory of Angie Lamb.

CONTENTS

Introduction

Biomediations

What kind of digital life did you have in the middle of the year 2013? Were you on Facebook? If so, had you started "checking in" to locations? (Disneyland had the most check-ins in the United States that year. In my home city of Melbourne, Australia, in the Kulin nation, it was the hallowed sports stadium, the Melbourne Cricket Ground.)[1] What kind of cell phone were you using? (The iPhone 5 had been out for eight months, and the Samsung Galaxy S4 had been out for three.)[2] Had you discovered the instant joys, and painful silences that come with communicating via text message instead of over the phone? Had you taken a selfie yet? ("Selfie" was the *Oxford English Dictionary*'s word of the year.)[3] Did you have a blog? (WordPress reported that in 2013, 5.7 new blog posts were posted every second.)[4]

There is a reason I begin a book about autobiography, materiality, and media by asking you to remember your digital life in 2013. By late June 2013, commentators and journalists were convinced everything about our digital lives was going to change.

In June 2013, Edward Snowden began releasing the now-infamous documents that revealed the extent to which the routine digital communications of everyday people—cell phone records, text messages, social media posts, e-mail, the files held in cloud storage such as Dropbox—were being stored, shared, and analyzed by the national security organizations of the United States, the United Kingdom, Europe, and Australia. As shown in the documentary *Citizenfour*,[5] Snowden went from working as a freelance systems administrator in the intelligence community to being a leading source of information and commentary on surveillance, revealing that "the communication records of millions of US citizens are being collected indiscriminately and in bulk—regardless of whether they are suspected of any wrongdoing."[6]

What has changed in your digital life since Edward Snowden disclosed that the governments of several countries have access to your e-mail?

This is a question I have been contemplating in the years since the Snowden revelations. Anecdotally, while we may be more aware of what we have signed up for, little has changed in my digital life or the lives of my friends, colleagues, and family. We still write to each other on Google's mail service, have contracts for our cell phones with large telecommunications companies, store our pictures and documents in Google drive or Dropbox, use the Google search engine to answer all our questions, and chat with each other over iMessage or Facebook messenger. Some statistics indicate that the use of the services and technologies implicated in the Snowden revelations has only expanded in the years since he explained to us how privacy has been eroded by networked digital technology.[7] Why, then, has so little changed in our digital practices?

In the subsequent years that he has lived in exile in Russia, Snowden has clearly become frustrated that the vast majority of everyday users of networked technologies think "they have nothing to hide" and they do not need to concern themselves with the practical or moral questions raised by mass digital surveillance.[8] The commentary on the issue of privacy, its renewed importance as a right that needs defending, continues to grow. In the fields of law, information studies, and communication studies, this problem is often referred to as the "privacy paradox." The privacy paradox names two seemingly irrational elements of our current use of networked digital technology. The first is the apparent discontinuous relationship between people's opinions and behaviors: when asked, people indicate they are deeply concerned about digital privacy, but it is clear that the way most people use technology indicates they do not act on these concerns.[9] Second, users appear to be willing to trade, or give away, their personal information for what scholars believe is very little benefit in terms of service provision or monetary gain.[10]

As a scholar of autobiography, I too am interested in the privacy paradox. However, I do not approach it as a failure of logic or of community standards, or as an inherent change in our ways of being social.[11] Rather, I see the privacy paradox as evidence that life is a dynamic experience of lived relations. Most often, we understand the intersection of privacy and relationality through the lens of the human subject, the desires humans have (however inconsistent and irrational), and the lives they lead. Yet recognition as a self-willing subject with the right to privacy has never been an experience shared by everyone. As surveillance scholars argue, the notion of privacy attached to that subject position was never universally available: some populations, and some individuals, have always been subjected to higher degrees of observation and management through racialized, gender-based practices, through the discourses of health, and through the social welfare policies that subject communities with fewer economic resources to heightened forms of contemporary biopower.[12] That privacy is a "right" that people should logically want to protect denies the long lived histories of many communities and individuals who have never experienced that right, or its logic, directly. Critics increasingly agree that contemporary surveillance is an issue of knowledge and power, rather than a question of what technology can or cannot do.[13]

The privacy paradox presents a problem because it names an inconsistent behavior that many policy makers and legal scholars find inexplicable: How can systems of governmentality create a consistent regulatory and legal environment when the behaviors they seek to protect and guard against are inconsistent and shifting? Recognizing the universalizing assumptions about who has had a historical claim to the right to privacy is an important starting point for understanding why people continue to use digital services despite the now widespread knowledge that the service providers engage in, collaborate with, and profit from mass surveillance of the population. However, in the years since the Snowden revelations, I have been trying to understand the more generalized discontinuity between the news he brought us about our surveilled status and the lack of widespread change in the use of networked communications technologies and social media. It is clear that the risks and vulnerabilities produced by this situation are unevenly distributed, and many scholars have argued that to think about this issue we must decentralize the subject and recognize that the issue is one of biopower as a means of aggregating individuals into populations to be managed. But this is also a shared moment of social, political, and institutional change that renews our need to understand the intersection of culture and power as it is materialized in those social and cultural practices where relationality—the intersection between the individual and the collective—so often finds purchase. As Shoshanna Zuboff argues of "big data" (an object and process produced by surveillance): "It originates in the social, and it is there that we must find it and know it."[14] To understand this moment, we must think about our use of media and materiality to make sense of our lives and to encounter the lives of others.

This book is an attempt to do just that. However, I do not approach digital communications technology, or the privacy paradox, head-on in *Stories of the Self*. Recent scholarship in media studies has produced in-depth accounts and new ways of thinking about those issues.[15] Instead, *Stories of the Self* advances a different approach to the question of why it is that so many people have not changed their behavior despite knowing that the material generated by their digital lives is being collected, analyzed, shared, and sold by governments and corporations. The answer developed to this question here is that the very categories of "a life" and "a self" emerge through mediation and the materiality of media, and respond to the inherent relationality of our being. Mediated communication and networked intimacy are unavoidable. We cannot wish away the privacy paradox by hoping that our desire, and impulse, to see others and be seen by them will cease. Because we cannot not be in relation with others, mediated living is uniquely vulnerable to being integrated into systems of communicative and surveillance capitalism.[16]

At the heart of our collective living is the reality of our shared reliance on each other. This reliance takes two forms. Ethicists, anthropologists, ecologists, and political philosophers have long noted we are dependent on each other for our existence because we must collectively share the material resources that support life. This brings with it the second element of our connection: we are reliant on each other in a social sense because, as Judith Butler argues, "a life has to be intelligible *as a life*, has to conform to certain conceptions of what life is, in order to become recognizable."[17] How we are apprehended by others, and how we apprehend them, is fundamental to our shared existence and is an urgent issue for contemporary politics in a globalized world and in local communities.[18]

Activists, readers, writers, artists, and critics share a common belief regarding the power of personal storytelling and its importance to the challenge of negotiating the ethics and politics of our shared existence.

Autobiography matters—culturally, politically, historically, socially—because it puts individual lives "on the record,"[19] and in so doing creates a scene of apprehension: it is a cultural and social practice that makes lives available for engagement by others and responds to the fundamental need to make ourselves legible in the social field. Once "on the record," lives can illuminate, challenge, and enhance our understanding of our shared reality. Autobiography, then, is an important cultural practice for negotiating the reality and responsibility of our shared existence. An investment in this idea has shaped the study of autobiography since its beginnings and has become a fundamental premise in popular culture, as well as in disciplines such as anthropology, where personal storytelling is framed as a powerful vehicle for knowledge making, community building, and social justice.[20] In popular culture, this is epitomized in the recurring refrain that telling and listening to "our stories" will help heal the wounds of social division. But the widespread investment in the power of personal storytelling, shared by scholars, cultural producers, activists, and audiences, comes with a range of risks, such as giving accounts of oppression that foreground its individual rather than structural conditions.[21] Or it may result in personal storytelling functioning as a tool for statecraft, or being recruited into national narratives that the individuals telling the stories might wish to contest.[22] Some critics have also expressed concern about the cultural dominance of personal storytelling,[23] and claims that it is a universal human practice,[24] suggesting that it reifies ways of speaking and thinking about human life that limit our understanding of what life is, or could be. The impulse toward self-narration and self-representation (often coded as a turn to narcissism) is also sometimes cited as a key factor in the development of the privacy paradox.[25]

Stories of the Self takes up the seeming ubiquity of autobiographical storytelling in order to argue that the cultural and political investment in the power of personal stories does more than demonstrate the power of narrative to establish, contest, reinforce, or destabilize dominant ideas about the world and lived experience. Rather, it evidences a larger and deeper interconnection between life, media, and matter that grounds our inherent relationality. Writing and reading personal stories brings us into relation with each other, but it also brings us in relation to matter—we are always also physically copresent with stories we tell and read through the handheld screen, the locatedness of an art exhibition, the screen in our home, the earbuds in our ears, the book in our hands.

Thus, to account for the inherent relationality of lived experience we must do more than focus solely on storytelling as a practice that is widespread because of its power as narrative. To do so is to risk conflating discourse and media. This risk means we may take for granted the complex media and material practices through which stories are inscribed and which make them available for reading, sharing, archiving, and commodification. To ignore media materialities in the process of autobiography is to underestimate the role of media forms in shaping the veracity of the claims that underpin autobiography as a cultural and social practice that purports to speak a truth about lived experience and foster the forms of recognition we require for a more just politics and social field. A narrow focus on narrative also fails to recognize that lived experience is always mediated experience: we cannot hope that people will return to localized, "private" forms of self-representation in order to ease the tensions of the privacy paradox. As I will discuss further, recent scholarship in the humanities and social sciences that extends our understanding of relationality to include matter asks us to think differently about the production and reception of personal storytelling because we cannot take a material base for cultural activities as a stable given, or as unrelated to their practices and meanings. We must, in the words of Anna Tsing, recognize that there are "no self-contained units" in any given encounter; indeed, "units are encounter-based collaborations."[26] This means thinking of the making and telling of personal stories as a process that occurs within an assemblage that is partly influenced by the agency of matter (including the seeming immateriality of digital media), both human and nonhuman. The conditions in which a given assemblage occurs are informed, but not determined, by a much larger structure: the discourses of capitalism and nationalism that shape the material world through the production of markets, identities, and borders; and discourses of gender, sexuality, race, age, and health that materially position individuals and populations in relation to the social and political field.[27] A consideration of media materialities—institutions, aesthetics, practices, and flows—provides one means of coming to terms with how these discourses are materialized in ways that shape whose life matters and how, at the level of the individual and the collective.

The discussion about digital forms of surveillance dramatizes this issue because, as theorists such as Jasbir K. Puar have shown, surveillance produces an assemblage in which media technologies and human life interact. The outcome of that interaction is an archive that renders specific populations legible and therefore available for control and exploitation.[28] The use of surveillance cameras for racial profiling, for example, demonstrates the importance of media forms in how we think about what a life is—what its value is—and how life becomes available to governments and corporations for the extraction of value in the form of information that can be aggregated, commercialized, and traded in the service of managing the population. Yet the reality that the records produced by our use of networked technology for autobiography come with vulnerability that is not evenly distributed must also be kept in view. For some of us, the risk created is as small as misinterpretation: the misalignment of our data double with our lived experience, resulting in an algorithm presenting a computer user with "an advertisement for baby formula when you're past menopause,"[29] while for others the vulnerability to misuse is far greater, resulting in racial, gendered, or sexuality profiling that has enormous ramifications in terms of access to education, health care, and freedom of movement. This unevenly shared vulnerability comes from the core of our state as relational beings: the ethics and politics that stem from our reliance on each other, the role of institutions as mediators in the social and political field, and the asymmetrical power relations that distribute the responsibility that comes from shared vulnerability.[30] We cannot avoid the need to give an account of ourselves, nor can we escape the ethical ties that stem from the vulnerability inherent in our reliance on others to apprehend us, or the ethical ties that come from our responsibility to apprehend them. Yet the scene of apprehension is not purely linguistic or symbolic—it occurs within material conditions. The insertion of our data doubles into automated predictive technologies that utilize algorithms to make decisions about health care, for example, may on the surface appear to absolve us of engagement in the scene of apprehension, as we hand this responsibility over to computers in our local hospital and computer servers located in server farms. However, as the work of scholars such as Puar and Safiya Umoja Noble demonstrates, we cannot ignore how the use of technology and media forms to store and sort information—including autobiographical acts—materializes existing inequalities in the social field.[31]

Stories of the Self is an attempt to think specifically about the role of media and materiality in this scene of presentation and apprehension, and to consider how specific forms of media materialize ideas about what a life is, and how and why it might matter. Its fundamental goal is to account for specific assemblages of human and nonhuman matter in autobiographical scenes, which are also scenes of apprehension. The scene of apprehension is, fundamentally, a scene of reading, and so *Stories of the Self* develops approaches to reading the intersection of autobiography, media, and matter that pays attention to how personal storytelling is materialized, and how individuals, publics, and institutions engage with the matter of life and respond to the agency of the matter they are colocated and coemerge with. In its full title, *Stories of the Self: Life Writing after the Book* links narrative and media as they are traditionally understood in literary studies (stories and books) in order to frame a fundamental reconsideration of our understanding of life writing, and the relationship between life writing and current changes in contemporary culture. So far in this introduction, I have been exploring these issues through the issue of digital surveillance and its textualities of scale. In the chapters that follow, I take as my focus texts and works created by artists and everyday people that specifically invite reflection on the importance of media materialities for our thinking about life. The book is arranged spatially: think of it as an exhibition made up of a series of rooms in which I present examples of different media that are used for autobiography, and offer an approach to reading them that might allow us to think about how life is materialized in narrative, mediation, and matter. In chapters 1, 2, and 3, I examine three uses of media forms and their affordances to demonstrate how we might read for media and materiality in acts of self-life-inscription. I have chosen ubiquitous but divergently understood forms as the first two exhibits: cardboard boxes and cameras are two common technologies used for gathering and reflecting on lived experience. One, the cardboard box, is not really thought of at all as a media form; the other, the camera, has been widely discussed in terms of the unique affordances it presents. The third form, crowdsourcing, allows us to consider how media forms *interact* to create collective scenes of apprehension. In that chapter, I consider a transmedial approach to producing collective autobiography and demonstrate the complex interplay between analog and digital forms for constructing and maintaining the legitimacy of autobiographical narratives. In the examples I consider, these narratives and media forms are then subject to strategies of commodification by cultural actors I call "confessional entrepreneurs."

Chapters 4 and 5 build on the earlier chapters to consider how media and their materialities are consciously repurposed to produce new perspectives on lives that are constantly interacting with the overdetermining discourses of sexuality and race. In chapter 4, "Collage," I examine how queer autobiographers use the voices of others to speak powerfully about the inventiveness and tenacity required to imagine flourishing in, rather than surviving, queer life. In chapter 5, "Dossiers," I consider two recent projects that stage public readings of the surveillance dossiers of mid-twentieth-century racial justice activists. In that chapter, I consider how public readings that draw attention to the materiality of the paper-based dossiers amassed during the Cold War might provide us with new ways of thinking about our enclosure within digital forms of surveillance through our use of mobile and networked media.

Across the rooms in this exhibition, my interpretive lens is focused on the link between what is to be valued and protected in who we are and how we live, and the media forms in which the information and stories relating to our identity and our lives are created and shared. But I am also interested in what we think doesn't matter—how information, feelings, ideas, actions might be given away or considered irrelevant to who we think we are. In terms of the privacy paradox, this is one of the key questions: Why are people prepared to accept a trade-off in which their personal communication and their files stored on the cloud are available for viewing, reading, downloading, and sharing by a range of actors who are not the intended audience for them in return for low-cost or free digital services? I aim to show that what we think matters in and about our personal experience, what is deserving of protection and, conversely, what can be treated with indifference, is partly shaped by the media forms the information and stories take. Rather than thinking of the millions of people who continue to use Google and Dropbox as people who don't take privacy seriously, we might consider the possibility that their actions reflect a much stronger cultural association between *matter* (material things) and life as a process of being and becoming. This raises the possibility that the *things* that connect us to others, and to our lived experience, play an equally powerful role in contemporary life as the telling of stories, and the documents and digital files that are the currency and detritus of everyday life in the twentieth-first century. Crucially, approaching the privacy paradox through the lens of autobiography and relationality forces us to recognize that we are not (and not even that often) conscious, willing subjects when it comes to our use of networked digital technology. The subtle cues, the affective lures and rewards, the desires for collectivity, and the feeling of being seen or heard are not always—if they ever are—solely rational choices made by individuals. They drive us as much as we drive them, and so our position in the assemblage cannot be understood by focusing on a sovereign subject who can always choose and act from a rational sense of their needs or intentions.[32]

Stories of the Self explores *why* it is that matter has significance for who we think we are and what we think our lives mean. It takes lived experience and our relationships with others as the bedrock of life and self, and considers how autobiographical practices in a range of media help us understand what people think is important about who they are and how they live. This mattering is physical and symbolic: it is tied up with the materiality of media in ways that shape which elements of our autobiography we value—and may seek to protect—and which elements, to return to the question of surveillance, we do not treat as requiring the "freedom from interference or intrusion" that privacy denotes.[33] In this sense, *Stories of the Self* does not take the right, or the desire, for privacy as a stable category or assume that everyone desires the same level of privacy. Rather, it works from the assumption that we have individual and collective responses to the need for privacy that are underpinned by norms relating to what gives a life value and (as I discuss in chapter 3 specifically) what desires, actions, or fantasies burden us with shame, or threaten our access to the social field, if they are revealed.

Indeed, beyond its primary definition of privacy as "the state or condition of being alone, undisturbed, or free from public attention, as a matter of choice or right; seclusion; freedom from interference or intrusion," the *Oxford English Dictionary* indicates how privacy is linked to exposure, propriety, and shame. Privacy denotes "being privy to some act," to "secrecy, concealment, discretion," to "personal matters," and to "intimacy." The term can also denote *space*: a place of concealment, or discretion. The obsolete term "privity" denotes the use of "privates" as a term for the genitals. Secrets, intimacy, sexuality, spaces, publicness— these are the terms that queer and feminist scholars have returned to so fruitfully in the critical analysis of contemporary life and politics during the rise of digital forms of communication. While often not explicitly responding to autobiography or the question of digital privacy specifically, the work of scholars such as Sara Ahmed, Lauren Berlant, Eve Kosofsky Sedgwick, and Michael Warner has renewed the theoretical interest in all the senses of the word "privacy." Berlant argues, for example, that the critical turn to intimacy has the potential to "engage and disable a prevalent U.S. discourse on the proper relation between public and private, spaces traditionally associated with the gendered division of labor."[34] These scholars have shown the extent to which who we think we are, who we are perceived to be, and what kinds of communities we can participate in are shaped by the issues that privacy denotes and the forms of subjectivity it assumes.

These privileged forms of subjectivity are shaped by regimes of value and ideologies that preexist the individual.[35] *Stories of the Self* argues that these regimes of value extend to forms of mediation. It's obvious that a memoir in a bookstore situates the life of its author in specific ways, and in ways that are different from the cardboard box of mementos and discarded objects that sits in their cupboard, or the photographs and videos they upload to their Instagram feed. Yet how we account for the way that the media used for making autobiography shape the significance we attach to lived experiences has not been consistently examined either in autobiography scholarship or in media studies. Judith Butler touches on this issue in her analysis of grievable lives in *Frames of War*, asking:

> What allows a life to become visible in its precariousness and its need for shelter, and what is it that keeps us from seeing or understanding lives in this way? The problem concerns the media, at the most general, since a life can be accorded a value on the condition that it is perceivable as a life, but it is only on the condition of certain embedded evaluative structures that a life becomes perceivable at all.[36]

Butler examines the urgent ethical and political question of why it is that the exposure of some populations to death is considered an acceptable political reality. Yet her point about the importance of the media in constituting a life extends beyond our ability to see others; our own lives are increasingly perceivable to ourselves and our intimates through the media in which they appear. In autobiography studies, there is a growing recognition that accounting for mediation will change the way the field undertakes its work. The question of *how* our work will change and how we can become more attentive to the role of mediation in autobiography is the subject of this book.

Before outlining how mediation and materiality are used in this project, I will begin by explaining how I am using the term "autobiography" here, instead of the more common terms "life writing" or "life narrative." This overview will demonstrate how important it is to keep a critical understanding of genre in focus when we think about contemporary culture. Genres are systemic strategies that mediate relationships between texts and readers, and they are "a shared convention with a social force."[37] How genres intersect with matter is a key concern of this book, and I will lay the foundation for the readings that follow in the chapters by arguing for the need to pay attention to self-life-inscription as a collection of flexible and systemic ways of making lived experience significant, and the importance of understanding how systematic structures of mediation (including media industries), and matter itself, contributes to our use of genres.

Autobiography as Self-Life-Inscription

In this book, "autobiography" refers to a cultural practice that seeks a public, an audience of imagined and unknown strangers who will interact with how a specific life has coemerged with specific media forms and practices.[38] In proposing that we rethink autobiography as self-life-inscription, I draw on thinking about technologies of inscription undertaken by Lisa Gitelman and N. Katherine Hayles. In *Always Already New*, Gitelman distinguishes between media that broadcast signals (such as radio) and media of inscription that are generally accepted as "stable and savable."[39] Hayles also marks out the power of inscription as a key function of certain types of media. In *Writing Machines*, she argues that "to count as an inscription technology, a device must instantiate material changes that can be read as marks."[40] Taking the "-graph" of "autobiography" to refer to the more general process of inscription rather than the specific practice of writing is in keeping with its modern use. The *OED* explains that "-graph" is a combining form, originating from the Greek γραφος. Most of the modern words that use "-graph" evoke "the general sense of 'that which *writes, portrays, or records,*' as actinograph, heliograph, hygrograph, ideograph, phonograph, seismograph . . . etc." Thinking of autobiography as a process that writes, portrays, *or* records addresses two issues regarding terminology that consistently trouble the field of life writing studies: the problem that "life writing" refers to a single form of textual production (writing) associated with a single set of aesthetic and critical practices (literature),[41] and the issue that "life narrative" places storytelling at the center of definitions of autobiography.[42]

Despite the qualification of "autobiography" as a genre associated with the Enlightenment, self-willing subject of Europe,[43] scholars in related fields continue to use the adjective to designate a broad set of practices and textual forms such as performance,[44] visual art,[45] and documentary film and video.[46] "Autobiographical" is also used to designate a specific type of memory in both memory studies and psychology.[47] Indeed, the field of life writing studies itself retains "autobiographical" as an adjective in the term "autobiographical acts."[48] This suggests to me that while autobiography as a noun referring to a specific genre of literature has been superseded by broader, and perhaps more progressive, interests in a range of practices of self-inscription, the term "autobiography" remains a useful one to people working in a range of fields who are interested in how reflection on the experience of living serves a wide range of purposes: from individual cognitive and affective states, to interpersonal, social, and cultural relations and political and historical aims.

Some readers may be concerned that by reintroducing the term "autobiography" I am bracketing the complex ways in which such "voluntary" acts are enmeshed in processes that preexist and structure individual identities, such as psychological processes,[49] neurological processes,[50] and the normative discourses that structure the social field in which the subject emerges.[51] By marking out autobiography as an act of self-life-inscription that seeks a public of potentially unknown people, I could be accused of returning to a "pre-theory" version of life writing criticism that largely understood autobiography as an aesthetic (or more specifically literary) project in which the author gives their life coherence, shape, and unity in order to put it into the public record.[52] Yet the case studies assembled in *Stories of the Self* demonstrate the complex ways in which autobiographers and the texts they create are conditioned by discourses of subjectivity and what it means to have a life. Indeed, rather than continue the established critical practice of paying attention to life writing as a discursive practice in which these dynamics are enacted, *Stories of the Self* extends our understanding of the forces that shape acts of self-life-inscription to consider the power of materiality and mediation (and their associated protocols and agency) in constituting the social field in which individual acts of autobiography take place. In doing so, I pay close attention to how particular media forms intersect with prevailing norms regarding subjectivity and what "a life" is. Thus, I evoke "self-life-inscription" by using the term "autobiography" *not* to designate the "self" as the author of the life (as early critics did, where the "self" was taken to be the one writing as well as the one written) but to refer to the inscription of self *and* life. In my proposed usage, "autobiography" refers to the making of texts that explore subjectivity *and* life: *auto* (self); *bios*, "the form or way of living proper to an individual or group"; and *zoē*, "the simple fact of living common to all living beings."[53]

In thinking about *auto-*, *bios-*, and *zoē* as enmeshed rather than discrete entities, *Stories of the Self* is working within the intellectual tradition established by Foucault's critique of biopower, and its various extensions in queer theory, political philosophy, and social theory. For Agamben, politics in the West is defined by the collapsing of the ancient distinction between *bios* and *zoē* that underpins many of the core values of Western democracy:

> Every attempt to rethink the political space of the West must begin with the clear awareness that we no longer know anything of the classical distinction between *zoē* and *bios*, between private life and political existence, between man as a simple living being at home in the house and man's political existence in the city.[54]

If the distinction between *zoē* and *bios* no longer holds, we must also consider how life itself is "an incomplete process of doing and being."[55] *Stories of the Self* considers how *zoē, bios,* and *auto* are enmeshed with media in day-to-day life, how those media shape our experience of life, and how we use media to imagine what life could be. From media studies scholars, such as Jay David Bolter and Richard Gruisin, *Stories of the Self* takes the position that "all mediations are themselves real. They are real as artefacts . . . in our mediated culture."[56] How can life writing scholarship account for this realness? If we take the complex media and material practices that constitute "the record" for granted, we risk overstating the power of autobiographical discourse and underestimating the role of media in shaping the veracity of the claims that underpin autobiography as cultural and social practice that claims to speak a truth about lived experience. This emphasis on language ignores the importance of matter and media in the function of biopower: the inclusion of *zoē* within the regime of power/knowledge.[57] Foucault's critique of the formation of biopower has been of primary importance for many of the theoretical approaches I draw on in this project, notably the work of Judith Butler and queer theory. Yet, as new materialist arguments demonstrate, the critical focus on *bios* that grew out of the linguistic turn and the resulting preoccupation with representation that dominated strains of humanities scholarship in the last thirty years have limited scholarly attention to *matter* and *material* as vehicles of life and analysis of how matter is complicit in the development of hierarchies delimiting forms of life and styles of living.[58] As Hayles suggested in 2002, "Perhaps now, after the linguistic turn has yielded so many important insights, it is time to turn again to a careful consideration of what difference the materiality of the medium makes."[59] In recent years, a range of critical approaches that deprioritize discourse as a purely linguistic phenomenon and turn attention to materiality and mediation have come to prominence to redress this perceived imbalance.[60] These approaches include material culture studies, new materialism, thing theory, and posthumanism across the humanities and social sciences. *Stories of the Self* is an attempt to think through how some of these recent developments in criticism and theory might reconfigure scholarship on autobiography and media. In the next sections I will consider how the recent turn to theorizing mediation and materiality informs *Stories of the Self* and suggest how these theories open up the possibility of thinking about the importance of media and matter in the social and collective practices we draw on to attach significance to our lives.

Autobiography and Mediation

Until recently, autobiography studies has had sporadic contact with media studies, because questions regarding the aesthetic, psychological, social, and political formation of autobiography have largely been treated within the context of literary studies.[61] The field has, however, drawn on important conceptual and archival work on the social function of life narrative in sociology,[62] and, as I demonstrate in more detail in chapter 4, philosophical understandings of selfhood, such as Judith Butler's conceptualization of subjectivity as performative. Yet the need for closer attention to how mediation and media institutions contribute to the practice of autobiography is increasingly felt in the field of life writing studies. A key update to the first edition (2001) of Sidonie Smith and Julia Watson's field-encapsulating *Reading Autobiography: A Guide for Interpreting Life Narratives* was the inclusion in the second edition (2010) of a chapter titled "The Verbal-Visual-Virtual Contexts of Life Narrative," which acknowledges that mediation can no longer be ignored in the study of life writing.[63] Media studies has always held an interest in how broadcast media is a resource and a force that shapes the intersection of the individual and the social. For example, as early as 1956, media theorists Donald Horton and R. Richard Wohl proposed that broadcast media had created a new form of relationship and experiences of intimacy.[64] Perhaps it is unsurprising that the study of autobiography and media studies have not meaningfully intersected earlier, however, as early media studies was largely driven by the challenge of how to theorize and account for concentrations of power and the reach of *mass* (broadcast) media, and an interest in theorizing the material processes of media production. The recent changes in media production, circulation, and reception brought about by networked and digital media forces the intersection of autobiography and media studies. Contemporary media studies is coming to terms with the central role of self-life-inscription in social media practices, and this has resulted in increased attention to networked media as technologies of identity and sociality, the shift from broadcast to participatory media cultures, and the changing conditions of media production, such as the rise of produsers. In *Stories of the Self* I hope to demonstrate how existing approaches, concepts, and ways of thinking in autobiography studies can usefully contribute to media studies accounts of the increasing importance of autobiography in the contemporary media environment by bringing together insights into mediation from media studies with ways of reading autobiography itself as a mediating process in the social and political field.

In *Keywords*, Raymond Williams suggests that "mediation" has had three distinct, yet murky, uses in English. The first is to refer to the political process of negotiation, often led by an intermediary.[65] The second refers to a negative process "where certain social agencies are seen as deliberately interposed between reality and social consciousness, to prevent an understanding of reality,"[66] a way of using the term reflected, for example, in concerns about the impact of social media on the experience of social life.[67] The third meaning of the term, which Williams traces to Adorno, refers to a "direct and necessary activity between different kinds of activity and consciousness," which "has its own, always specific forms."[68] This final definition is closest to how "mediation" is used throughout *Stories of the Self*, which seeks to model ways of reading texts that remain attentive to the reality that autobiography is constituted through acts of mediation. Another way of saying this would be that all autobiographical acts are also acts of mediation to which we must attend. Moreover, we must recognize that the increasingly diverse media environment provides an unprecedented array of choices regarding mediation that autobiographers, and audiences, negotiate. In this negotiation, mediation—the necessarily specific forms given to autobiography—may also act as means of negotiating between competing social or ideological forces. José van Dijck articulates this understanding of media as a technique of mediation between self and society when she defines mediated memories as "*the activities and objects we produce and appropriate by means of media technologies, for creating and re-creating a sense of past, present, and future of ourselves in relation to others.*"[69] She goes on to state that "mediated memory objects and acts are crucial sites for negotiating the relationship between self and culture at large, between what counts as private and what as public, and how individuality relates to collectivity."[70] Shifting the focus from memory to the question of the present and the future, this dual function of mediation is explored in *Stories of the Self* by examining the use of collage for queer life writing, the use of the camera as a device of detection in recent documentary, and in chapter 5 where the remediation of surveillance documents is examined.

Williams concludes his entry by stating that each of the three senses of the word "mediation" would be better served by an alternative word: "conciliation"; "ideology or rationalization"; and "form."[71] Yet Lisa Gitelman argues that media studies critics "have long noted" that "the success of all media depends at some level on inattention or 'blindness' to the media technologies themselves (and all of their supporting protocols) in favor of attention to the phenomena, the 'content,' that they represent for users' edification or enjoyment."[72] Media is successful when a process of reconciling its users to its protocols and materiality renders its form invisible.[73] Gitelman's argument that the process of representation being channeled through specific media (the process of mediation) becomes "self-evident [and invisible] as the result of social processes" demonstrates that attention to mediation requires analysis of the interplay and interconnectedness of conciliation, ideology, and form that will also inherently draw our attention away from representation to questions of affect, desire, and the inherent dynamism of lived experience as a materially grounded, and mediated, flow.[74] Her suggestion that "media become authoritative as the social processes of their definition and dissemination are separated out or forgotten, and as the processes of protocol formation and acceptance get ignored" has led me to conclude that to come to grips with how *all* forms of media shape our ideas about life and self, we must read the digital and analog together.[75] Like media and memory theorist José van Dijck, I reject a "preliminary distinction between home and mass media" because it hampers our ability to "account for media shaping our sense of individuality *and* collectivity,"[76] limiting our ability to account for our positions as subjects entangled with media apparatuses, media texts, and media industries from our very beginning. Thus, *Stories of the Self* thinks about handmade postcards that get posted online and published in books, cardboard boxes, personal documentaries, zines, and the material legacies of racialized surveillance to map some of the diverse intersections of life, matter, and media in the contemporary moment, in order to attend to mediation as a process through which life and self emerge.

"*We have always been mediated*," Sarah Kember and Joanna Zylinska argue, drawing on the work of Martin Heidegger and Bernard Stiegler.[77] In *Life after New Media: Mediation as a Vital Process*, they propose "that mediation can be seen as another term for 'life,' for being-in and emerging-with the world."[78] This provocative redefinition of mediation *as* life directs our attention away from autobiography as a process through which lived experience is narrated and therefore represented, to recognizing that our use of media—and our engagement with its material potential and limitations—is a fundamental process in life itself. Taking up this provocation allows us to radically expand our understanding of what kinds of artifacts count as autobiographical—cardboard boxes of objects, postcards submitted to a crowdsourced project, surveillance dossiers—and to acknowledge how the extraordinary diversity of lived experience and life is materialized in diverse and inventive media materialities.

To do this, however, requires that scholars and critics develop strategies of viewing, responding to, understanding, and framing self-life-inscription that can be responsive to the diversity, innovation, seeming banality, and, sometimes, the just-plain-strangeness of mediated life. Considering "to what extent and in what way 'human users' are actually formed—not just *as users* but also *as humans*—by their media" puts current ways of reading and understanding autobiography and media use under pressure.[79] When we pay closer attention to media forms and the power of materiality in the process of making life, not just making representations of it, the scholar must learn—to adapt Karen Barad's phrasing—to meet the work halfway by suspending, or at least altering, established ideas about the utility of personal storytelling, the role of genre, and the position of audiences. Each chapter in *Stories of the Self* is an attempt to do just that, and so rather than advancing a singular argument for *how* we can interpret media and matter in autobiography, each chapter enacts a mode of reading that responds to the case study itself. In chapter 1, I explore the agential materiality of Andy Warhol's *Time Capsules* to consider how it forces a reconsideration of the primacy of narrative to our understanding of autobiography by practicing the reading strategy of rummaging. Chapter 2 considers how two contemporary documentaries (*Catfish* [2010] and *Stories We Tell* [2012]) demonstrate the power of the moving image camera to produce the identity of the autobiographer-as-detective by reading the camera as an actor in the documentary scene. In chapter 3, I read the remediation of handmade objects in the crowdsourced confessional project *PostSecret* as a form of collective autobiography that deploys the authorizing power of objects, rather than narratological features, to convince its audience of the nonfictional status and affective truth of its texts. Chapter 4 reads for collage in the creation of queer autobiography, in order to disrupt the assumption that autobiography requires that we give an account of ourselves in our own voice. Chapter 5 attends to the remediation of surveillance documents through public reading to consider what they might tell us about the will to master that surveillance enacts.

While closer attention to the power of mediation is a key component of *Stories of the Self*, media studies accounts of mediation are insufficient for grounding a way of reading that can attend to the role of matter and material in autobiography and the cases assembled here. In proposing the methodology of media-specific analysis, N. Katherine Hayles demonstrates that any attention to mediation entails attention to materiality, to matter.[80] For this reason, *Stories of the Self* also draws on recent theorizing of material culture and materiality.

Self-Life-Inscription and the Material Turn

Matter and materiality have become a topic of interest in a range of humanities and social science disciplines in recent years. Material culture has become an influential approach in anthropology, archaeology, and sociology spanning historical studies and contemporary ethnographies. Christopher Tilley, an influential theorist of material culture and an archaeologist who brings phenomenological approaches to his work on landscapes and stone, articulates the shift in thinking that a focus on materiality brings to the closely linked social science fields of anthropology and archaeology: at its core, a material culture approach takes "material worlds as seriously as language or socio-political relations as a medium through which people come to know and understand themselves, a means of creation and self-creation, one in which a consciousness of the thing was a fundamental part of social being."[81] The study of material culture and human and nonhuman assemblages in anthropology is an attempt to reposition the material artifact as the starting point for a consideration of culture and society, rather than as a piece of evidence upon which linguistic and symbolic accounts of the social rest. Material culture studies also rejects the tendency to read material objects as "quasi-texts," as a structuralist or poststructuralist approach might do. As Daniel Miller argues, the focus on materiality in anthropology involves a critique of "approaches which view material culture as merely the semiotic representation of some bedrock of social relations."[82]

At the same time a reinvigorated field of material culture studies has emerged in the social sciences, philosophy and political science have also become interested in the agency of matter and materiality through the lens of new materialism, thing theory, and object-oriented ontology. *Stories of the Self* engages with the feminist, queer, and posthumanist thinkers in this field, particularly the work of Judith Butler and Karen Barad, and demonstrates how its strongest work can be utilized to resist reading materiality as a "quasi-text." This increasingly influential line of theorizing extends the early deconstructive work by feminists such as Donna Haraway and the feminist retheorizing of corporeality. It also often draws on the theories of nonhuman agency developed by Bruno Latour and is influenced by the European philosophical tradition through Spinoza, Foucault, and Deleuze and Guattari. These theories respond to the contemporary moment by arguing "that foregrounding material factors and reconfiguring our very understanding of matter are prerequisites for any plausible account of coexistence and its condition in the twenty-first century."[83] This turn to matter productively challenges a focus on autobiography as a narrative act by inviting us to think differently about how autobiographers are engaged by and engage with the materiality of their lives, and the material properties of the media they choose and that chooses them. "Inscriptive media represent," Gitelman argues, "but the representations they entail and circulate are crucially material as well as semiotic."[84] This materiality is partially stabilized through protocols, "a vast clutter of normative rules and default conditions, which gather and adhere like a nebulous array around a technological nucleus."[85] Yet these protocols, as I explore in chapters 1 and 2, are only momentary instances of giving form and structure to the ongoing flow of *auto-bios-zoē*. As Gillian Whitlock writes, the combination of new materialist and posthumanist critiques of the sovereign human subject provides an exciting challenge to the field of life writing studies as "life narrative is caught up in the social history of this sovereign self: it has been central to understandings of what counts as human and why, to the constant and relational making of 'human' and 'nonhuman.'"[86] In addition, the ways of thinking and analyzing matter proposed by new materialist approaches strengthen our ability to account for the fundamental materiality of *auto*, *bios*, and *zoē* and to pay attention to how autobiographers are engaged in and respond to the wide variety of material flows and interactions that constitute life. Whitlock's work on an Australian archive of letters and objects shared between refugee advocates and refugees in detention demonstrates that considering the "testimony of things" opens life writing studies up to the possibility of accounting for the diverse array of *nonnarrative* practices that shift across analog and digital spaces and proliferate in environments of media and material diversity, abundance, and scarcity.[87]

The question of how we might account for the agentic dynamic capacities of matter and media is a recurring one in *Stories of the Self*. Key case studies that support this line of inquiry include Andy Warhol's *Time Capsules*, the collaging practices of queer zine makers, the work of documentary filmmaker Jonathan Caouette (explored in chapter 4), and the remediation of the outsized materiality of Paul Robeson's FBI file by artist Steve McQueen (in chapter 5). Through these cases, I explore how paying attention to materiality and mediation destabilizes the critical method of reading for human subjectivity (no matter how fragmentary or performative). In the case of the *Time Capsules*, an artwork made up of more than six hundred boxes of material taken from Warhol's life (sometimes by Warhol, sometimes by his assistants), the agency of the materiality is undeniable both in its scale and in the way it actively disrupts and resists existing methods of interpretation, storage, preservation, and display. Also interested in scale, McQueen remediates the enormous physical legacy of the FBI's surveillance of Robeson to frame the materiality of the file as a surrogate for the body of the surveilled subject. In the case of the collaged autobiographies explored in chapter 4, the remediation of a variety of popular forms of media creates an assemblage that challenges the centrality of the original voice of the narrator-author as the guarantor of autobiographical fidelity. *Stories of the Self* attempts to demonstrate how we can learn to read these texts as creative responses to the challenge of giving an account of oneself within the constant generative flow of matter and time that characterizes *zoē*, *bios*, and *auto*.

* * *

The turn to questions of materiality, in archaeology, anthropology, and associated social theory, and mediation, in media studies and other strands of cultural theory, are two strong currents in contemporary scholarship that seek lines of inquiry beyond the question of representation. In some areas of literary studies—my "home" discipline—a similar search for new lines of inquiry has resulted in a burst of critical activity around (among other things) the archive and affect, and the blooming of a new kind of empiricist research through the application of digital humanities approaches that treat texts as data sets. For a field such as life writing studies, which has been heavily invested in thinking about questions of representation, the times are also dangerous ones. The field must, I argue, strike out beyond its established approaches of thinking and writing about the representational component of the texts we choose to analyze. From media studies, we have much to gain that will help us extend our largely singular focus on writing as a form of representation to considering how subjectivity and the process of living are formed and reflected upon in mediated environments. From studies of material culture and theorizing of materiality, we can productively extend our thinking about narrative as a process of self-making to consider how the *making* of media objects (of films, selfies, zines, websites, postcards, and art installations) is equally powerful, and in some instances given precedence over the work of telling a story. From a more consistent engagement with the arguments of media studies, we can gain impetus to think with more precision about how individual autobiographical acts participate in media flows, understood as "flows of production, circulation, interpretation or reception, and recirculation, as interpretations flow back into production or outwards into general social and cultural life."[88] Yet the relationship between mediation and materiality is complex and is difficult to hold as a stable formulation across the long history of culture. This is made clear by Wendy Hui Kyong Chun, who provides a brief overview of the history of the relationship between the terms "medium" and "media" in the introduction to *New Media, Old Media: A History and Theory Reader*. As Chun succinctly explains, "medium" (in Latin) refers to an intermediary; in English, the definition of "medium" "as an intervening substance" "emerged" in the fifteenth century.[89] The *substance* referred to in her definition is where theories of media and matter intersect.

Stories of the Self demonstrates what autobiography scholarship might look like if it takes seriously the insights from the theories and approaches I have surveyed here. It also demonstrates the continued relevance of attention to autobiography for understanding fundamental questions about the intersection between the individual and the social in the contemporary moment. In one sense, then, this book is an attempt to convince my life writing colleagues to spend less time in bookshops. To my colleagues in media studies, it is an argument intended to demonstrate the utility of autobiography as a primary driver for analyzing forms of media participation and production. My commitment to offering critical engagements with digital and analog texts stems from a combination of motivations very common to scholars who practice textual analysis: sometimes it stems from an appreciation for the artistry and nuance of the text itself, and sometimes it is motivated by a desire to understand why others find the texts or practices in question so compelling. The quirky textual examples that characterize *Stories of the Self* are also intended as something of a celebration of the wide variety of forms that autobiography can take, and how different media and approaches to materiality can make lives seem significant in vastly different ways. But reading and thinking in this way, responding to autobiography as occurring within an assemblage made up of a located, material intersection of discourse and human and nonhuman actors, also changes how, and what, we read. *Stories of the Self*, in this sense, is a continuation of my interest in trying to learn how to respond to cultural forms and practices that are marginal, weird, too big, or too small, that do not fit neatly with existing paradigms of interpretation that shape how we respond to texts in cultural and literary studies. "Response," Anna Tsing suggests, "always takes us somewhere new; we are not quite ourselves any more—or at least the selves we were, but rather ourselves in encounter with another. Encounters are, by their nature, indeterminate; we are unpredictably transformed."[90] With this in mind, let us turn to the first encounter, which is with a widely used, but rarely discussed, autobiographical media form: the cardboard box.

1

Cardboard Boxes

Tennessee Williams saves everything up in a trunk and then sends it out to a storage place. I started off myself with trunks and the odd pieces of furniture, but then I went around shopping for something better and now I just drop everything into the same-size brown cardboard boxes that have a color patch on the side for the month of the year. I really hate nostalgia, though, so deep down I hope they all get lost and I never have to look at them again. That's another conflict. I want to throw things right out the window as they're handed to me, but instead I say thank you and drop them into the box-of-the-month. But my other outlook is that I really do want to save things so they can be used again someday.
—Andy Warhol, *The Philosophy of Andy Warhol: From A to B and Back Again*

Sitting in your home somewhere, there's a cardboard box. There might be more than one of them. It might be a shoe box or a box that you brought home from the liquor store filled with wine for a party. Or perhaps you do not remember where you got the box. Inside that box are all kinds of things: letters, greeting cards, photographs, ticket stubs from concerts, odd little figurines who used to speak to your children or your lover in a funny voice. There are probably some receipts in there too. Maybe a stray cigarette or lighter from your wilder days, or a mint that was left on the pillow of that expensive hotel you splurged on. It might be where that copy of *Jane Eyre* is that you were looking for the other day. There might be some old bank cards or an expired passport in there too.

If the people you live with, or who know you well, asked about the contents of that box, you'd probably be a bit evasive. "Don't ask *me* what's in it," you'd say, admitting that despite carrying it around all these years, you're not entirely sure of its contents. You don't look in it very often. You might have moved it from place to place for years without opening it and unpacking its contents. Why do you have this box? Why do you keep those things?

This chapter attempts to understand why it is that the cardboard box has become a ubiquitous technology of self-documentation. While putting life into a story is the most commonly studied means for people to reflect on their lived experience and relationships, objects also play a vital role in our experience of who we are. They connect us to the past and can provide a powerful sense of the continuity of our experience. We can also feel burdened by objects, or bound to and by them when they represent elements of our life we have not come to terms with. Yet, we often keep objects in cardboard boxes long after their connection to a place and time has dissolved in our memories.

For help in understanding the role of the cardboard box in self-life-inscription, I have turned to Andy Warhol. When he died on February 22, 1987, Warhol left behind the *Time Capsules,* his largest and most complex artwork, consisting of more than 610 containers of material, 569 of which are cardboard boxes.[1] From 1974 until his death, Warhol placed a dizzying array of objects from his life in the boxes. The contents are exactly like the contents of your box (but also, not). This chapter reads the *Time Capsules* in order to build an understanding of why the cardboard box has become a prosthetic for our memories and sense of self. Why and how does the box allow us to "capture time"?

* * *

Like many of us, Warhol turned to the cardboard box as an autobiographical technology when he was moving. The *Time Capsules* began when Warhol and his team were relocating The Factory (his studio) from 33 Union Square West in New York City to 860 Broadway. After the move was finished, Warhol added to the work continuously until his death in 1987. Consisting of hundreds of thousands of objects, and unreadable by any one individual, the *Time Capsules* present an unprecedented challenge to a biographical reading that would connect the work to a narrative of the artist's life. The *Time Capsules* are not a narrative, nor can they be shaped into one. The question of whether they can be *read*—in a way that approximates what we mean when we refer to reading as a critical or creative practice—is one that has only arisen in the last few years. At the end of 2013, the archives team at the Andy Warhol Museum in Pittsburgh completed the task of opening each of the boxes and cataloguing its contents. The vast majority of the boxes had remained sealed since Warhol, or a member of his entourage, taped them closed, sometime between 1974 and Warhol's untimely death.

While there have been exhibitions dedicated to the *Time Capsules*—including one in Melbourne, Australia, in 2005 that piqued my interest in them—they are a very challenging work both to exhibit and to view. In their scale and content, the *Time Capsules* are overwhelming. They are a wonderful example of biomediation: they make use of the mundane material form of the cardboard box to stage an encounter with a life. What can we *do*—if we *do anything*—with this encounter? How might we read a work that is stubborn in its refusal to be accessible or legible, to let any one thing, or group of things, be representative?[2] And what might an encounter with the *Time Capsules* tell us about the role of media and materiality in autobiography?

The ability to unsettle and overwhelm the potential viewer, to disrupt their usual way of looking or reading, is the source of the power of the *Time Capsules* as an autobiographical work. Their bulky mass sits in stark and defiant contrast to many of the well-known works of Warhol's oeuvre. While the silk screens, the wallpaper, and the *Brillo* boxes are iconic images and objects that we value for their simplicity and lucidity, the *Time Capsules* offer only excess and mess. They repel the way of seeing that has become associated with Warhol in many accounts of his work.[3] With the *Time Capsules* there is no punctum, indeed there is nothing for the gaze to settle on.[4] In this way, they are closely aligned with Warhol's early (in)famously plotless film works, his use of cassette tapes to record conversations, and text-based works such as *a: a novel.*[5]

The *Time Capsules* cannot be looked *at* because they are intertwined with the institution that houses them—they are like an invasive weed that chokes the plumbing of your house. This intertwining with the institution points us to the work's theme. Like many other Warhol works, the *Time Capsules* are a comment on fame. Unlike other Warhol works, however, the *Time Capsules* make *use* of fame. They are literally kept intact by it. Without the ongoing work of the archivists at the Andy Warhol

Museum, the *Time Capsules* would have succumbed to decay: the enormous amount of food distributed across the work would have fed insects and rodents that would have, once the supply of chocolate and candy ran out, turned their hungry mouths to the paper, the T-shirts, the glitter and sequins, the small reels of Super 8 film, the loose pieces of cassette tape, the photographs, the canvas, the hats, and the boxes themselves. Left alone in even the most stable and well-maintained archival environment, the *Time Capsules* would have created a microclimate and decayed. The work demands the resources and constant attention of the staff in the archives department of the Andy Warhol Museum, who through their continuous conservation efforts slow the effects of the passage of time. The *Time Capsules* exist in the magnetic field created by the poles of fame and death. You cannot read them without reading the institution and the practices in which they are located: like the fame they use as a resource, the *Time Capsules* require constant maintenance and attention if they are to endure.

Fame and Death: Institutions and Life

The *Time Capsules* began in 1974, at the height of Warhol's fame. At that time, he had barely survived his encounter with its animus, having been shot by Valerie Solanas in 1968. In the mid-1970s, Warhol made several works about death, notably the skulls series of silk screens (including a self-portrait) in 1976. But death—like fame—had been established as a Warholian theme early in his career. In 1962, he began the *Death and Disasters* series and produced the iconic diptych of Marilyn Monroe, shortly after her death. The *Time Capsules* are a place where Warhol's two primary themes intersect in a unique way: the intersection is not orchestrated in his highly developed visual language; instead, he uses a medium far less common in his oeuvre, making a work that sits somewhere between sculpture and installation.

There is an audaciousness that might be admired in Andy Warhol's belief that if he labeled 610 containers of stuff an artwork that it would be preserved.[6] He was not the only artist of his generation to make work out of unorthodox materials that challenged the sanitary conditions of the gallery and the practices of art preservation and which, through use of fragile materials such as food and dirt, sought to reconnect art with the messy, material realities of lived experience.[7] Yet in my reading, the *Time Capsules* are not a refusal of the orderliness and sterility of the gallery, or an attempt to connect the art object to the "real world" by means of the found object; they are a work that is designed to develop a parasitic relationship to the institutions of art. The *Time Capsules* are Warhol's most pointed and profound comment on the codependence of fame and its institutions. While his most famous utterance on the topic foregrounds the brevity of fame—everyone will have their fifteen minutes—the *Time Capsules* are his clearest use of materials to illustrate the labor required to *maintain* it.

Alongside the work's use of fame as a resource, Warhol's boxes give us insight into how the cardboard box can produce an excessive mundanity that ultimately works as a shield against the demand that lived experience or identity be organized into a coherent narrative in the service of social recognition. The cardboard box, therefore, can be a means of resisting and critiquing the requirement to organize life, to edit it down to a size that makes it suitable for consumption, interpretation, and institutionalization. In a short speculation on the *Time Capsules* in his biography of Warhol, Wayne Koestenbaum articulates the paradox at the heart of the work in terms of Warhol's desire for visibility and disappearance: "The unopened time capsule—its stories inaccessible until the seal is violated—offered him a perfect compromise between tomb and body; he could occupy space but also empty it, and he could be a body but also vanish."[8] Koestenbaum considers what the closed box offered Warhol. My question is: What might an open one offer us?

In reading Warhol's boxes, I am trying to determine the protocols and affordances of the cardboard box. How does it circulate? What relationship does it have to systems of preservation, or capturing what makes our life *ours*? And how might these capacities in turn shape our quotidian use of it as a medium for autobiography?

Warhol's *Time Capsules* are an instructive limit case for such an investigation. While alive, Warhol gave a master class in presenting a consistent and instantly recognizable persona. In many ways, his way of being in public epitomizes Judith Butler's arguments that identity is constructed by the repeated performance of characteristics that, through their reiteration, develop the appearance of stability and inherence.[9] Yet, as many critics have noted, Warhol's persona was also explicitly self-conscious and, in so being, refused to naturalize what Butler refers to as the "fiction" of stable identity.[10] It was always clear—because Warhol made it so—that the version of Warhol presented in public was a version he had developed for the purposes of satisfying the need to have a legible identity.[11] To those who encountered Warhol through the parasocial relations of the media, that identity was akin to a brand, anchored by the wig, the entourage, the halting speech and flat affect. To the people who knew him personally, that identity was more nuanced, and yet just as reliable, particularly after he recovered from the shooting: Andy went to church every Sunday, and he adhered to a "weekday 'rut.'"[12] This included a daily painting schedule,[13] as well as daily phone conversations with Pat Hackett to dictate his diary. However, attempting to understand the relationship of the *Time Capsules* to Warhol's biography or his identity is a doomed undertaking. The boxes disrupt any attempt at synthesis. They will not be molded to a story of Andy Warhol, nor can they be adapted to support an existing account of who Warhol was, or is. They remain a largely untapped resource in scholarship and biography on Warhol for the very reason that if you want to "learn something about Andy Warhol," the *Time Capsules* will tell you nothing.[14]

That does not mean, however, that the *Time Capsules* are pointless or useless or that they fail to signify or matter. Indeed, after five days of looking at them, I concluded that they are an autobiographical artwork whose significance is unrecognized. They trouble existing categories of reading because they work with and against the revered cultural category of the archive. By mixing unique and highly charged objects from his life with cigarette butts, half-eaten boxes of chocolates, bottles of shampoo from hotels, and newspapers, Warhol "dispenses with most conventions of good composition and proper spectatorship alike."[15] The *Time Capsules* demand that we rethink our approach to looking at and for autobiography. Warhol has used the mundane technology of the cardboard box to challenge the hunger for personal information that is a product and fuel of fame. The boxes will deliver on their promise of offering genuinely moving and rich insights into Warhol's lived experience, but only if we discard established ways of reading, and devise new ways of engaging with Warhol's self-life-inscription. They can also tell us a lot about the cardboard box as a form of self-life-inscription.

Massive Presence: Warhol's Replicas and Originals

My reading of the *Time Capsules* should not be misconstrued as a work of biography. Nor does it add to the long-standing art historical conversation regarding Warhol's contribution to the project of contemporary art. One reason it cannot do either of these things is that in accessing and engaging with the *Time Capsules* I am forced to read the institutional structure and protocols that surround them. In that sense, art history and biography are two discourses that the work activates and disrupts. As I explain later, the *Time Capsules* cannot be distinguished from the work of preserving, cataloguing, and exhibiting them. When I traveled to the Andy Warhol Museum in 2014 to spend five days viewing the *Time Capsules*, the six-year process of opening the containers and cataloguing their contents had recently been completed. My aim was a relatively humble one: Was it possible to read the *Time Capsules* as an autobiographical artwork? If so, how would such a reading proceed?

My interest in the work had been sparked nine years earlier by a 2005 exhibition of the *Time Capsules* hosted by the National Gallery of Victoria in Melbourne, Australia, in the Kulin nation. Taking up several rooms in the gallery, the exhibition displayed the contents of fifteen containers, totaling around three thousand objects. Like many people attracted to the exhibition, I was enchanted by the idea of all that *stuff* from Warhol's life being on display. When I visited the exhibition, however, I was surprised to discover that most people viewed it with the aid of a free printed guide, akin to a newspaper, handed out with the entry ticket.[16] This guide listed *every* object displayed in the dozens of display cases in the exhibition. Each item in the cabinets was numbered, and each number corresponded to a listing in the guide. People relied heavily on this guide to structure their viewing of the *Time Capsules*—they spent their time reading, rather than looking. This was a sensible way to exhibit the material and make it accessible to the public, but I also felt that the physical presence of the excess of objects and the serendipity that might come from the juxtaposition of items were diminished. The decision to exhibit the work in this way made a certain kind of sense, but I left the gallery feeling that I had missed something important by viewing the work in this way.

This experience in 2005 of *reading* the *Time Capsules* through their textual remediation was not my last. When my application to visit the archives at the Andy Warhol Museum was approved in early 2014, the then chief archivist began e-mailing me the finding aids the museum shares with researchers. The standard protocol for receiving the finding aids had been that researchers identify the subject of their research on Warhol, and the archives team advised which of the *Time Capsules* containers could be of interest. The researcher then received finding aids for the specific containers that related to their research. Because I was the first person to apply to look at the *Time Capsules* as a complete work, the chief archivist began the process of e-mailing the finding aid for every container. Over the course of several weeks, I received more than six hundred documents, each one a finding aid for a specific box (or filing cabinet or trunk). Managing these documents was my first challenge in trying to read the *Time Capsules* and was a powerful introduction to the scale of the artwork and the logistical issues it involves. Each e-mail from the chief archivist had ten to twenty individual Microsoft Word files attached—each document several pages long.[17] This was my second encounter with the processes of remediation that the *Time Capsules* have generated. The finding aids are intended to make engaging with the *Time Capsules* easier for researchers, curators, and archivists, but the aids turn hundreds of thousands of objects into more than six thousand pages of text.

Perhaps naively, what I had wanted to do when I decided to try to read the *Time Capsules* as an autobiographical work was to apply to it the reading method that the protocols of the cardboard box seem to encourage: rummaging. As a sturdy, relatively stable and cheap means of storage and transportation, what we know as "cardboard boxes" are referred to as corrugated fiberboard cartons or boxes in the packaging industry.[18] Corrugated fiberboard boxes, which Warhol famously depicted in his box sculptures of the mid-1960s, are intimately connected to the rise of national brands and the mass distribution of consumer goods that began in America in the late nineteenth century.[19] While the individual packaging of food items in branded cartons, bottles, and tins cemented the place of branded food in American life in the early twentieth-century,[20] the manufacturers' easily identifiable cardboard boxes surely played an important role in the organization of the large stockrooms of the "self-service" supermarkets that revolutionized America's relationship to food in the interwar period.[21]

Warhol had made his mark—and achieved an important milestone in his career as an artist—reproducing the cardboard box and the supermarket storeroom in the early days of Pop Art. In 1964, for his second exhibition at the Stable Gallery, Warhol exhibited the now-famous *Brillo boxes* as part of a series of grocery boxes.[22] According to the catalogue raisonné, "There are seven series of box sculptures: *Brillo (3¢ Off), Mott's Apple Juice, Del Monte Peach Halves, Kellogg's Cornflakes, Heinz Tomato Soup, Brillo,* and *Campbell's Tomato Juice*."[23] When Warhol exhibited these boxes, they were arranged according to their brand identities, and the "space was filled, floor to ceiling, with grocery boxes" in order to re-create a stockroom.[24] This exhibition cemented Warhol's place in defining Pop Art and resulted in the career milestone of his move to Castelli Gallery, the gallery of other Pop artists Roy Lichtenstein, Jasper Johns, and Robert Rauschenberg.[25]

According to Arthur C. Danto, Warhol's grocery boxes and silk screens introduced "a deep discontinuity into the history of art by removing from the way art was conceived most of what everyone thought belonged to its essence."[26] The box sculptures illustrate and comment on the role of the cardboard box in the rise of brands and mass production and the increasing centrality of products of machine-enabled repetition and consistency in American life in the twentieth century. All these things were primary subjects in Warhol's work and in the modes of production he used to make art. As Danto points out, the exhibition of grocery boxes as sculpture is one of Warhol's most profound contributions to the debate regarding the ontological status of the art object to which each generation of artists after Duchamp/von Freytag-Loringhoven attempts to make its contribution.[27] But the grocery boxes are not true-to-life replicas of their subject: they are not usable (they have no opening, but are made of four solid sides), and they are made not of cardboard but of wood.[28] They are sculptures.

While the *Brillo* box is now synonymous with Warhol, the individual box was not the focus of Warhol's artistic intention in 1964. His goal, at least according to biographers and assistants who worked with him on the project, was to create an effect through the presence of *many* boxes.[29] Danto, who saw the original exhibition, believes that "it was really undeniable that he wanted them piled on the floor, and to have a massive presence."[30] Like the silk screen works, the grocery boxes and the *Time Capsules* are works that utilize scale and repetition. In the 1964 work, the massive presence of like objects was the aim, in order to "undermine conventional orders of number, composition, and visual distinction."[31] The *Time Capsules* continue this sculptural, spatial exploration of the striking physical presence of 610 boxes. But their physical presence when grouped together is but the first layer of many possible encounters with outsized materiality. Unlike the box sculptures, which are empty, each *Time Capsule* is stuffed with individual objects. We might be tempted to refer to the thousands of objects within the *Time Capsules'* massive presence as *excess* or *excessive*, yet I argue that the *Time Capsules* are a work that powerfully demonstrates the fullness of Warhol's life. Through materiality they inscribe the diversity, strength, and duration of his relationships. The cardboard boxes make physically present the abundance of Warhol's life.[32] For Jonathan Flatley, Warhol's use of the cardboard box as medium is explicitly tactile, "a particular way to store experiences of touching, holding, and otherwise interacting with the surfaces of things" that Flatley associates with "reading, writing, and drawing" as modes of interaction.[33] However, my encounter with the work, and its remediation, suggests that a less explicitly textual style of interaction is evoked by the *Time Capsules*: that of rummaging as a response to a massive presence that obscures the individual object.

With Warhol's box sculptures in their exhibited form, the individual box is largely irrelevant. Similarly, no shop assistant is sent to the stockroom to fetch a *specific* carton of *Brillo* pads: they can grab whichever one is easiest to select from the stack. (Although they may need to pay more attention to which carton of cornflakes they select.) In the design and construction of cardboard cartons, the principle that individual boxes be interchangeable requires that every box must be able to withstand the physical pressure of static force should it be positioned at the bottom of a stack.[34] Paper engineers refer to this as the "stacking strength" of the box,[35] and it is one of the unique properties of the cardboard box as a medium: in its design and construction, the fiberboard shipping carton is made to be the strongest individual among a collective, regardless of whether it will ever be called on to play that role.

Regardless of *which* box ends up at the bottom of a stack of boxes, every box is designed to withstand the force of the weight of the others.

A cardboard box, then, is a material container whose affordances make each individual interchangeable: if required, any given box can play a load-bearing role in relation to the weight of the collective. Andy Warhol was rarely seen without an entourage and, if his diaries are any reflection of his lived experience, spent most of his time in groups of people. As Wayne Koestenbaum observes, Warhol was interested in the "assemblage of ephemeral social atmospheres."[36] We might think of the large collection of containers that make up the *Time Capsules* as a materialization of such atmospheres: taken together, the boxes are a crowd. Before we can rummage in an individual *Time Capsule*, we must think about them as a whole; in their massive presence, and their togetherness.

As a collective, the *Time Capsules* make considerable demands on the institution that houses them. They take up space, they are inexorably bound up in the process of decay, and their materiality is unstable: they contain liquids that can seep, foodstuffs that can rot, and fragile artworks that can be destroyed. While some individual boxes contain mainly paper—newspapers, magazines, letters, books, catalogues, and so on— many of them include less stable materials; there are dozens of bottles of shampoo and conditioner taken from hotel rooms, bars of soap, chocolate bars, Easter eggs, cigarette stubs, cans of pop, cans of soup (Campbell's, of course), and cookies spread across the work (there is also a loaf of bread in the shape of a dachshund, and half a baguette painted blue).[37] The only box no longer intact is the *Time Capsule* made up entirely of raw pizza dough; this box decayed much quicker than the others, but when Warhol was alive it was stored among the crowd.

Unlike the wood used to make the box sculptures in 1964, the corrugated cardboard of the *Time Capsules* is highly responsive to its environment: the paper fibers used in corrugated fiberboard "absorb moisture from their surrounding environment . . . and release moisture" when the air is dry.[38] The strength and durability of individual boxes is considerably impacted by the atmosphere created by the presence of other boxes. When stacked together (as they are intended to be), cardboard boxes affect each other through "creep"—the damage caused by long periods of static force that come with storing and shipping boxes in stacked units.[39] The static force resulting from the continued presence of others generates creep. This effect among humans—the force we exert on each other in groups—was, as Koestenbaum observes, of keen interest to Warhol.[40] As a medium cardboard boxes are designed to withstand the pressures of collectivity and relationality, at least in the short term.[41]

Like getting access to Warhol when he was alive, reading the *Time Capsules* as an autobiographical work begins by negotiating the crowd.[42] For researchers and curators, this negotiation is done twice over. It begins with traversing the data, the enormous volume of raw information presented by the finding aids before one can even begin to negotiate the objects themselves. Warhol famously worked with media of inscription—cassette tapes, film, the book—to produce works that appeared to reject the process of selection in their documentation of lived experience.[43] As with these other works, the seemingly "unedited" nature of the *Time Capsules* is just a ruse, however: as I was to discover, there are many things from Warhol's life that did not make it into the work, but which exist in the Andy Warhol archives.[44] Despite appearances, there is a process of selection behind the work. So, when faced with the *Time Capsules* as a whole, where does one begin?

Looking for Jed Johnson

In 2005, when I first felt the urge to rummage in the *Time Capsules*, I imagined engaging in a "thorough but unsystematic or untidy search."[45] But the institutional protocols of the archive require that I know what it is that I am looking for. Before I arrive at the museum each day, I must submit a prioritized list of *individual objects* that I wish to view. The thousands of pages of finding aids make it clear that there is no hope of a thorough search of the *Time Capsules* in five days. Warhol's fame prevents me from following my instincts among his many objects, the way I might casually browse a friend's things as I help them pack up their house to move, or rifle through the back room of a thrift store. The *Time Capsules* are enmeshed in the institution, and so you must choose a place to start. The only possible choice is an arbitrary one. Choose a place to begin, a thread to follow, activate the search—start to rummage—and see what turns up. In the five days I had with the *Time Capsules*, I thought of them as a hybrid between a text, a game, and an instrument: you have to *play* them, in every sense of the word, for the autobiographical content to be discovered.

Each day I chose a different entry point and duly submitted a list of objects that might start me on a rummaging (reading) of the work. Rather than pursue a consistent position regarding what might "reveal" the autobiographical in the *Time Capsules*, my approach changed every day. I played the *Time Capsules* five different ways:

Day 1: A relationship: someone from Warhol's life
Day 2: The shooting
Day 3: One whole *Time Capsule*
Day 4: Mail art
Day 5: The food

On day one I go looking for Jed Johnson. Johnson was Warhol's lover, and they lived together in the company of two dachshunds (Archie and Amos) for twelve years.[46] There was a twenty-year age gap between them. Born on December 30, 1948, Jed and his twin brother, Jay, arrived at Warhol's Factory in 1968. Jed Johnson died in 1996, at age forty-seven: he was a passenger on TWA Flight 800, which exploded shortly after takeoff from JFK International Airport en route to Paris on July 17.[47]

How is Warhol's longest romantic relationship represented in the *Time Capsules*?[48] When I went looking for Jed Johnson, I discovered that intimacy can be registered in the presence of mail. The shared living of Johnson and Warhol is evidenced in a long and complex trail of envelopes (and their contents) that is spread out across the boxes. In living together and in sharing, among other things, a postal address, Warhol and Johnson created a scene of "domestic privacy."[49] This was both the site of *their* intimacy—their shared everyday experience—and the destination for mail that serves their intimate relationships with others. The *Time Capsules* are densely populated by Jed Johnson's mail. There is a letter from Johnson's doctor, sent to 1342 Lexington Avenue (their home before the move to East Sixty-Sixth Street), reminding him that he is due for his annual checkup. A birthday card for Jay Johnson from their sister Susie is sent in care of Jed (the brothers received separate cards—Jed's is there too). Postcards to Jed from Jay as he travels the world. One, sent from Rio di Janeiro postmarked December 24, 1976, reads in large, boyish handwriting: "Just too crazy here even for me. If I don't see you before you leave have a wonderful Christmas. Love to Andy, Archie, Amos, etc. JAY." A card from the casting agent Lynn Kressel addressed to Jed in 1977 reads: "Dear Jed, I have just read Vincent Canby's comments on *Bad* [the film *Andy Warhol's Bad*, which Jed Johnson directed] in today's times [*sic*], and found them interesting and a credit to you and Pat. Hope we can work together again sometime soon. Best, Lynn." Jed Johnson is also the addressee for the regular bills from the grocery store Gristedes and the bills for the cable television subscription.

Through Warhol's inclusion of mail in the *Time Capsules*, we see "intimacy meet the normative practices, . . . institutions [in this case, the mail] and ideologies that organize" Warhol and Johnson's world.[50] The delivery of mail to the home inserts people into the complex communications network of the postal system by means of a geographic location (an address).[51] The sharing of an address is one of a multitude of points where intimacy intersects with institutional practices. As David M. Henkin argues, "The spread of the post transformed the individual name into a legitimate site—an operational address—in the new communications network" overseen by government and corporate interests.[52] Individuals became locatable nodes in the communications network of the postal system when delivery of mail to the home came to large US cities in 1863,[53] and the mail has also long been used to address groups of people bound by intimate connections (couples, families, groups of friends).[54] The presence of Johnson's mail in the *Time Capsules* archives the shared node of a home delivery address, where Warhol and Johnson were addressed as an intimate pair, or as part of a larger intimate group (including Warhol's mother, Julia Warhola, and the dogs). The *Time Capsules* include many items of mail addressed to Jed Johnson and Andy Warhol, or to Andy Warhol and Jed Johnson. These include a postcard addressed to "Jed Johnson/Andy Warhol and Nana" (possibly a reference to Warhol's housekeeper, Nena),[55] as well as invitations addressed to the couple (sometimes "Jed and Andy," sometimes "Andy and Jed") to drinks and parties.

The *Time Capsules* record a site where intimacy meets institution in the privileged site of the home.[56] It also raises the question of Warhol's approach to assembling the work: as I encountered Johnson's personal, professional, and administrative mail in the boxes, I wondered whether he knew of, or consented to, its inclusion in the work.[57] I imagined Warhol's wandering eye and hand moving over a hall table where the mail delivery lay, or selecting items from a pile of opened mail on the kitchen bench.

This evidence of a domestic, cohabiting intimacy challenges the view of Warhol as detached and asexual, epitomized by the nickname "Drella" (bestowed on him in the Factory days, a portmanteau of Cinderella and Dracula), which emphasizes the voyeuristic and standoffish in his persona.[58] Like Jonathan Flatley, I am interested in an alternative reading "against a certain commonsense view that understands his art (and its machine-like use of repetition for instance) as a defense *against* being affected."[59] The *Time Capsules* archive the everyday intimacy of Johnson and Warhol's shared life in the arrival of the mail and the comixing of individual identities (Jed Johnson, Andy Warhol) in the couple form (Jed and Andy)—a physical trace of how each man was both himself and a member of the two.

The view of Warhol and Johnson's life presented by the mail in the *Time Capsules* also expands the accounts of Warhol that stress the alienation, trauma, and isolation at the center of his queer identity. The readings that focus on Warhol's queerness often do so in a justifiable attempt to reinscribe Warhol's homosexuality and queerness into the account of his life and art.[60] That the *Time Capsules* could be read as a trace of an everyday cohabitation and durational intimacy is not an argument for a homonormative reading of Warhol and Johnson.[61] In the *Time Capsules* there are many objects that cannot be subsumed into the normative lens of the couple form, with its attendant logics of monogamy, stabilized desire, and clearly established roles.[62]

While there is a lot of mail linking Johnson and Warhol in the *Time Capsules*, it would be a mistake to view this trace in isolation and read it within a romance narrative that leads to Jed and Andy's/Andy and Jed's domesticity.[63] A far more complicated view of Warhol's relationship with Johnson emerges through the presence of a particularly resonant individual object, which can be found in *Time Capsule 66*.[64] But to get to this object, we must return to the institutional setting of the *Time Capsules* and consider how the use of archival categories in the catalogue of the work compounds Warhol's use of scale and massive presence to invite and thwart a reading of the work as self-life-inscription.

Archiving Ambivalence

The finding aids for the *Time Capsules* organize the material contained in each box by type: subheadings such as "Correspondence," "Books," "Mail art," and "Manuscript material" give a structure to the contents of each box that is not reflective of the way the boxes were originally packed (items were generally just put in the box until it was full) or how the boxes themselves are organized in the archive. Thus, a complicated material gesture that may or may not have passed between Andy Warhol and Jed Johnson is listed as a "Book," subcategory "Exhibition catalogues." The book is one of the many catalogues that can be found in the work, but it is also a trace of attachment offered and withdrawn, a remnant, possibly, of Warhol's encounter with the "scene of intimate risk" that Lauren Berlant argues is the disorganizing affect of attachment that "love" seeks to give form.[65] For Berlant, what we refer to as "love" is a genre that allows us to find a safe passage out of the incoherence that comes with attachment. We say we love someone because being around them disorganizes or disrupts us. To call this feeling love gives it form, and the form provides relief from the anxiety of being disorganized.

Who knows what language Andy Warhol and Jed Johnson used between them to negotiate the disruptive affect of their attraction and desire. There is a hint to the struggle Warhol had with the language of attachment scrawled in a 1971 exhibition of his work at the Tate Gallery in London. The description of this object in the finding aids reads: "exhibit catalogue for Warhol at the Tate Gallery 17 February–March 1971 with inscription in front of catalogue 'To Jed' [Darling is blacked out] Andy Warhol and signed on p. 3 by Andy Warhol with A.W. initials © 1971." I request *Time Capsule 66* from the archives, intrigued by the description.

When the archival assistant brings a *Time Capsule* into the room for me to view—I can only see one at a time—she becomes my prosthesis. I came to the museum to see if rummaging is a method for reading cardboard boxes, and it is a very respectful, cautious version of rummaging that produces the *Warhol* 1971 Tate catalogue from *Time Capsule 66*. Protective gloves are worn. The assistant begins by removing the cardboard box from what I have come to think of as its body bag: a clear, thick plastic sleeve that each box sits in to protect the cardboard. There is no way of knowing in what order things are placed in a box: the assistant must look for the item I have requested by patiently unpacking the *Time Capsule* until she finds it. Individual items, or folders of correspondence, are placed carefully on a long table as the archival assistant searches for the book.[66] She rummages as my proxy: while I don't handle a box myself, I get to watch as rummaging unfolds before me.

The surprise of what comes out next is fresh with each object. Indeed, the seemingly endless possibility for distraction and tangents that occurs as each object is taken out of a *Time Capsule* powerfully demonstrates an important affordance of the cardboard box that may explain its utility as a common tool for autobiography. The cardboard box is uniquely capacious, able to hold a wide variety of objects, including many media forms (letters, photographs, reels of film). When we rummage in a cardboard box, whether looking for a specific thing or seeking to catalogue its contents, our attention is split in different directions as each object is revealed: Why is *this* here? Oh look! *That's* where this is! What was I/she/Warhol thinking when they put this here? This invitation to be surprised, to allow each object to suggest its original context and spark questions regarding its origin, is an unfolding serendipity that evokes something of a lived experience among an entourage. Six hundred and ten densely populated boxes, like 610 visits to Warhol's Factory, or the thousands of gallery openings and parties he attended in his life, offer the viewer an ever-expanding field: by rummaging in the boxes, we encounter this expansiveness, the social connectedness, the movement between scenes of sociality. The *Time Capsules* demonstrate Koestenbaum's suggestion that a key characteristic of Warhol's work is to "transpose sensation from one medium to another."[67] As we rummage through *Time Capsule* 66 in search of the book (remember why we're here?), the sensation of the crowded room is remediated in the crowd of objects.

Yet underneath the pleasant surprise that comes with watching a *Time Capsule* be unpacked, there is a less positive feeling. The slow stream of objects creates what I come to think of as anxiety. As time passes, it becomes clear that the object I am seeking is far down in the box; the assistant will have to repack the box when I am finished, before the next one can be brought from storage. Repacking a *Time Capsules* is a far more difficult process than unpacking one. This trick of capaciousness is an important part of the protocol of the cardboard box: when we use cardboard boxes for storing or shipping personal items, we can always get more into them than we expect. When packing a box for the first time, we experience an illicit joy when we discover we can squeeze in one or two more things. This stolen space comes back to haunt us if the box is not entirely unpacked and discarded when it completes its role as protective container for transportation, such as when it is used for long-term storage or as a makeshift cupboard. I watched over and over again as the archives team at the Andy Warhol Museum wrestled with how much Warhol had crammed into a box. More than once they jokingly cursed Warhol, or the box itself: "The TCs [*Time Capsules*] don't like me today!" the assistant said in frustration after struggling to repack a particularly full box.

The problem of the capaciousness of cardboard cartons is key to the *Time Capsules*' parasitic relation to the institution. Individual boxes that make up the *Time Capsules* have spilled over into multiple "overflow" containers: print drawers that store the more fragile original artworks, clear plastic boxes that quarantine the food and liquids from the dry contents of the boxes, separate new boxes that house Julia Warhola's hats. The process of cataloguing the contents of the *Time Capsules* draws on the practices of archiving as a science: a set of protocols that can make matter manageable, knowable, and accessible.[68] The cardboard boxes—as both the containers for the objects and part of the artwork in their own right—trouble the science of organization with their capricious spatial affordance. All of these things came out of *this* box: but then we face the problem of getting them back in, and whether or not they *should* be stored together. Leaving a chocolate bar in a box with a disposable protective jumpsuit customized for Andy Warhol by Jean-Michel Basquiat is to condemn the auratic art object to decay through its proximity to the mundane reality of Warhol's sweet tooth.[69]

Waiting for the institutional protocols of the archive to locate the object is part of the *Time Capsules* as a work. This waiting draws our attention to the working of institutions—the vectors of power/knowledge that authorize them, the protocols that authorize their claims to be sites where knowledge is created—and the *Time Capsules* are a work that overwhelms those protocols and discourses and their quest for knowledge. In 1974, when Warhol began the work—began, that is, selecting objects to be included in the *Time Capsules* from the vast array of things he purchased and was given—his fame was secured. He knew we could never throw out his stuff (no matter how banal), that at least some of us would become his "mad widows,"[70] destined to protect every paper clip, every cigarette butt, every piece of ribbon, and every empty envelope *because* they had some connection to *Him*. But Warhol had also experienced bruising encounters with the forms of authority and recognition bestowed by the institutions of the art world, including his early struggles to be accepted as a fine artist because of the negative associations often attached to his successful career as a commercial artist, accusations that he was a sellout for making commissioned portraits, his personal disappointment regarding his lack of recognition by the Museum of Modern Art, and the dismissive reviews of his collaboration with Basquiat. To rephrase Derrida's formulation: the *Time Capsules* sit between two poles, two versions of Andy Warhol.[71] The proper name of Andy Warhol is the figure of fame: the canonical figure in the invention of Pop Art, a key player in revolutionizing how contemporary art is made and seen, an actor in the project of institutionalizing that revolution, the subject of art historical knowledge production.[72] The other pole is Andrew Warhola, what in autobiography studies we would call the "historical 'I'" (or who Koestenbaum refers to as "Andy Paperbag").[73] The person who ate lunch, made the paintings, went to church every Sunday with his mother, loved to talk on the phone, who lived, who was shot, who feared the hospital. In autobiography, as in the archive, "what is in question is situated precisely *between the two*."[74] And so we wait for the book to appear.

Walter Benjamin argued that "the existence of the work of art with reference to its aura is never entirely separated from its ritual function."[75] From the religious ritual to the secular worship of beauty, Benjamin believed that the revolutionary potential of works of art that use mechanical means of reproduction (film, silk screens) was that it freed the works from the discourse of ritual into the realm of politics.[76] Central to this movement is the increasing emphasis on "exhibition value" that comes with art that is mechanically reproducible;[77] the work has no specific location, and it can be viewed by more members of the public. One of the reasons the *Time Capsules* have proved difficult to integrate within the existing narrative about Warhol's work and life is the trouble they pose to methods for creating exhibition value. While it is logistically possible to transport all 610 containers for exhibition (if you can get stale food through customs or quarantine), exhibiting them is another matter. As the exhibition in Melbourne in 2005 demonstrated, the *Time Capsules* require significant remediation for their exhibition value to be extracted. When I left the exhibition in 2005 wishing I had had the opportunity to rummage, I had failed to see one of the key meanings of the work: that rummaging is incompatible with fame's role in creating and organizing exhibition value. One of the strongest elements of Warhol's oeuvre is to show us that fame is desire—we want to rummage in Andy Warhol's boxes *because* they are his. Yet, we cannot rummage in Andy Warhol's *Time Capsules*; they are too valuable to let just anyone nose around in them, and they are too large to be exhibited together, and so we are left longing. The best we can hope for is a glimpse of what is deemed worth looking at, or if we are very lucky, as I was, that a qualified, certified archival assistant can rummage for us.[78]

The *Time Capsules'* combination of limited exhibition value (the result of the scale) and objects from Warhol's life (rather than replicas) dramatizes the tension that drives audiences to autobiographical works—the desire to encounter something of the reality of lived experience. It also exemplifies the modes of production of celebrity, where the institutional protocols associated with public relations and media reporting heighten our desire for contact with the star, while also inserting themselves as the mediator of that contact.[79] Thus, watching an archival assistant carefully unpack a *Time Capsule* is to watch the archive in action, to be reminded that, as Carolyn Steedman argues, in the archive "the object (the event, the happening, the story from the past) has been altered by the very search for it, by its time and duration; what has actually been lost can never be found. This is not to say that *nothing* is found, but that thing is always something else, a creation of the search itself and the time the search took."[80]

And then, finally, the book appears (figure 1.1).

I suggested earlier that the presence of mail addressed to Jed Johnson, to "Jed and Andy"/"Andy and Jed," could be read as a material trace of the intimacy shared by Johnson and Warhol in the twelve years they lived together, and as evidence of the role of others in constructing that intimacy. One might be tempted to use the mail to mount a redemptive narrative of Warhol's adherence to the couple form, to recuperate not only his homosexuality but also his queer desires (his fondness for

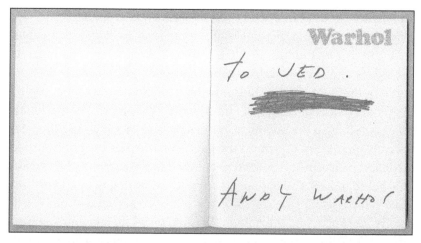

Figure 1.1. Andy Warhol, *Warhol* (Tate Gallery, London, February 17–March 28, 1971), signed by Andy Warhol from *Time Capsule* 66. Accession number TC66.20.1.

photographing genitals, for example, or the erotic voyeurism celebrated in films such as *Blow Job*, *Sleep*, and *Kiss*) to take the *edge* off the genuinely challenging and subversive treatment of desire and sexuality in his work. Such a reading might see Warhol's cohabitation with Johnson— and their shared parenting of the dachshunds Archie and Amos (they shared custody after Johnson moved out in 1981)—as a normative truth that lay beneath the veneer of Warhol's celebration of nonnormative sexuality (surface and depth being modes of interpretation strongly associated with Warhol as a postmodern figure).[81] For Flatley, Warhol's praxis "is queer, and queer as distinct from gay";[82] Warhol's approach to assemblage and repetition made space for him "to conceive of attraction, affection, and attachment without relying on the homo/hetero opposition so central to modern ideas of sexuality and desire."[83]

Within the *Time Capsules* we find a complex, and personal, archive of materials that suggests Warhol's relationship with the disorganizing, ambivalent experience of attachment.[84] We also find the utopian promise of being a misfit that Flatley identifies in Warhol's liking and his queerness.[85] While the mail addressed to Jed Johnson and "Andy and Jed" spreads out across the *Time Capsules* to form an archive of the soft rhythms of home life, the 1971 Tate catalogue renders a moment where Warhol experienced deep ambivalence regarding his attachment to Johnson. Warhol inscribed this moment on the front page of a book documenting his international status as a visual artist and then deposited it in a *Time Capsule*. "To Jed. Darling," Warhol utters and regrets. He offers and then withdraws the sentiment, obliterating the word under a flurry of lines, hiding it with an emphatic retraction, replacing it with a visual record of ambivalence. We cannot know whether Warhol retracted the utterance immediately—scribbling over the word directly after it took form on the page—or whether the book with its dedication sat among other objects for days, weeks, or years before Warhol took back the statement and put the catalogue in a *Time Capsule*. What is left are the names on the page; two are handwritten ("Jed," "Andy Warhol"), one is printed ("Warhol"), and the blacked-out mess of Andy's feelings about *how* these names are connected hovers in the white field between them. What is the relationship between "Warhol," "Andy Warhol," and "Jed"? When he used a black marker to map this relationship by personalizing a catalogue, presumably as a gift for Jed Johnson, Warhol stumbled into the disorganizing affect of attachment that Berlant argues we formalize through the love plot.[86] Was Warhol confronted by the starkness of his attachment to, desire for, and vulnerability to Jed Johnson when he wrote "Darling" as the linking term between "Jed" and "Andy Warhol"? Or did he erase it as a form of retraction, to take it back because he did not, in fact, believe that Jed Johnson was his darling? Here we might see Warhol as unable, or unwilling, to believe in the stabilizing powers of love's formalism, or we might read the retraction as a record of ambivalence about Johnson himself. The personalized catalogue does not have a place in an existing narrative of Johnson and Warhol—no such narrative exists; neither do the *Time Capsules* provide a narrative sequence in which this moment of feeling is placed. There is no "before" or "after" Andy Warhol's attempt to call Jed Johnson "Darling" presented in the work. Instead, we have an object produced by Warhol's encounter in 1971 with the disorganizing power of his attachment to Johnson.[87]

And what of the institutional status, the fame, denoted by the printed name? If the handwritten text, and its obliteration by scribbling, is an imprint left by Andy Warhol's experience of ambivalence in attachment, who, or what, is represented by the "Warhol" that sits on the page above the site of handwritten inscription? The printed name represents the insertion of Warhol as a figure into the institution—it is the printed name of Warhol that facilitates and authorizes the dedication of resources to maintaining the *Time Capsules*.

The *Time Capsules* are an archive, but they invite critical engagement with the archiving impulse that attends celebrity and the forms of knowledge production associated with biographical criticism. They work on the question of the archive as conceptualized by Derrida, "a question of the future, the question of the future itself, the question of a response, of a promise and of a responsibility to tomorrow."[88] A large-scale work that mixes mundane items (grocery bills, a reminder that Jed Johnson is due to visit the doctor) with unique objects that record the importance of people such as Johnson in Warhol's life, the *Time Capsules* engage with the odd futurity that attends fame: being of the zeitgeist brings with it the burden of standing in for the present in some future moment. This is what Warhol acknowledged with his memoir of his "Pop" years and continued to explore through the *Time Capsules*.[89] Yet rather than leave a tightly curated version of his life and the times, the *Time Capsules* demonstrate a level of ambivalence toward the futurity of fame. The scale and material complexity of the *Time Capsules* inscribe Warhol's ambivalence about the future—the future beyond his death, where the *Time Capsules* would find their value as a product of Warhol's celebrity. By transposing the sensations of the entourage and the ambivalence of attachment into an excessive materiality, Warhol stages the scene for a rich encounter with his lived experience. For Jonathan Flatley, this is one element of Warhol's pedagogical approach to liking, whereby collecting is a means to see and enjoy similarity (not to be mistaken with being identical): "Warhol's collecting vividly dramatizes a mode of attraction based not on lack but on an accumulation and plentitude."[90] Koestenbaum reads these transpositions as a means for Warhol to "highlight how the act of conversion, from one galaxy to another, disembodies and alienates the material—embalms it, expunging the soul."[91] Rummaging in (rather than reading) the *Time Capsules* suggests that despite its massive materiality, the current of sensation that flows through the massive presence of the work can be accessed, as I hope to show with my final example.

Death and Destruction

Warhol's ambivalence toward fame-after-death is staged through the most mundane and destructive elements included in the *Time Capsules*: the food, cigarette butts, dirty coffee cups, half-empty chocolate boxes, and toiletries that are spread out across the boxes. With these objects, Warhol inserted decay into the archive. These materials are a form of built-in obsolescence in the most analog of artworks.

For Derrida, the archive carries within it the drive to destruction, the possibility of annihilation,[92] and Warhol's inclusion of food and liquids in the work materially inscribes destruction into the *Time Capsules*. The passing of time changes the work: the food rots and grows mold and the liquids leak, solidify, or evaporate, changing the atmosphere of the fiberboard boxes, whose porous qualities trap and release moisture. By separating the unstable materials from the work, the archives team at the Andy Warhol Museum have put the *Time Capsules* on life support. The processing of the *Time Capsules*—the cataloguing and storage of them within the archives department of the museum, the separation of the food and liquids from the other materials—slows their passage through time. The *Time Capsules* will travel further into the future now the food and the liquids have been removed and their inevitable decay can no longer hasten the decomposition of other materials, including the boxes themselves. The atmosphere created by all that stuff in boxes, and the creep of all the boxes piled together, is dissipated by the processes of preservation and cataloguing. Within the overlapping logics of fame, archival science, and art history, this is what *should* happen. If we are interested in speculating about Warhol's intention in making the work, we might suggest that Warhol knew it *would* happen. And perhaps he took some pleasure or amusement in imaging how some future team of professionals would approach the task of archiving Andy Warhol's pizza dough. But in my last day looking at the *Time Capsules*, through a powerful intermingling of smell and sight, a different reading of the *Time Capsules* emerged, one that suggested how the capacious storage affordances of the cardboard box offer the autobiographer the opportunity to stage a striking encounter with the ephemeral vicissitudes of lived experience and relationality.

On my final day in the archives, I looked at the food and other perishable materials that are included in the *Time Capsules*. Stored separately from the cardboard boxes in large sealed plastic tubs, all perishable items are clearly marked so that their original location in a specific *Time Capsule* can be traced. Every single item is stored in at least one ziplock plastic bag, to contain the smell of rotting organic material and reduce the seepage and spread of mold. Despite these efforts, when a plastic storage box is opened, the smell of decay is very strong. I spent several hours exploring these boxes—with the help of an archival assistant—and the dense, sweet-sour smell was pervasive and unrelenting. A particularly acrid smell was given off by an Easter egg, unbroken and encased in its bright foil wrapper and two ziplock bags. The smell emanating from the food and other perishable items is nondescript; your nose tells you things are decaying, but not precisely what they are. When inhaled for long periods, it is nauseating. The joy of serendipity in looking at these items is overlaid with the constant sensory stimulus of organic matter past its prime. The message the smell sends is simple: the workings of time on these ephemeral items cannot be stopped or slowed. They can only be contained.

After many hours of viewing and smelling the perishable items, the archives team offered to show me one final *Time Capsule*. *Time Capsule* 522 is a doozy, and a favorite among the team. It is loaded with auratic objects; the finding aid lists some of them as "drawings by Keith Haring and Jean-Michel Basquiat, a hand painted turtleneck by Kenny Scharf, and a Tyvek suit on which Basquiat has written in green oil stick." The *Time Capsule* also includes a copy of Basquiat's birth certificate and copies of Warhol's parents' marriage certificate and their naturalization papers. The box holds an invitation to the second inauguration of Ronald Reagan as president of the United States and invitations to exhibitions by Basquiat and Haring. It also contained a chocolate coin and a bottle of Guerlain eau de cologne (now stored separately). *Time Capsule* 522 is a box with high exhibition value, but it was in viewing two photographs from the box with the smell of rotting food in my nose and on my palate that I came to understand how Warhol had used the cardboard box to occasion a reflection on his life as one made excessive through the presence of intimacy and death.

Among the objects housed in *Time Capsule* 522 are two black-and-white photographs of a young man taking a shower. In the first photograph, he looks out at us, into the camera from behind the plain shower curtain. A light smile is on his face, and his mouth is partly open. Soap bubbles sit in his dark hair. His left arm is raised; his right hand rubs soap around his left armpit. His body throws a shadow on the white tiles of the shower. There is an unguarded, happy look on his face. In the second photograph, the smiling face is obscured by a towel—the man is out of the shower now. Standing just on the other side of a doorway, he dries himself. His erect penis points downward toward a toilet. In the room where he stands, there is a large painting on the wall—a portrait of Alphanso Panell from Warhol's *Ladies and Gentleman* series (1975).[93] In the foreground, in the room where the photographer stands, a shelf that holds roughly folded towels frames the doorway. Together the two photographs almost form a sequence: the man washes and dries himself, and the narrative possibilities of what comes before, or after, this moment spin off in myriad directions.[94]

Like the book that bears the obliterated dedication to Jed Johnson, these two photographs puncture the tangential, nonsensical experience of rummaging in the cardboard box. On the one hand they are snapshots—one of the hundreds, if not thousands, of pictures of male nudity Warhol took, but rarely exhibited, over his lifetime.[95] But the precision of the framing and the exquisiteness of the timing of both photographs also belie the visual acuity that made Andrew Warhola Andy Warhol. It renders intimacy momentarily freed of ambivalence. The photographs evoke sexuality as a merging of the sensual and the visual. They record a moment in time—who knows precisely when—and their presence in the *Time Capsules* is, to me, a powerful indication of how the *Time Capsules* offer a glimpse into the *zoē* of Andy Warhol: the being of Andy Warhol in this moment. To have the camera ready to record something as simple as Jean-Michel Basquiat having a shower.[96]

But to view these two photographs with the smell of rotting food lingering in your nostrils is to view Basquiat in the prime of his life through the knowledge of his death. *Time Capsule* 522 includes Basquiat's birth certificate and numerous personal items relating to Basquiat and Warhol's friendship, including two portraits of Warhol drawn by Basquiat (one titled *Andy Sleeping*) and name cards from one of the many dinners the two attended.[97] Warhol died eighteen months before Basquiat, who suffered a heroin overdose at age twenty-seven in 1988. *Time Capsule* 522 is a memorial assembled while Basquiat was still living, albeit living in such a way that made many people who knew him fear for his life. The rotting food and degrading organic materials register the ephemeral nature of Warhol and Basquiat's friendship, and viewing these photographs more than thirty years after the men's deaths, the images and the smell together evoke the brevity and fullness of their shared lived experience. Warhol's relationships with men like Jean-Michel Basquiat and Jed Johnson were one, important, element of his life. The sensations—the ephemerality of being with them—is transposed through the open-ended material affordances of the cardboard box.

The insight offered by the *Time Capsules* into the life—the *zoē*—of Andy Warhol becomes tangible when one looks at items such as these. How was the "quick, vital" "simple act of living common to all beings" experienced by Andy Warhol?[98] Well, sometimes it meant that you stood ready with your camera to render your friend, your fellow artist, in his liveness. In the case of his friendship with Basquiat, this joy in looking and rendering goes both ways, as Basquiat's sketches in *Time Capsule* 522 and works such as *Photographer (Jean-Michel Basquiat being photographed by Andy Warhol)* (1983) attest. It also meant that the joy of that mutual seeing was underpinned by a recognition of the ephemeral nature of your relationship, and of your lives.

Conclusion: The Cardboard Box Is the Holder of Intimacy

The reference to the *Time Capsules* in *The Philosophy of Andy Warhol* that opened this chapter is, in many ways, a classic Warholian statement. Using the hook of an anecdote about a celebrity, Warhol narrates the practice of making the *Time Capsules* as a solution to a problem. The contradiction—"I want to throw things right out . . . I really do want to save things"—gives expression to ambivalence; about objects, about being the recipient of gifts, about time, about death. The *Time Capsules* suggest that Warhol lived a life of the potlatch, constantly receiving things from friends and collaborators, fans, organizations, people seeking his attention. The *Time Capsules* are an inventive solution to the very material problem of too much stuff created by too many connections.

For Flatley, Warhol's collecting (including the *Time Capsules*) is "a practice for creating a space of commonality shared by all the objects in the collection, constantly changed by the relations of resemblance they participate in."[99] The act of collecting all these things together in cardboard boxes brings them into a relation and invites the collector, and a viewer of the collection, "to relate to the everyday world of objects in terms of their similarities and correspondences."[100] As the line I have traced through the *Time Capsules* shows, they were also a way for Warhol to register the sensations of intimacy that were a vital part of his lived experience. The cardboard box is a place to put things that can't be thrown out, but which are not regularly used or suitable for display. The messy elements of attachment, the material excess it creates, can be housed and stored in "same-size brown cardboard boxes." Warhol's use of the cardboard box in the work emphasizes that as a form of mediation, they are a great leveler: they do not elevate their contents, and the way objects are placed in them gives no indication of their relation, or their meaning.[101] All we know is that they have been kept.

The interpretation of the *Time Capsules* that has emerged from playing them—as a game or instrument—establishes the cardboard box as a unique medium for the making of autobiography. I have shown how the material traces of intimacy are held together by the fiberboard cartons of the *Time Capsules*, and how the boxes themselves stage the drama of the duration of relationality through their affordances and their susceptibility to creep. In the five days I spent looking at the work, dozens of other lines of interpretation suggested themselves as I was allowed to rummage by proxy through Andy Warhol's stuff, and as I shared in and benefited from the extraordinary knowledge and generosity of the archival team. I have chosen to record the trace of intimacy's materiality here because I think it suggests something important about the cardboard box as a medium of self-life-inscription.[102] We keep things in boxes because they materialize our ties to other people. In its design the cardboard box invites us to hold on to our connection to others, without the requirement that we organize the feelings associated with those ties into narrative.

But the keeping also becomes an opportunity for some future rummager, or player, to explore the vibrant materiality of the cardboard box. The potential for the material that is kept to be found, played, handled, and in so being to forge some new relation is the greater potential of the transposition offered by the cardboard box. Koestenbaum's reading of Warhol's transposition of the ephemeral sociality of conversation into *a: a novel* leads him to conclude that transposition results in death and embalming, producing a "novel [that] communicates the tragic gap . . . between a living act and its transcription on the dead page."[103] Unlike the novel, the cardboard box is a means of storing, but not storying, lived experience. Our own cardboard boxes, like the *Time Capsules*, are a means of forming and re-forming sensual assemblages and opportunities for others to come into contact with the material trace of our lives. The cardboard box is a medium of inscription that stores the latent potential of the ephemeral objects that populate our lives for others to encounter at some future moment.

2

Cameras

There is a body of work in media studies that tracks how the democratization of access to the technologies of media making and distribution is reshaping the role of media in social and political life. *Stories of the Self* is concerned, specifically, with the role of media in how we think about what a life is and how it might be lived. I am proposing that we approach autobiographers not as writers of stories that are mediated in one form or another but as subjects formed and re-formed with media technologies. Sarah Kember and Joanna Zylinska argue that this is our common reality: that media forms are "not just a series of objects (computer, iPad) or broadcasting practice (TV, radio, the Internet), but . . . dynamic processes of emergence in time."[1] Understanding mediation requires that we understand "our coemergence *with* media,"[2] not how we use specific devices or platforms. In this chapter, I consider our coemergence with media by thinking about the media apparatus as an active agent in the emergence of life.[3] I consider a specific genre of personal documentary as an example of how media technologies create specific opportunities not just for reflecting on lived experience but for living in its own right. What happens when we live with the camera? And what ways of being does the camera help bring about?

Of course this question is very general, and so it must be narrowed down to give us a better opportunity of understanding specific instances of coemergence between life and media. Given the centrality of identity to relationality, outlined in the introduction, I have chosen two documentaries in which the autobiographer goes in search of the truth of identity. In the narratives of these films, the autobiographer plays the role of a detective in search of a truth. The camera frames and documents the search. In *Stories We Tell*, making a film allows the filmmaker to ask difficult questions about her paternity and to assert control over the story of her conception and its meaning.[4] In *Catfish*, making a documentary about online dating turns into a mystery about identity that must be solved.[5] In both texts, life, the possible significance it might have, and the autobiographer's agency emerge through a relation with the material possibilities of the camera apparatus.

I am thinking here of the cinema apparatus theorized in film theory and more specifically about media technologies as apparatuses in the sense developed by Karen Barad—as "open-ended practices" that have an agential role in determining the outcome of a moment of observation.[6] In Barad's formulation, apparatuses are not deterministic, but introduce specific capacities and possibilities into a given instance of relationality. This potential is not unbounded; an apparatus also forecloses certain kinds of interactions and possible outcomes. The relational scene of observation is inherently indeterminate, which means the outcomes of a given relation are not predetermined. Thus, thinking about the apparatus in a Baradian sense is not a return to technological determinist ways of thinking about media and culture. Rather, apparatuses are active contributors to a given scene of relation and to the significance or meanings assigned to its outcome.[7] What might this mean for our thinking about the role of media in shaping ideas about what a life is?

Autobiography as Observation

Thinking about the role of the camera in the search for truth, in this chapter I am reading autobiography as a materialization of an assemblage.[8] Approached this way, self-life-inscription is a set of actions that occur in a situation where humans, nonhumans, machines, objects, and matter are interacting. Thinking about autobiography this way raises the possibility that autobiographical texts demonstrate that we are both the inscribers and the inscribed: that mediation and materiality are the resources on which we draw when thinking about what our lives are, and the dynamic context in which the living itself happens. We do not have complete control in this scene; we initiate actions but also respond to the unique characteristics of people, texts, and things around us.[9] Therefore, autobiography emerges out of the "relations of force, connection, resonance and patterning" of the assemblage,[10] rather than being a mediated space where identity is represented or signified.

In thinking this way, I run the risk of bringing a concept (assemblage) that has been influential in dislodging the subject as the locus of analysis in cultural and social studies[11] to bear on a cultural practice that is largely understood as being *all about* the subject (autobiography). But, as Barad has argued, recognizing the active agency of materiality in constituting the world and its meaning involves acknowledging the primary coconstitution of the "'observed object' and 'agencies of observation.'"[12] While we have become accustomed to thinking of identity and sociality as relational—that we become who we are through our interactions with other people—Barad asks us to extend this perception to the material world itself: "'We' are not outside observers of the world. Neither are we simply located at particular places *in* the world; rather, we are part *of* the world in its ongoing intra-activity."[13] That is, we are part of the ongoing emergence of the world, of life (*zoē*), its possibility and potential significance: the scene of our coemergence with media is one in which the human is but one of many active, material forces. For Barad, the human subject is just one of several actants that make up the scene where the doing defines what *is* (including what is human), rather than an agent possessing or assuming definitional power by narrating the doing after the fact.[14]

While approaches to autobiography have long emphasized that the meaning of a life is produced through the act of self-narration (rather than preexisting it), Barad asks us to think more precisely about how an autobiography is made, and to think about the text as something other than an end product of a process that we can ignore or bracket. Rather, we need to consider the conditions under which the text becomes materially possible: turn our attention to "practices, doings, and actions" rather than representations.[15] This shift in attention can help us understand the role of media in shaping lives and how they matter. It asks for a different reading strategy, one that considers the assemblage in which the text was formed—reading backward from the final product to the conditions of its emergence—and to think of that assemblage as agential, rather than willed and managed by the autobiographer. Let me demonstrate this point with an example from Alison Bechdel's widely celebrated autobiographical comic, *Fun Home: A Family Tragicomic*, a double-helix narrative that reconstructs Bechdel's father's closeted homosexuality in order to figure the queer relation between father and daughter. Like the documentaries I consider here, the plot of *Fun Home* treats identity (in this case gender and sexual identity) as a truth about Bruce and Alison that can be tracked down and understood.

Alison Bechdel describes the process of piecing together the truth of her father's "hidden life" depicted in *Fun Home* as involving "pretty standard detective work."[16] *Fun Home* exemplifies the power of the co-emergence of a life and media—Bechdel's painstaking labor in research-ing and composing the text occurs in an assemblage characterized by specific media forms and their material properties and affordances.[17] When Bechdel becomes an autobiographer, she becomes entwined with a variety of media materialities, such as the light box on which she spends hours tracing images, the computer and its drawing programs that she uses to assemble the pages of the comic, the notebooks that hold her childhood diaries, and the original prints of family photographs. Self-life-inscription is a conscious engagement with the media and ma-teriality in which her living takes place. In Bechdel's case, she narrates her emergence as an autobiographer as occurring in response to the pos-sibility presented by a media object: a photographic print of her father's lover discovered after his death. Bechdel describes *Fun Home* as being "spawned" by this photograph.[18] She is drawn into an assemblage with it and goes to work seeking a truth about her father's lived experience that can explain its existence. The text of *Fun Home* emerges out of the rich scene of possibility of that specific assemblage: Bechdel's discovery of the media object of the photograph. Indeed, this specific meeting between artist and object is a key reason why the finished product of *Fun Home* enchants us: the book carries a fidelity to the assemblage that spawned it through the complex depiction of the generative, sustaining assemblage of humans, media, and the material environment in the family home. The narrative—filled with instances of reading, acting, playing instru-ments, and drawing—is underscored by Bechdel's complex and precise remediation of media forms into comics and the book object.

We see the importance of the coemergence of media, matter, and life exemplified in Bechdel's famous redrawing of the photograph of her fa-ther's lover as a double-page spread at the center of the book. As many critics have noted, this image includes two hands that hold the photo-graph, an image that is framed by the book and the reader's own hands as they hold the page.[19] *Zoë*, "the simple fact of living common to all living beings,"[20] in Bechdel's text is sexuality and desire—Bruce Bechdel's sexuality and desire inscribed in the photograph, Alison Bechdel's drive to understand her father and herself through its remediation. *Fun Home* demonstrates that life, as well as the meanings we may attach to it or the significance that might adhere to experience, is not distinct from the media forms and objects with which it is entangled. Rather, it is found in the process of the intra-action between the specific media apparatuses Bechdel and her family have been entangled with as they live and observe their lives, including the materials used to make and circulate *Fun Home*.[21] The Bechdel family is persistently engaged with media and matter: the camera that produces the photograph of her father's lover; the books constantly handled and shared between Alison and Bruce; the childhood diary in which Alison records the date of her father's arrest; the embodied practice of learning lines and movements and the sewing of costumes that constitute Bechdel's mother as an actress; the letters that travel between Alison's parents during their courtship, and between her and them when she goes away to college, to mention just some of the many media forms and practices presented in the narrative.[22]

A materialist reading of assemblage in autobiography does not produce a determinist account of the autobiographical process where the end product (the autobiographical text) is thought of as a result of the affordances and capacities of the apparatuses used to make it. Nor is it a continuation of the idea that the text mediates between the reality of lived experience, the autobiographer, and the reader (as discussed in the introduction), or that autobiographies are representations of identity. A key component of Barad's theory of materiality is that "apparatuses play . . . a crucial, indeed constitutive, role in the production of phenomena" at the material, rather than the representational level.[23] Combining a quantum perspective with feminist philosophy, notably Judith Butler's theory of performativity and Donna Haraway's critique of objectivity, Barad has developed a new framework for considering the active role that matter plays in the world and in discursive formations. "The relationship between the material and the discursive is one of mutual entailment. Neither is articulated/articulable in the absence of the other; matter and meaning are mutually articulated."[24] What makes Barad's theory particularly relevant for thinking about self-life-inscription is the centrality of the apparatus in constituting the moment in which elements are brought into relation and the dynamic role it plays in shaping the meanings that emerge from that relation.[25] Alongside the physics experiments that ground Barad's argument, autobiography is a great example of the introduction of an apparatus into a scene in the search for knowledge, significance, and meaning.

The Scenes of Observation

Many autobiographers tell stories based on the premise that the truth is *out there*—a discoverable fact that must be located and accounted for. This search for the truth takes place in the context of a genuine lack of knowledge about a fact or gaps in a narrative that reduce its explanatory power. For Sarah Polley in *Stories We Tell* the question relates to genetic identity: Who is my father? For Nev Schulman in *Catfish* it is more complicated: Who am I falling in love with?[26] These autobiographers have something in common with the physicists described by Barad in *Meeting the Universe Halfway*; they draw on media apparatus in order to aid their quest for understanding.[27]

In *Meeting the Universe Halfway*, Barad tells us that physics is the study of matter and motion, and a primary interest for physicists has been to understand light. Over the course of many experiments and calculations in the early twentieth century, physicists discovered that light behaves differently depending on the apparatus scientists use to observe it: light exhibits "wavelike behavior" when observed one way, and particle-like behavior when observed in another way. Yet any attempt to see the wavelike and particle-like behavior simultaneously is impossible, a problem referred to in physics as the "wave-particle duality paradox."[28] In Barad's account of his work, physicist Niels Bohr explains this behavior by positing that light's properties are produced by the engagement between light and the apparatus used to conduct the measurement. There is no objectively stable characteristic of light (wave or particle) that exists before the attempt to measure it. Light has specific capacities that can be observed through specific engagements with it—thus each process of observation, each instance of the interaction between the apparatus and the materiality of light produces "local material resolutions to the inherent ontological indeterminacy" of light.[29] Crucially, this insight is not a continuation of the relativism sometimes associated with constructivism—that we see only what we want, or are able, to see. For Bohr, the interaction between light and the apparatuses used to observe it produces objective knowledge about the dynamic agency of light. Indeed, that light can behave like both waves and particles *is* profound knowledge that can be verified through repeated experimentation. The knowledge we gain is of light's radical indeterminacy, dynamism, and agency, rather than some understanding of its fixed properties. This knowledge includes knowing that the behavior of light emerges in our attempts to observe it. Barad's connection of Bohr's insights to social theory leads me to ask: Might living act something like light? Does the meaning of lived experience emerge when living intersects with attempts to observe it? And might the different apparatuses we use to observe living—cameras, postcards, cardboard boxes, chat boxes, and mobile phones—produce different insights into the diverse properties of life's dynamic agency?

In *Catfish* and *Stories We Tell*, as well as in *Fun Home* and countless other autobiographies, an autobiographer goes in search of a truth about something in their life. They initiate a process in which they seek an explanation: they set in motion a "local material resolution to the indeterminacy" regarding some element of their lived experience, or the lived experience of someone close to them. At the level of narrative, in this type of documentary autobiography, the autobiographer plays the role of detective: they introduce the camera as an apparatus that will assist them in their search for certainty.[30] Both films offer compelling examples of how a media apparatus (the moving image camera) participates in an assemblage in which media, matter, and humans interact and generate a possible result in the scene of observation. I will begin by considering how specific properties of the camera contribute to the narrative form adopted in both films. In the conclusion to the chapter, I will consider the larger ethical questions that result from the attempt to find the truth about identity they enact.

Observation of the Truth

The importance of the apparatus of the camera in shaping a narrative logic that revolves around detection and cases is evident in *Catfish* and *Stories We Tell* in three ways: (1) in the presence of the camera in the diegesis; (2) in the presentation of the autobiographical subject as a detective working on a "case"; and (3) in the failure of the autobiography and the detection narrative to provide the autobiographer with an adequate framework in which to respond to the complex ethical terrain that is revealed when the solution to the case brings them to the borderland of the assemblage that enables the film. While the detective-autobiographer seeks the truth of identity, the case is solved by the revelation that the truth they seek is shared, relational, and emergent. In each case the scene of observation opens onto another assemblage and to more indeterminacy, in which the autobiographer is no longer a central figure but an agent in a new assemblage centered around another scene. Let me begin with the first two points.

In *Stories We Tell* and *Catfish*, the autobiographer begins with a belief that the truth of experience is "out there" and the cinematic apparatus—the camera and technologies of sound recording—is chosen because of the indexical relationship with historical reality that is assumed to inhere in the medium.[31] Thinking with Barad's argument that apparatuses performatively enact concepts, we might say that the media chosen by the autobiographer shapes not only what form the autobiography will take (a film or, more precisely, a documentary) but also the epistemology and metaphysics of the process itself.[32] We see this insight, too, in documentary studies. As Bill Nichols argued in *Representing Reality*, the use of the camera to record "real life" (rather than staged, fictional events) in documentary reinforces the indexical relationship between what is recorded and historical reality in documentary film.[33] Documentary studies has been concerned with theorizing and understanding the relationship between the camera as an apparatus of seeing and recording associated with scientific forms of knowledge production, as well as an apparatus with poetic and aesthetic affordances.[34]

This connection between the camera and epistemology is a factor in the assemblage from which an autobiographical documentary emerges. In Barad's terms, the apparatus of the camera is a materialization of the discourse that posits truth as existing in the world and having properties that can be objectively documented. The camera is an apparatus that can record the stable properties of the world because it is located in the same physical and temporal location as the activity it records. For a camera to record something, it must be physically present at the scene. The makers of personal documentary take up the camera because of its assumed ability to record an indexical image from reality as it unfolds in front of the apparatus. This primary affordance of the camera—the way it materializes a discourse of truth seeking through physical copresence and simultaneous recording—empowers those who hold the camera to become truth seekers. We see this at the level of the narrative, where the filmmaker uses the presence of the camera to ask people to speak the truth (discussed further later). It also structures the scene of observation as one in which a particular kind of truth will emerge, one that can be captured by the audiovisual technology of the camera: one rendered visible through the bodily responses and expressions of the subjects filmed, the environments (interiors, public spaces, streetscapes) in which scenes are located, and which produce sound frequencies that can be captured by the recording apparatuses that accompany the camera in the scene (whether that be an in-built microphone or a separate sound recording system using boom microphones that is synchronized with the moving image footage in postproduction). The choice of media designates more than the specific technology of inscription that is used to produce a text. The *graph* is a materialization of specific ontologies, metaphysics, and epistemologies: in the case of the camera, the truth will come via matter that can be inscribed as something that can be seen and heard (rather than, say, what can be smelled, tasted, felt on the skin or through the body, or perceived in three-dimensional space).

Taking up an apparatus that inscribes by being physically copresent with a scene enables the autobiographer-filmmaker to move into scenes in the service of the device itself: they take the camera places and interact with spaces, people, and objects *in the service* of the camera's need for copresence. As we shall see, the agency of the camera merges with the agency of the autobiographer to produce the role of investigator.

But first I want to pause to reinforce the importance of reading (and therefore thinking) aesthetics and epistemology together. We risk a great deal if we sideline the question of the importance of aesthetic choices and dynamics in acts of self-life-inscription to focus solely on what kinds of knowledge claims autobiographies make. In the case of autobiographical documentary, we must consider how the power of the camera to generate an indexical and seemingly authentic representation of reality is always buttressed by "larger textual effects" such as narrative, editing, tone, and style.[35] But also, as I explore later, we must consider how the camera itself suggests narrative possibilities (and fore-closes others) in scenes in which it is introduced. The camera might be a materialization of the discourse of a specific kind of truth, but it is not solely responsible for enabling the autobiographer to act as a truth seeker. Narrative structures, commentary, editing, and visual style em-phasize and reinforce the power of the camera and its agency as a tool of observation. This in turn is reinforced again by the marketing and critical responses to the documentary, where the logic of truth seeking is largely reiterated, or may be subject to challenge—as was the case with *Catfish*. Thinking about the documentary as an assemblage requires that we read production, reception, and distribution differently and as con-nected: that the decision to make a film (rather than a blog, a memoir, a comic, or some other autobiographical text) not be treated as incidental (if it is treated at all), and that we consider how the film—once made and distributed—creates new assemblages where meaning is produced. Therefore, we have to begin by considering how introducing the camera into a situation structures the scene in particular ways. What narrative possibilities, what ways of being, what forms of agency are possible once the camera designates the scene as under observation? And what forms of agency or ways of being are foreclosed? The question becomes: How do these processes of production, and our reception of them, material-ize the paradigm that the truth of identity is a fixed reality that can be located through the application of the appropriate tools? What oppor-tunities for understanding relationality are possible in such a scene, and which are foreclosed or cannot be registered by the specific apparatus in use? I will demonstrate how we might read one kind of autobiographi-cal documentary in order to answer these questions by describing the camera as a means of forming a case.

The Case

The process of observation—in which an apparatus is introduced into a scene in order to determine what is happening—is material and dis-cursive. Indeed, Barad insists that our ability to understand discourse as a process of materialization must be more attentive to the active role of matter in the scene of observation. What does this mean exactly? Unlike the physicists whose use of instruments is motivated by the pursuit of understanding a world believed to be beyond the human subject's capacity for observation (light, energy), autobiography is a cultural practice that generally pursues understanding of human lived experience. All autobiography has some relationship to objectively verifiable facts: dates, paternity and maternity, real names, places, and events.[36] When an autobiography takes the search for these facts as its modus operandi, it becomes grounded in the epistemological practice of what John Forrester calls "thinking in cases."[37]

Thinking and reasoning in cases is a specific means of producing knowledge and meaning about an event. At the core of this practice is the evaluative process of judgment. The practice of thinking in cases is "a means of judging,"[38] rather than a judgment—a process of doing, not of representation. As Lauren Berlant puts it, "The case is always pedagogical, itself an agent,"[39] rather than an empty, convenient form through which to approach an event or scene. In the example of the documentaries I am considering, the event has two components: one is the assumption that identity is something static, grounded by immutable facts such as name and genetic material, and is a concept that can be materialized in the apparatus of the camera. The case is a site of agency that enables the search for and evaluation of evidence in support of the search for that truth. Berlant argues that the case is neither merely "out there" waiting to be solved nor simply a matter of arranging what one finds—retrospectively—into the form (or narrative) of the case in order to present what one has found. To make a case is to make a specific environment in which judgment can occur. Cases create a scene of observation that will facilitate judgment. The knowledge made by case logic differs from knowledge made by other means because, as Forrester elucidates, thinking in cases is uniquely attuned to the problem of how knowledge of the individual (the specific event in the case) might relate to knowledge of the world more broadly; how it might function as an exemplar.[40]

In personal documentaries that seek a truth that is assumed to preexist the making of the film, the process of thinking in cases is initiated when the camera is taken up as the apparatus for an autobiographical project. We see the residue of that logic in the finished product, but we must also consider how the decisions and processes that precede the completed text shape the life that emerges alongside the making of the text. This means our reading must recognize that the narrative choice to present the search for identity as "a case" and the autobiographer as a detective does not indicate the point at which the association between the camera and discourses of science are disrupted by fictional narrative techniques. Rather, approaching identity through the narrative frame of the case is enabled and reinforced by "the camera's status as a scientific instrument" and its use in designating scenes of observation, some of which appear in the film that is screened.[41]

Unlike other examples of case logic, both the films I am considering here offer us a means of thinking about the process of their production because they use a self-reflexive style. In *Catfish*, the filming is simultaneous to the action, while in *Stories We Tell*, Polley mixes archival footage from home movies (shot by her father) and staged images of the past to reconstruct elements of family history. This self-reflexivity about the documentary process invites a reading of the apparatus while also, at times, covering over deeper investments in autobiographical agency as emerging in an assemblage with the camera that materializes a search for the immutable truth of identity.

Observational Assemblages in *Catfish* and *Stories We Tell*

Released in 2010, and the foundation of a subsequent reality TV program made for MTV, *Catfish* tells the story of Yaniv (Nev) Schulman, who at the time of filming is twenty-four years old. Nev, his brother Ariel (Rel), and friend Henry Joost share an office in New York City where they work as photographers and filmmakers who document the performing arts. Cameras are everyday objects for the filmmakers, as well as tools of their trade. The opening credits of the film foreground the materiality of the digital image: the screen is filled with pixels, which slowly scroll past the eye, producing color fields that make up a larger image that is never revealed to the viewer. The role of the pixel as the material ground for digital forms is foregrounded and juxtaposed with a direct and open exchange between filmmaker (Rel) and subject (Nev) in the opening of the film, which is presented as free from the interference associated with digital mediation.

This scene also frames the documentary as being enabled by Nev and Rel's brotherly relationship—as occurring within their preexisting relationality and its specific tenors, habits, and possibilities. It is structured by a recognizable form of intimacy and antagonism between the two, which is rendered in dialogue and Nev's facial expressions. The opening line of the documentary is delivered by Nev, to someone who sits behind the camera filming him. In what follows, I remediate this exchange into prose:

"You know if this is your documentary, you're doing a really bad job," Nev pronounces.

"Why?" asks the voice off camera.

"Because you just keep catching me when I don't want to talk about things."

The person behind the camera asks how the documentary should be made, and Nev advocates a move away from the observational approach:

"Set it up. Organize a time with me. Put together some materials, e-mails, we'll get the Facebook conversations printed out, and we'll really talk about it."

"But do you want to be the subject of this documentary or not?" asks the presence behind the camera while Nev takes a bite of his lunch.

"No, I don't," Nev laughs in disbelief, as though he has said this before. "It's about Abby," he explains.

"Well do you want to be the co-subject?" asks the filmmaker.

"No. I don't see why . . . I don't think I'm that interesting."

"I am making a documentary about Abby through you, can you understand that?"

Nev concedes the point with a begrudging nod. "I understand, I'm just saying," he rolls his eyes.

In this opening dialogue, Nev's discomfort with the dynamic agency of the camera is registered: when it observes him, he appears as the subject of the documentary (like light acting as a wave in response to the wave-observation apparatus). His desire to be interviewed in a more formal arrangement indicates his preference for being consulted as an expert—the much maligned "talking head" of documentary—in a film *about* someone else. The brothers negotiate the scene of observation as it unfolds, concluding with Nev's grudging acquiescence to Rel's suggestion that Nev himself is an apparatus of observation ("I am making a documentary about Abby *through you*"). But this tentative compromise is quickly undermined by the establishing montage that follows their exchange, where Nev is repositioned as a subject of the film. This conversation dramatizes a material question: Can Nev act as anything *but* the subject of the documentary when the camera is pointed toward him?

In scenes such as this and in its plot, *Catfish* dramatizes how intimacy and relationality are materialized through a variety of media forms. The plot hinges on a series of events that are motivated by the exchange of media objects in the service of friendship and romance, while the film itself emerges out of the kinship and friendship of the filmmakers and extends their identities as media makers (Nev, a photographer, Rel and Henry are filmmakers). The montage that reestablishes Nev as a subject of the film tells us that the plot begins with Nev receiving a painting from a stranger in the mail. The painting is a remediation of one of his photographs that had been published in the *New York Sun*. Nev is touched by the response to his work and becomes intrigued and enthusiastic when he discovers that the painter is Abby, an eight-year-old girl who lives in the town of Ishpeming, Michigan. Nev and Abby strike up what Nev describes later in the film as "an extraordinary correspondence"; Nev e-mails Abby more of his photographs, which become source material for her paintings. More and more paintings arrive in the mail, and Rel and Henry "document Nev and Abby's friendship." As the narrative progresses, we follow Nev as he becomes friends with Abby's mother, Angela, and other members of the family on Facebook. Nev is filmed talking with Angela on the phone and excitedly rereading e-mails he has received from Abby.[42] Soon another family member joins the mediated scene: Abby's nineteen-year-old sister, Megan, writes to Nev to thank him for being so kind to her sister. A flirtation between Megan and Nev begins, and soon Nev is speaking on the phone to Megan and trading texts and e-mails with her. Nev is in the throes of a crush—which registers in his body language, blushing, and smiling—and he begins to speak openly to Rel and Henry (and the camera) about the possibility of a romantic relationship with Megan.

Throughout the first act of the narrative, *Catfish* consists of observational and interactive footage of Nev. He is the central character and narrator—the camera is an inscription device that records his regular updates on the things he has learned about Abby and her family. The audience for these updates is the apparatus itself, Rel and Henry, and the audience of the documentary. In this first act, the apparatus of sound and image recording are not visible in the frame. Henry and Rel are not visibly present either, but they are occasionally heard off camera asking Nev a question, laughing at his jokes, or confirming that Abby and her family do indeed seem extraordinary. Henry and Rel and the apparatus of observation are all positioned outside the scene of observation as constituting, invisible presences.

A dramatic change in the narrative and visual style of the film comes when Nev, Rel, and Henry travel to Colorado to work as filmmakers and photographers at the Vail International Dance Festival. Nev sees the trip as an opportunity to meet Megan and her family in person and tries to arrange an appointment with them. This brief second act brings about the change in the direction and purpose of the film. A key scene marks the shift in the nature of the assemblage made up of Rel, Henry, Nev, the camera, mobile technology (Nev's iPhone), e-mail and instant chat, and Abby's family. In a hotel room in Vail, the three young men sit around a small table while Nev chats online with Megan through a laptop computer. Megan—who has described herself as a singer and dancer, who also works with animals—sends Nev a sound file of her singing a song for him "on the spot." In a rapid transition from trusting enjoyment to suspicion, Nev, Henry, and Rel (all three now visible on screen) discover that the file is a fake: it is not Megan singing but a sound file extracted from a YouTube video of another woman's performance. With this revelation, the narrative takes up the discourse and narratology of detection: Nev is shocked and visibly hurt; Rel and Henry's interest is heightened. A rapid reassessment of the situation and renegotiation of the purpose of the documentary unfolds, and the three agree that Nev deserves to know "the truth" and that they will continue to engage with the family and try to discover who it is Nev has been talking to. Nev, Henry, and Rel become detectives: seeking the identity of the people, or person, Nev has spent the last eight months getting to know. The third act, to which I shall return, follows the three men as they go to Megan's house, and then Abby and Angela's hometown, in search of answers.

Unlike *Catfish*, where the majority of the plot and the filming of the documentary occur simultaneously, *Stories We Tell* presents a retrospective narrative of Sarah Polley's discovery that the man she was raised to think of as her father is not her biological father. The film quickly establishes that the genetic identity of Sarah Polley, youngest child of Michael and Diane Polley, had, from her late teens, been the object of playful speculation among her father and siblings. Diane Polley died of cancer when Sarah was eleven years old, and Sarah was the only one of the children living at home when Diane died. As members of the family recount it in the film, Sarah's siblings and father would jokingly comment that "Sarah looked nothing like her father." In *Stories We Tell* Sarah Polley assembles her family, and friends of her mother, to tell their version of how the questions about Sarah's parentage emerged, the speculative answers that they developed, and their assessment of the aftermath of the revelation that Sarah was indeed the result of her mother's affair with film producer Harry Gulkin.

Catfish moves to a self-reflective mode in which the cinematic apparatus appears on screen after it is revealed that there is identity fraud at the center of the romantic story between Nev and Megan. *Stories We Tell*, however, explicitly establishes the importance of cameras and sound recording to the narrative in its opening. A more self-consciously professional aesthetic project than *Catfish*, *Stories We Tell* begins by establishing storytelling as a retrospective activity through a montage of archival footage in its opening sequence. This footage is grainy and marked by an unevenness in the visual field and in shot construction that connotes the use of a handheld film camera. This montage is accompanied by a voice-over of Michael Polley reading an excerpt from Margaret Atwood's novel *Alias Grace* that reflects on narrative as a retrospective act: "When you're in the middle of a story, it isn't a story at all. But only a confusion, a dark roaring, a blindness." The confusing violence of experience, Michael continues, is "a wreckage of shattered glass and splintered wood" that only gains form through the act of "telling it" as a story "to yourself or to someone else." With this self-reflexive opening, the documentary comments on the performative role of narrative in making sense of experience. This truth-making power of narrative is anchored by the truth of identity, which is established in the second self-reflexive sequence in the opening of the film.

The second sequence involves Michael, again in voice-over, reading from a letter he wrote to Sarah:

> I am unique. From that precise moment when I was dragged out of my mother's womb into this cold world I was complete. An amalgam of the DNA passed on to me by my mother and father. And they too had been born finished products, with their DNA handed down by their respective parents and so on back *ad infinitum*. It is clear to me that I was always there, somewhere in my ancestor's DNA just waiting to be born. So this unique "I" has always existed in the mystery of nothingness. So, where to start . . .

In these twin self-reflective scenes, Polley marks out narrative as an explicitly retrospective practice that reworks the calamity of lived experience, which is akin to "a boat crushed by the icebergs or swept over the rapids and all aboard are powerless to stop it." It is the identity of those aboard the boat that is the constant: a "unique 'I' that has always existed" who enters the world "complete" in their genetic identity. The violent mess of living is experienced by individuals who are "finished products" the minute they board the boat of life by being born. *Stories We Tell* unfolds within these parameters, and the urgency and seriousness of the question of Sarah Polley's parentage gains traction through this framing. The documentary posits its core problem as one of narration: How can Sarah Polley tell the story of her lived experience if she does not know the genetic source of her "unique 'I' that has always existed"?

The certainty in the power of narrative and the fixity of identity are juxtaposed with a scene that hints at the importance of the camera as a materialization of the discourses of truth that underpin Polley's project. Following the opening sequence establishing the retrospective nature of narrative, a short scene unfolds in which Sarah and Michael Polley arrive at a recording studio where Michael will record the voice-over the audience has just heard. Michael's distinctive English accent immediately identifies him as the narrator who read the excerpt from Atwood's novel that started the film. As they prepare to begin the work of recording, Michael says to Sarah: "One day I hope you'll explain to me what it is you're hoping to achieve with all this." His question appears to be sparked by the presence of two cameras that are recording the session in the studio. Michael observes that this is "not how it's usually done"—implying that voice-over work is not commonly the object of visual observation. "I told you it's a documentary," Sarah responds. "It's an interrogation process we've set up." Michael says nothing in response. With this statement, Sarah introduces herself as detective and interrogator, and the mixing of detective and autobiographical narrative modes in the documentary is set in motion. More significantly, the importance of the camera as an apparatus that facilitates truth seeking (and the seeking of a specific kind of truth) is established.

This revelation of the camera's role in materializing a discourse of truth seeking (or interrogation) is reinforced as Michael's second monologue unfolds over a montage that intercuts footage of Sarah and Michael in the recording studio with footage of Polley's siblings preparing to be interviewed for the documentary, and black-and-white footage of a woman (later revealed to be Diane Polley) preparing for a screen test. We watch as various people look nervously at various cameras, arranging and preparing themselves for what is to come, as microphones, lights, and cameras are trained toward them. Like Nev's unease at being positioned as a subject of observation in the opening of *Catfish*, this montage underscores the power of the cinematic apparatus to unsettle people: the montage consists largely of nervous laughter, and images of people with discomfort lingering briefly in their eyes, making nervous jokes and wriggling. Under these conditions, Polley will ask her four siblings, her "Dad" Michael, and later in the film her biological father, Harry Gulkin, and her mother's friends "to tell the story of the whole thing" in their own words. Polley is the detective who seeks the truth of her identity by soliciting and gathering the accounts of those involved and those who witnessed events leading up to her conception. The role of the camera as the apparatus that enables this search is clear from the beginning.

Within this assemblage, *Stories We Tell* demonstrates how the apparatus splits the life into two phases. There is "Sarah," the subject of the mystery of genetic identity and Polley, the director-autobiographer-interviewer-detective. Polley's agency to ask the difficult questions about Sarah's identity coemerges from an assemblage with the camera. The camera's presence brings with it a discourse of the indexicality and objectivity that we see registered in the discomfort of the interview subjects in the earlier sequence. Just as Nev Schulman's agency moves from subject of observation to detective (observer) when he discovers that the song he was sent via e-mail was not an original recording but a sound file extracted from an existing online source, in *Stories We Tell* what a life is—and what living itself is—coemerges in an assemblage with the material affordances of the apparatus.

The Mutual Entanglement of Observer and Observed

I began this chapter by noting that taking up an apparatus of observation has a low barrier to participation in the twenty-first century. We might say that there has been a rapid increase in the accessibility of apparatuses with which we can coemerge. Unlike the physicists in Barad's account, who must laboriously construct the scenes of measurement and tinker with the apparatuses they use,[43] establishing a scene of observation of everyday life requires less time and ongoing resources than ever before. Looking around us, we see these scenes being initiated almost constantly: a photograph or short video recorded here, a description provided by text message to an absent interlocutor there, an overheard fragment of conversation reported on Twitter or Facebook, a closed-circuit camera recording the flow of foot traffic through a railway station. Given her consistent use of scientific situations to extrapolate how apparatuses materialize concepts, Barad's account only gets us so far in understanding this mundane proliferation of surveillance and self-life-inscription. Recent work on the racial biases of facial recognition technology and algorithms, and Wendy Hui Kyong Chun's study of new media and habit point to the myriad ways in which media studies can extend the recognition that our technologies are not tools of objectivity whose influence in developing findings about the world can be minimized or discounted.[44] Barad's insight that *"there is no unambiguous way to differentiate between the 'object' and 'the agencies of observation'"* asks us to think beyond representation, however, to the issue of how objects, humans, and technology intra-act within the scene of observation.[45] This, for Barad, requires a new understanding of life as inherently relational at the material as well as the psychological, emotional, social, and political level. The recognition that in the scene of observation "some things come to matter and others are excluded . . . possibilities are opened up and others are foreclosed" is inherently an ethical one.[46] If every moment of observation is one that includes the need to act ethically in regard to the relationality that we cannot escape, what does that mean for the autobiographer, and for us as audiences who engage with their work?

Spoiler alert: in *Catfish*, Abby and Megan are indeed too good to be true. Abby is in fact an eight-year-old girl, but she does not paint. Angela, her mother, does. But Angela is a lot of other things besides. She is the carer of her husband's seriously disabled twin sons, whose complex disabilities put enormous demands on the family and Angela's time. When Nev, Rel, and Henry finally arrive on Angela's doorstep ready to confront her about her ruse, they enter a scene in which Nev's crush and his feeling of having been lied to take on an entirely new meaning. When brought into relation with the everyday reality of Angela's life, Nev's emotions are no longer center stage. Knocking on the door of Angela's house armed with their camera in search of the truth, the detectives encounter a different formulation of "the simple fact of living common to all living beings."[47]

In its final act, *Catfish* establishes that Nev has been important to the doing of Angela's everyday life. Her relationship with him is part of what sustains her in the situation she is in and is a tool for managing her frustrated artistic ambitions in the context of her day-to-day living. Her entanglements with paint and paper, and with Nev's source images and his conversation, are a material practice of sustenance and flourishing. Nev quickly realizes that his photographs are his point of entry into *this* assemblage, which connects him to Angela's children, her house, her art, her marriage—and the camera observes him as he comes to terms with this entanglement.[48] Nev consents to sitting for a portrait, recommitting and perhaps finally accepting, his position in the assemblage of observer and observed. This time the tool of observation is Angela and her art materials, but the camera watches on of course, creating a double scene of observation in which the significance of the scene is refracted. At the narrative level, *Catfish* uses the case logic to draw a conclusion about relationality and living as a process, rather than identity. The apparatus of the camera ultimately does not materialize the static truth of identity but documents the complex materiality of *auto-bios-zoē*: of seeing and being seen, of the significance of life coemerging alongside the media through which the living happens. While criticized by some for appearing exploitative of Angela's situation,[49] *Catfish* enacts an ethics that reflects that "responsibility entails an ongoing responsiveness to the entanglements of self and other, here and there, now and then."[50] In this sense, while taking a completely different route in my analysis, I agree with Zara Dinnen's conclusion that "in *Catfish* . . . the precarity of the social script is . . . shown to be at risk or at stake."[51]

The final act of *Stories We Tell*, on the other hand, demonstrates the foreclosures introduced by the performative materiality of the apparatus, the way in which *"apparatuses are boundary-making practices"* that enable the materialization of some kinds of meaning while precluding others.[52] Toward the end of the film, Polley reveals that Harry Gulkin wrote a personal essay in which he detailed his affair with her mother, Diane, and his joy at discovering Sarah as a living reminder of that affair. Harry intends to publish the essay, but Sarah intervenes to prevent him from telling his story. Sarah threatens to cut ties with Harry if he publishes his version, and so he reluctantly retracts it. How are we to understand this refusal?

The coplacement of the camera and paper and pencil facilitates a shift in the epistemology and ontology of the scene in *Catfish*—what can be registered and how, and what that means for the significance of the scene—is altered when Angela's position in a different material and mediated environment is put alongside the filmmaker's investment in the apparatus of the camera. Harry's introduction of another form of observation (the writing of memory and feeling, the personal essay) and its attendant ontoepistemologies is framed as a threat to the truth seeking that has motivated Polley's documentary. There are some stories we cannot tell, it seems, and it is those that refuse the mediation of the camera. This generates a complex ethical moment that Sarah and Harry must negotiate because what is and what matters emerges out of their very attempt to observe, and by observing understand, their connection. This connection is an entanglement that exceeds and underscores the scene of observation Polley initiated. The film *Stories We Tell* is one outcome (using the camera apparatus) that produces a set of meanings associated with their relationality. Gulkin's essay—which the audience is told exists, but which they cannot access—produces another set of meanings through a scene of observation enacted using a different apparatus (the word processing software on his computer and the genre of the essay). The possibility of a discontinuity between these accounts does not threaten the validity of the truth either process might uncover; rather, it confirms that the meaning of their linked genetic identity emerges differently from different scenes of observation. Yet, this is not the weak pluralism of constructivism; instead, it confirms the dynamism of matter and the ethical responsibility that Barad contends attends to "the lively relationalities of becoming of which we are a part."[53]

The final act of both films sees the detective-autobiographer participate in the resolution of the scenes of observation and emerge into a new scene where the mystery of identity opens out onto another complicated, indeterminate scene involving other apparatuses. There is no denouement, in the strict sense, as the indeterminate, ongoingness of life (*zoē*) exceeds the structures of the case by leading into new scenes of connection, entanglement, materiality, and relationality. Sarah sits in Harry's apartment as he expresses his disappointment that his written version of events has been suppressed. Nev drives away from Angela's house in Ishpeming to return to New York and his collection of her paintings—and the film ends with him receiving in the mail the portrait she began during his visit. Objects emerge from the scene of observation with new meanings, and the documentary itself must be edited to tell a version of the transformation that was observed. In the final act, the audience, too, emerges from the narrative flow of the detective story—the accumulation of clues, the slow accretion of theories that can explain events—to consider their own position in the assemblage. The documentary was made to be shown, the audience is an end point for the observation process that the autobiographer initiated. But the autobiographer is also produced by the process in which they participate. As I noted in the introduction, autobiography is a cultural practice that seeks a public, an audience of imagined and unknown strangers who will interact with the matter and meaning of a particular life. The scene of reception is also a scene of observation in which media technologies play a role: the projector, the screen, the DVD player or streaming service that delivers the film to its audiences. This returns us to the cinematic apparatus as theorized in film theory: as an assemblage of technologies, matter, environment, and humans that extends from production to reception.[54]

Reading autobiography as a practice of relational materiality, then, invites us to read both with and against the case logic and ontology and epistemology which underpin acts of self-life-inscription that treat the truth, or significance, of lived experience as *out there*, and which position the autobiographer as a detective. Reading the assemblage as a scene of both possibility and foreclosure that produces life, rather than merely records or represents it, strengthens our understanding of the role media materialities play in lived experience and the ongoing relational process of assigning value and significance to life. The challenge, of course, is to push beyond thinking of the power of Henry and Rel's camera, Angela's pencil and sketch pad, and Nev's laptop and instant messaging software as merely reinforcing or authorizing the social, ontological, and epistemological reality of identity as a fixed truth.[55] Rather, they are the means by which this fixity and its truth are materialized. Barad's, and indeed Butler's, arguments about materiality do not incorporate matter into discourse in order to reify discourse as possessing totalizing definitional power. The interaction between the apparatus and the matter that it observes—like bodies that perform and enact the discourse of gender—is always a scene of possibility. Each scene of observation is the scene of potential where discourse finds material purchase, and recognizing the role of the apparatus in creating the scene where this potential unfolds is but one step in reading autobiography as a material and mediated practice. In the next chapter, I will return to a focus on how matter itself contributes to the scene by examining how anonymously produced handmade postcards have formed a collective narrative and an intimate public organized around secrets that stages lively relationality as a collective, dispersed, and ultimately commodified practice.

3

Crowdsourcing

In 2004, Frank Warren invited people to write a secret that "is true and you have never shared" on a postcard and mail it to him at a street address in Germantown, Maryland, USA. Participants were encouraged to "let the postcard be your canvas" and were invited to "see a secret" by visiting the project website, a blog hosted by Blogger, where scans of recently received cards were uploaded weekly. *PostSecret* was conceived as an art project and began with a batch of three thousand custom-made cards that Warren distributed by leaving them in art galleries and in library books, and by handing them out at subway stations.[1] While the original stock of cards was exhausted in three weeks, for well over a decade Warren has received handmade cards in the mail every week.[2] He has amassed a collection of more than half a million cards,[3] and HarperCollins has published six books showcasing secrets from the project.[4] *PostSecret* is transmedial: individual postcards are remediated onto the blog and into books and are discussed by fans on the *PostSecret Community* website, where people can share secrets by uploading videos (and are encouraged to "become a supporting member" of the community by purchasing a book via Amazon). Warren also presents the secrets on speaking tours that often visit American high schools and university campuses, and cities outside the United States such as Melbourne and London.

PostSecret is clearly an example of what media studies scholars have described as the rise of participation and free labor in networked culture.[5] Free labor is marked by increased visibility and participation by audiences in networked cultural production, and the erosion of cultural labor as a paid profession by new labor practices such as internships and crowdsourcing. My interest in crowdsourcing as a practice intersects with these discussions but inquires after something slightly different: Why and how has networked culture produced a new form of collective autobiography that is transmedial, affect driven, and, perhaps surprisingly, grounded by nondigital personal artifacts such as childhood diaries, handmade postcards, and face-to-face interviews?

The projects I consider here demonstrate the importance of nondigital objects and practices in anchoring claims to authenticity in networked autobiography, particularly when autobiography becomes a group rather than an individual activity. Autobiography is usually associated with the individual. Indeed, the *self* of self-life-inscription comes first in our thinking about autobiography for many reasons. As research into book history, authorship, and copyright has shown, our need—as readers—to imagine a single creative intention behind the work is tightly linked to the performative power of the book as a material base for knowledge distribution and validation.[6] Yet, the resilience and success of *PostSecret* in building an intimate public around secret keeping *because of* the anonymity of individual contributors raises a number of questions about the impact of online models of participation on the cultural practice of self-life-inscription. The crowdsourced anonymity of the project attracts large numbers of people to a textual archive that is presented and largely read by audiences as genuine—despite violating the most basic primary condition of autobiography: that the narrator be identifiable as an individual. On the one hand, the commercial success of *PostSecret*, with its sellout performances and publications that regularly appear on best-seller lists, demonstrates how media forms materialize the commodification of autobiography, as Julie Rak has demonstrated in the case of the book.[7] Indeed, *PostSecret* exemplifies the continued importance of the book as marketable (and bankable) cultural commodity in transmedial projects. In confessional entrepreneurship, the book often functions to archive and authorize the autobiographies the projects solicit, and the sales figures (as well as attendance numbers at live events, and the number of downloads of podcasts or apps) are presented as consecrating the project's claims to creating a vehicle for a preexisting need to share personal stories. With this kind of crowdsourced autobiography, self-life-inscription is a transmedial commodity and practice: gaining traction in the cultural zeitgeist because it combines the unique materialities and affordances of specific media forms to create an intimate public that is then put up for sale in books and performances. There is a mix of narrative and media elements at work in *PostSecret* and other projects like it that demonstrate how collective forms of self-representation "can look normative and disciplinary, a scene of instruction in the proper formalism of the person."[8] This disciplinary function creates formal expectations at the level of media and matter by delimiting which types of media, and their unique affordances and material properties, are the appropriate site for self-life-inscription. They also, as Berlant has observed, create scenes where what constitutes an appropriate style for autobiography is taught.[9]

The first section of this chapter examines the anonymous handmade postcard as the affective and material base of the *PostSecret* intimate public and considers how the remediated postcard grounds the truth claims of the project when it moves online and into books. The second section examines the economic and cultural model the project enacts, considering the transmedial affective world aesthetically and commercially. I consider the websites, the terms of service agreements, the self-presentation of the entrepreneurs, and the importance of different media forms—the blog, the book, the performance, the postcard or interview—in *PostSecret* and projects like it. I propose that the wide-ranging use of mediation and materiality in these crowdsourced projects can be understood as confessional entrepreneurship:[10] the coaxing and remediating of crowdsourced life narration for the financial and symbolic benefit of an individual or small team of people. Crowdsourced autobiographies coaxed by confessional entrepreneurs demonstrate the power of collective life writing to commodify affect, and the role of lighter forms of community—with low barriers for participation and responsibility—in the contemporary social field.[11] Central to their success is deft deployment of mediation and materiality on the social web to generate coherent, indeed tightly curated, experiences of intimacy online, in books, and in performance. These projects, which create transmedial scenes of encounter between strangers open to commodification in a variety of ways, are instances of what Jodi Dean describes as communicative capitalism: a form of capitalism where "contemporary communications media capture their users in intensive and extensive networks of enjoyment, production, and surveillance. . . . Just as industrial capitalism relied on the exploitation of labor, so does communicative capitalism rely on the exploitation of communication."[12] Alongside *PostSecret*, I consider other projects that exemplify confessional entrepreneurship as a form of crowdsourced autobiography such as *The Moth*, *StoryCorps*, *Six-Word Memoirs*, and *Mortified*.

Each of these projects functions as an intimate public and is grounded by short life narrative fragments that are contributed by members of the public. These micronarratives are packaged together to create a product that is available across a range of media, offering access to highly generalized feelings of community.[13] In the case of *PostSecret*, the public is constituted by micro life narratives presented on single postcards to collectively form a metanarrative about secrets and the need to share them. What is striking about confessional entrepreneurial projects is that the meaning that grounds the intimate public's claim to authenticity is materialized in the interplay between analog and digital forms. Closely reading this interplay illuminates the ongoing importance of materiality in digitally networked social and narrative spaces. Following Berlant, I am interested in "the kinetics of aesthetic form . . . [as] a way to open up an analysis of the mechanisms that enable the reproduction of normativity not as a political program, but as a structure of feeling, and as an affect."[14] Reading *PostSecret* reveals the diverse materialities and economies that produce and circulate transmedial autobiography. The chapter will conclude with a consideration of the larger practice of confessional entrepreneurship of which *PostSecret* is a prominent example.

Importantly, reading *PostSecret* as an intimate public allows us to examine the continued influence of confession on a variety of popular autobiographical modes, and how confessional discourse is materialized in transmedial collective autobiography. The power/knowledge formation of confession mapped by Foucault—where subjects confess to an individual who has the power to heal or forgive them by hearing the truth—has undergone democratization through the widespread uptake of digital technologies. This in turn has recoded the meanings associated with analog forms such as the postcard, the live performance, and the book. In *PostSecret*, participants witness (i.e., read) each other's confession through the blog and the books, and confess themselves on postcards and in audience participation at the performances. They undertake this witnessing and confessing to gain access to an experience of belonging and to confirm their emotional literacy in the keeping of secrets. It is this literacy that Warren—as the entrepreneur behind the project—promises to teach. This literacy is also leveraged to produce an audience for the blog and, perhaps most important, a market for the books and public events that are commercially successful.

Intimate Publics and Markets

In the preface to *The Female Complaint* Berlant suggests: "The autobiographical isn't personal. . . . In the contemporary consumer public . . . all sorts of narratives are read as autobiographies of collective experience. The personal is the general. Publics presume intimacy."[15] Berlant's theory of the intimate public reads the intersection of the personal and the collective as one freighted in affect. As an analytic frame, it also draws attention to political economy because intimate publics arise "when a market opens up to a bloc of consumers, claiming to circulate texts and things that express those people's particular core interests and desires."[16] The production and consumption of autobiography can *produce* a public who "*feel* as though [the project] expresses what is common among them."[17] Individuals read the texts of an intimate public, and these texts generate a feeling in their audience-consumers that

Figure 3.1. Postcard on *PostSecret* from January 2011. www.postsecret.com.

the common experiences *preexisted* the creation of the public, "that even before there was a market addressed to them, there existed a world of strangers who would be emotionally literate in each other's experience of power, intimacy, desire and discontent."[18] This affective resonance and identification is accompanied by the shared feeling that the group was always already bound together by experiences before texts were made to express those experiences. The convergence of identification and the feeling that the texts express preexisting feelings explain how crowdsourced autobiography deprioritizes the individual as author of their existence, in favor of a feeling of consolation in collective experience and faith in stable unifying relationality among like-strangers. But how, exactly, is this achieved, and what role do media and matter play in the production of this feeling?

In the case of *PostSecret*, the possession of a secret is the resonant, normative core of the intimate public. What it *means* to have a secret and how it *feels* to share it are materialized by the affective, social, and discursive work of Warren's curation of the participants' contributions and responses. At the most basic level, the postcards, as individual life narrative fragments, do not undertake the representative work traditionally associated with autobiography (particularly in the United States), where the individual life story functions "within a representative structure where one stands for many."[19] Rather, each postcard works as a testament to the variety of ways that the structure of feeling at the core of the public ("we all have secrets") can be true and unifying. At first glance, the broadness of the claim that "we all have secrets" may seem too flimsy and general to function as the normalizing claim of the intimate public. Yet it brings to stark attention the resilient normative power of the confessional form as a means for constituting subjects.[20] *PostSecret* demonstrates how the form of the confession is used to normalize a structure of feeling—relief, a feeling of being seen and recognized for who one *really* is, what Berlant describes as "fantasies of belonging and reciprocity"[21]— that is vital to memoir as a genre and its effects in some of its most popular modes.[22] As feminist theorists of autobiography have argued, confession has been fundamental to autobiography as a literary genre and its role in maintaining a model of the self as something stable, and amenable to being structured and expressed.[23] What *PostSecret* exemplifies in its transmedial use of the postal system, Web 2.0, performance,

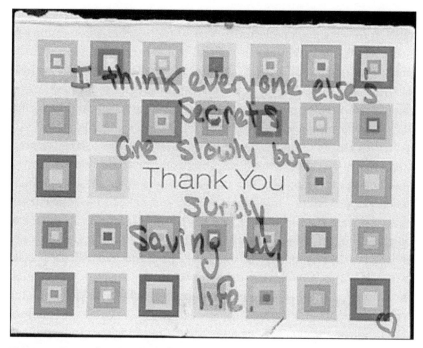

Figure 3.2. Postcard on *PostSecret* from June 2010. www.postsecret.com.

and book publishing is the extent to which confession works to produce and structure affects of connection and reciprocity that unify a public not through fostering an identification with the content of the narrative, or with the form of subjectivity the text presupposes, but *through the formal organization of feeling that encountering certain types of media produces.*[24]

Authentic Forms

For an intimate public to flourish, its texts must feel authentic to its participants. In *PostSecret* the anonymous handmade postcard meets this need. *PostSecret* is materially grounded in a range of media—Web 2.0 modes of publishing, handmade texts, performance, and commercial book publication—and a range of strategies are deployed to establish and maintain the narratives as real and genuine across the cycles of remediation. This involves extending the "strategies of the real" that present content and identities as authentic online.[25] These strategies are built in to the software platforms that bring together a community of users, as seen in Facebook's use of policy statements and algorithms to police the use of "real" names. These strategies also function at the level of rhetoric and narrative, where existing strategies of authentication familiar from older genres and forms are utilized in new online forms, such as the prevalence of first-person point of view in blogs.[26]

In the case of *PostSecret*, the authentication strategies used must overcome the barrier that anonymity presents to the reader identifying the autobiography as genuine; that is to say, unlike other autobiographical acts presented online, individual cards are not linked to user profiles or authorial identities of any kind. The *PostSecret* blog is housed on the free blog site Blogger (purchased by Google in 2003), and the only identity attached to the blog or any other media forms associated with the project is that of Frank Warren, a factor I will return to. The postcards cannot, then, function within the realm of the autobiographical pact—where the reader, in the act of selecting an autobiography to read, links the name of the author on the cover of the text with the narrator and protagonist in their mind, an act that helps shape the horizon of expectation regarding the truthfulness of the text and its relationship with lived experience.[27]

Instead, the authenticity of the postcards is secured through two distinct strategies that demonstrate the importance of materiality in constituting autobiography, and the centrality of confession as a discourse that materializes legible subjects. In both cases, anonymity actually works *for* authentication, rather than against it, by drawing on the audience's preexisting literacy in confession and coupling it with the evocative materiality of the handmade cards.

The postcards constitute their authenticity as individual autobiographical fragments by presenting physical traces of their authors. The idiosyncrasies of handwriting, the inclusion of objects (such as house keys, sewing threads, and flowers), and the use of cut-and-paste collage buttress Warren's claim that he is the recipient of the cards by providing physical evidence of their production. By looking *handmade* and hand inscribed, rather than mass or digitally produced, the remediated postcards exhibited on the blog work mimetically with the body, and subjectivity, of their implied authors.[28] Mimesis in remediation works, Bolter and Gruisin argue, "intersubjectively in terms of the *reproduction*

Figure 3.3. Postcard on *PostSecret* from June 2010. www.postsecret .com.

of the feeling of imitation or resemblance in the perceiving subject."[29] Thus, mimesis is an act of *reading*, not of writing. The materiality of the postcard offers a trace of the physical labor required to produce each card, and this material trace is framed in the project as evidence of the truthfulness of the secrets.

The handmade nature of the texts also reinforces the confessional metanarrative of the *PostSecret* project: secrets are written down, presumably leaving no digital trace in the life of the author as a saved file on a computer or in the cache of the internet browser. Nor do the secrets have a physical presence in the life of the person who owns them. They cannot be found by prying hands, like the other confessional forms they evoke such as a locked diary or a collection of letters in a cardboard box. This points us to a key element of *PostSecret*'s success: using the anonymity afforded by the materiality of the postal system to authenticate the secrets. The holders of the secrets—the thousands of authors who have contributed to the project—have made and shared fragments of lived experience in such a way that anonymity is protected, but the texts they have produced are powerfully connected to *some body* through the materiality of the postcard. *PostSecret* creates an intimate public predicated on the possession of the secret, and while secrets are "shared" via the project, the individual authors remain anonymous, and thus the secrets *remain secrets* within the everyday lives of their authors. *PostSecret* "is a space of mediation" in which the personal condition of having a specific secret is "refracted" through the generalized condition of secret keeping.[30] Confessing through *PostSecret* shields the individual contributor from the risk of exposure and consequent fallout associated with "going public" with one's secret to friends or family, or in an online space such as Facebook where the stakes of unintended publicity are well known. This alters the role that confession plays in the construction of the individual autobiographical subjects, who remain unidentified in the project but who, through confessing via *PostSecret*, gain access to the feeling of community and gain membership in a community of feeling. Sending in a physical claim to membership (a secret on a postcard), posting to the forum on the *PostSecret Community* website, or commenting on the Facebook page confirms one's literacy in the affect of secrets and confession.

Readers and contributors are drawn to this practice because the intimate public of *PostSecret* is underscored by a strong subtext regarding the healing power of confessing in the context of an empathetic public scene. This subtext is materialized in the cards themselves and in their power as personal mementos, which Susan Stewart describes as "souvenirs of individual experience" often produced through "the salvage crafts."[31] Stewart argues this particular form of souvenir is "emblematic of the worth of that life and of the self's capacity to generate worthiness."[32] The making of personal mementos through salvage crafts is a means of making a life matter: materializing both the value of the life and the value of the making. The materials used to make salvage crafts ground an experience of one's own worth (as a maker) and the worth

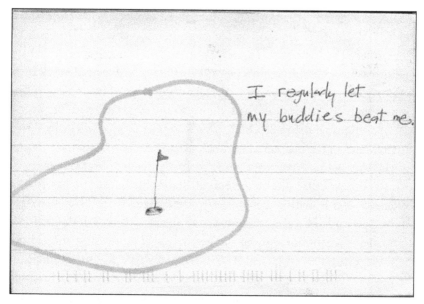

I regularly let my buddies beat me.

Figure 3.4. Postcard on *PostSecret* from June 2010. www.postsecret.com.

of others (as a reader). In *PostSecret* an experience of self-worth—of mattering—is made by constructing personal mementos that bear (and bare) secrets. *PostSecret* evidences that an intimate public that utilizes personal mementos as vehicles for self-life-inscription has transnational appeal. Its model repurposes and combines two widely practiced—though still culturally inflected—practices (the sending of postcards and the confession of secrets) with the deeper role that things and objects play in producing a feeling of personal and collective significance.

Warren's instructions for coaxing the secrets play a pivotal role in setting up the materialization of significance through the personal memento, and an ongoing role in authenticating the secrets circulated in the intimate public. The instruction is clear and direct: "Reveal *anything*—as long as it is true and you have never shared it with anyone before." By insisting that the contributions be *true* and *new*, Warren places responsibility for the authenticity of the project back on the individual contributors. This creates an explicit frame for what all intimate publics seek to confirm: that the subject of the texts and objects the project circulates express affective states that *preexisted* the creation of the public itself.

People possessed "true" secrets before there was *PostSecret*. They possessed a desire to share those secrets and to know the secrets of others. The project, the logic goes, (merely) presents itself as the space in which the secrets can be shared, producing "an affective scene of identification among strangers that promises a certain experience of belonging."[33] The importance of such framing statements to the larger practice of confessional entrepreneurship of which *PostSecret* is indicative will be explored further later in the chapter.

But, first, let us linger over some other elements of Warren's instructions—in particular, the requirement that confessants "be brief" and "creative" and how this is materially emphasized by the small surface of the postcard. This alignment between the affordances of the material template and a philosophy of the aesthetics of confession should not be underestimated in terms of its power to shape the form and content of the secrets Warren wishes to receive. As "America's most trusted stranger," Warren's template for confessional autobiography has considerable formal and material limits, and leads its author-contributors to particular kinds of confession.[34] A visit to the *PostSecret* blog shows that certain kinds of secrets are more suitable than others. Formally and materially, the postcard lends itself to short, often sentimentalized confessions that seek to confirm similarities rather than differences, and that largely forgo context in favor of statements that reiterate key affective characteristics of secret keeping. Shame, pain, disappointment, and regret are recurrent (see figure 3.1). So too are cards expressing release, relief, and freedom from the negative affect associated with the unshared secret (see figure 3.2). A third mode, which provides an important counterpoint to these weighty affective states, involves confessions of small everyday secrets, such as the card in figure 3.4. Cards of this nature confirm that literacy in confession and secret sharing is not dependent on personal experience of trauma, significant betrayal, or regret. The possession of *any* secret, and a willingness to share it and "hear" others, is what counts in the intimate public the project creates. As I have argued elsewhere in relation to digital storytelling, requests by the coaxer—the entity who asks another to engage in life narration—for brevity and creativity (usually defined in terms of aesthetic coherence and simplicity) often result in texts that privilege commonality over individuality.[35] The card in figure 3.4 demonstrates that participation and adherence to this requirement does provide lighter moments in the exhibition of the post-cards. Moreover, these lighter moments confirm the logic that "we all have secrets" that reveal "something" about us as individuals.

The card in figure 3.2 confirms the success of *PostSecret* in uniting a genre and form and offering it to the intimate public as something to which their desire to confess, to be heard, and to be literate in each other's experiences of secret keeping can be attached. That the project can achieve a seemingly upward affective drift despite the often negative, difficult, or traumatic secrets that are shared is of interest to media and autobiography scholarship seeking to understand the current forms of collectivity, relationality, and being political that online spaces engender. On the one hand, the complex dynamic between the sentimental, the negative, the general, and the intimate, Berlant argues, defines the terrain of the intimate public. Through the texts of the intimate public an inherent conflict is held in tension: the desire to remain attached and proximate to normative subject positions that have proved disappointing or even damaging to the individual. This tension is explored as a collective issue through the use of sentimental and melodramatic genres.[36] This is why so many secrets in the project are about the failure of the individual in relation to normative concepts that traditionally anchor a life (and life narrative): the biological family, reproductive heterosexuality and its attendant institutions, work, financial security, secure and stable attachments of friendship and romantic love (see figures 3.1 and 3.3).[37] The melodramatic form is fundamental to the intimate public because the "density of a style of being" it provides *is* the consolation offered for the failure to achieve the fantasized "good life" of stability.[38]

The importance of remaining attached to life even in the face of disappointment is emphasized in the *PostSecret* project through its sponsorship of the *International Suicide Prevention Wiki*, which was created as a resource to be embedded in the *PostSecret* app.[39] While the provision of mental health resources within the project is important, it also reinforces the imperative to confession and sharing that the project leverages—we all have secrets, and our secrets can kill us. The powerful tension between the disappointments brought about by failed attachments to normative ideas about life and the need to remain attached to them is rendered as a life-or-death struggle. Thus, the statement that "everyone else's secrets are slowly but surely saving my life" (figure 3.2) is both a clear affirmation of what the members of the intimate public *feel* is at stake, and an adherence to the formal conventions of the public.[40] This is a truth its members are encouraged to feel, and that Warren promotes, when he discusses and frames the project in performances, written texts, videos, and interviews—as I discuss later.

The *PostSecret Community* website addresses the importance of affective truth to the public explicitly in the frequently asked questions section, which addresses whether or not every secret is true.[41] The answer provided emphasizes that the cards are *artworks* rather than autobiographies. By evoking the amorphous category of "art" rather than the more limited genre of autobiography, Warren can respond to the question of the "truth" in *PostSecret* by positioning it in terms of the capacity to inspire epiphanies in readers. This framing, which brackets the question of whether or not the cards' authors are confessing a secret they truly hold, places the emphasis back on the feelings the project seeks to inspire. This confirms the importance of the affective intent of the project, which does not seek to document or even narrate the diversity of secrets held by the community it creates, but rather aims to provide a structure of feeling around secrets and confession that normalizes the act of confession in the formation of subjects.[42] It is a means of structuring the complex scene of attachment and disappointment Berlant suggests is a condition of an intimate public. In the intimate public of *PostSecret*, subjectivity is organized around the collectivized affective pleasures of confessing the ownership of a secret (*"Yes,* I too have a secret") and the redemptive power of uttering it. It appears to confirm Foucault's suggestion that Western society is populated by confessing animals.[43] In successfully transforming a confessional art project into an intimate public, Warren produces a market for the book collections and speaking events by promoting these items as key points of community membership.[44]

As a transmedia project whose success began with postcards and a blog, *PostSecret* is difficult to account for if we prioritize a single speaking subject as the originator and guarantor of autobiography (something I explore from a different perspective in the next chapter), or if we focus on one media form as the place where an intimate public is materialized. On its own, an individual *PostSecret* card is too slight to put an individual's voice "on the record," and like an individual tweet on a Twitter account, it is too short to present a story that might be marshaled as evidence or give insight into the meaning of lived experience. Nor is *PostSecret* a text that anyone (no matter how dedicated) can finish reading—like other texts explored in *Stories of the Self* (the *Time Capsules, End Credits*), it is a project that works with excess and duration. Thus, while it builds an archive of autobiographical fragments, it also resists ways of reading that privilege completeness, stability, and the singular voice of autobiography. In this sense, the project is live—dynamic and changing, like *zoē*—yet the ways of making meaning it offers remain stable and consistent; its formula has rarely changed in more than a decade. As a transmedial intimate public spread across multiple media, the textuality of *PostSecret* is networked and partial, yet it has proved to be very resilient, powerful, and commercially successful. The success and the stability of the model it has provided for crowdsourced autobiography suggest that there are underlying strategies and techniques in the project that—if identified—help us understand the changing nature of self-life-inscription in the light of a dynamic and connected media environment in which the interaction between the semiotic and material specificity of analog and digital forms plays a central role.

Confessional Entrepreneurship

While the affective circuits created by *PostSecret* are unique and uniquely successful, the model for crowdsourcing autobiography it uses is not. To understand how *PostSecret* works, we must look beyond the cards Warren receives and remediates, to the structural, material underpinnings of the project. Postcards and curatorial commentary are not the only texts that underpin *PostSecret*: like many other autobiographical projects that source their material online, *PostSecret* relies on the legal framing of the terms of service agreement. In looking beyond the single case study of *PostSecret*, we can consider a range of other projects that seek to coax, curate, and remediate autobiography from the general public, a practice of "confessional entrepreneurship." I propose this term as a way of conceptualizing the practice of individuals, or small teams of individuals, who initiate projects that are dependent on the willingness of the general public to generate and contribute autobiographical content: life stories on a particular theme, photographs, or everyday textual fragments like notes and lists. Projects organized by the logic of confessional entrepreneurship do not collect *confessions* in the narrow, generic sense; rather, they deploy confession as a technology of self that gives people access to an intimate public. In theorizing this practice in what follows, I examine how the affordances and cultural shifts heralded by Web 2.0 are generating autobiographical texts and practices that connect the individual to the collective through storytelling, material practices, and new subject positions.[45] These practices are not distinct from the discourses and practices of memoir in print culture. Confessional entrepreneurship intersects with the political, social, affective, and economic uses of memoir in contemporary culture that have been referred to as "the memoir boom." The boom has seen the rising profitability and cultural influence of personal storytelling as a unique cultural commodity that readers expect to offer particular kinds of reading experiences. That experience, Julie Rak argues, "gestures to the sense of belonging that the state [and functional conceptualizations of citizenship] cannot provide."[46] For Leigh Gilmore, the memoir boom presents a narrative of individualism that "replaces an American dream rendered unavailable by vast inequalities in the distribution of material resources with an endlessly renewable narrative template" of personal redemption.[47] Both of these critics link the rise of memoir—as a publishing and media phenomenon—with a crisis in citizenship, particularly in the United States.

We can recognize confessional entrepreneurs as attempting to create and mediate intimate publics because they "promise a certain experience of belonging and provide a complex of consolation, confirmation, discipline and discussion about how to live" and because their products circulate as commodities.[48] In my research on these publics I have identified four key characteristics of these projects, each serving a particular purpose in positing, structuring, and materializing the intimate public that underpins the intention to commercialize the content contributed by the community. These features are:

1. a web presence that is a site for both the coaxing of autobiographical content and the exhibition of submissions,
2. framing statements that stipulate both the content and the form of the autobiographical material that is solicited,
3. a terms of service agreement that grants the project operator "a perpetual, royalty-free license to use, reproduce, modify, publish,

distribute, and otherwise exercise all copyright and publicity rights with respect to that information at its sole discretion, including storing it on servers and incorporating it in other works in any media now known or later developed including without limitation published books," and

4. a persona of the project originator that authentically situates them in relation to the community they facilitate and curate.

A key marker of the success of these projects, from the entrepreneur's perspective, is their ability to repackage the material that is collected and curated online into forms of media, particularly books and ticketed live performances, that can be financially profitable and ensure the longevity of the project. In the case of the publication of books, this reflects the book's reliability as a commodity and its continued status as a marker of cultural attainment that can confer cultural capital on the confessional entrepreneur. As with the blog-to-book phenomenon, a book deal for these projects both confers and recognizes the success of the online project, as well as giving it an archival status that still largely eludes online and performance texts. In the case of live performances, the importance of the body of the storyteller as a material guarantor of the authenticity of the narrative is key. This echoes developments in the music industry, where digital streaming and downloading have eroded the viability of media of inscription (the vinyl record, the cassette tape, the compact disc) as the bedrock of artists' financial security, with a resulting turn to live performance as a key revenue stream.[49]

Archives of Universal Feeling

Confessional entrepreneurship uses networked media as technologies of intimacy and amplification. While there are many examples of people soliciting and curating autobiographical narratives from members of the community *offline* through the techniques of oral history and interviewing—as in the work of Nobel laureate Svetlana Alexievich—the online context is a site of exhibition and recruitment that provides extended reach and, importantly, radically expanded context in which the autobiographical texts are exhibited. Confessional entrepreneurship strives for and claims a level of universality for the autobiographical fragments coaxed and curated by the project that is not achieved, or is rejected by, many oral history projects. The impetus in confessional entrepreneurship is toward commonality and universality, rather than uniqueness established through the narration of geographic, cultural, and historical specificity. For example, *StoryCorps* describes it mission as

> to preserve and share humanity's stories in order to build connections between people and create a more just and compassionate world.
>
> We do this to remind one another of our shared humanity, to strengthen and build the connections between people, to teach the value of listening, and to weave into the fabric of our culture the understanding that everyone's story matters. At the same time, we are creating an invaluable archive for future generations.[50]

This universalizing discourse is rooted both in the realities of the global reach made possible by the internet and in a utopian belief in the authenticity of analog forms (oral storytelling). We also see here a remnant of the utopian investment in the power of the internet as a great unifier that has waxed and waned since the World Wide Web was first released to the public in 1991. In confessional entrepreneurship, the affordance of unlimited audience offered by networked technologies materializes autobiography as a universal human practice. However, this universality and potential for reach are tempered by the entrepreneur's need to control what people contribute to the project to ensure the consistency of autobiography as a product that constructs the very universality it claims to merely be a vehicle for.

While confessional entrepreneurs claim that autobiography is a universal human practice that they merely "facilitate" or "showcase," universality itself is the product of extensive strategies of curation in the templates, the coaching provided to contributors, and the web presence of the projects. The quantity of submissions is important here, and I will return to this in a moment. But first I will outline two common modes of curation that buttress claims to universality in crowdsourced confessional entrepreneurial autobiography. These curatorial strategies ensure that consistency produces the textual effect of universality.

The most common strategy used by confessional entrepreneurs is to select contributions for exhibition on the site and update it regularly. In the case of *PostSecret* the blog is updated every Sunday; *StoryCorps* and *The Moth* upload new podcasts every week. Another strategy is to have open contributions to the site and for the confessional entrepreneur to use the affordance of "highlighted" or "featured" contributions to elevate content that reflects elements the curator is seeking to foster. We see this strategy in sites like *StoryCorps* and *Six-Word Memoirs*. This method allows audiences to be aware of all the content while allowing the curator to prioritize engagement with contributions that best exemplify the form and content they are seeking. And what it *is* that confessional entrepreneurs are seeking is outlined in the templates they provide, and the narrative they offer about the importance of sharing stories from lived experience through their framing statements.

You Are Unique, Like Everybody Else: Templates and Framing Statements

Templates and framing statements outline the form and content requirements for contributing to a confessional entrepreneurial project. They articulate the confessional entrepreneur's vision for the *kinds* of content that will be contributed. Framing statements include articulations of the meaning produced by the content solicited—to build community, celebrate "universal" aspects of lived experience—and the importance of the formal constraints for materializing impact and meaning. The use of framing statements establishes the scope of the intimate public: the preexisting experiences that texts articulate, and the affective responses to those experiences the texts *express*. For example, on the site for the *Six-Word Memoirs* project, the "about" section tells us:

> In November 2006, Larry Smith, founder of SMITH Magazine, gave the six-word novel a personal twist by asking his community to describe their lives in exactly six words. . . . Hundreds of thousands of people have shared their own short life story at smithmag.net, as well as in classrooms, churches, and at live Six-Word "slams" across the world. The Six-Word Memoir exemplifies the best of SMITH Magazine's storytelling mission: populist, participatory, inspirational, and addictive. From speed dating to parlor games, to conferences and staff retreats, Six-Word Memoirs have

become a powerful tool to inspire conversation around a big idea, and a simple way for individuals to break the ice.[51]

Here we see the claim for universality focused around the social goods of "conversation, imagination and breaking the ice"—goods equally as vague as "sharing secrets" and therefore suitably porous to attract large numbers of contributions. Unlike *PostSecret* and other projects such as *The Moth*, *Six-Word Memoirs* have no thematic requirement—six-word memoirs can be about anything and are linked to suggested categories on the website. The focus instead is on form: six words that need to be "short, sharp" stories from your life that, when shared, enhance our social bonds. As Laurie McNeill argues, the open-ended nature of *Six-Word Memoirs* in both content and the demand for ongoing contributions results in "online auto/biographers reinscribing very traditional social functions that the different forms of 'autobiography' have served for centuries, including self-monitoring, therapy, and meaning-making."[52] This is no accident, as the *Six-Word Memoirs* framing statement makes reference to traditional offline sites of community and sociality associated with print culture—"classrooms, churches"—yet its relationship *to* these physical sites where the sharing of life narrative is practiced to maintain community is not made clear. The evocation, however, indicates that an intimate public is the confessional entrepreneur's goal: being active in the *Six-Word Memoirs* community by producing and sharing micro life narrative is, the framing suggests, not dissimilar to the embodied social practices we have been engaged in all "our" lives. Indeed, the formal constraint of six words might relieve us from some of the more problematic aspects of face-to-face sociality: people who *should* keep their stories to six words, for example. There's a reduced threat of being bored by these forms because of brevity (a *Six-Word Memoir*, a postcard) and the insertion of professional cultural producers into the production chain of many projects (as I discuss in detail later).[53]

The more coherent and tightly linked the form/content relation, the stronger the claims for universality and affect the confessional entrepreneurial project can make. *PostSecret* takes the universality of secrets as its foundation; *Mortified* takes shame. While Frank Warren advises how a postcard *should look* (it should be your canvas), he does not edit the cards he receives. He manages the form and content solely through curation—we see only the cards Warren himself selects for books, for exhibitions and projection during his live shows, and on the blog. *Six-Word Memoirs* and *StoryCorps*, through their apps, do not prescreen or edit material that is submitted (unlike *The Moth* and *Mortified*). Thus, curation of content is an ongoing and vital task in maintaining the coherence of many confessional entrepreneurial projects. Other confessional entrepreneurs, however, take a more proactive approach to shaping the texts they receive. In adopting shame as its universalizing core theme, *Mortified* aims to "share the shame" by curating and documenting live performances where the audience is invited to "witness adults sharing their most embarrassing childhood artifacts (journals, letters, poems, lyrics, plays, home movies, art) with others, in order to reveal stories about their lives."[54] *Mortified* is an example of considerable intervention by the confessional entrepreneurs, who manage the final text like producers in the film or television industry. This method is also used by *The Moth* and *StoryCorps*.[55] The framing statement for *Mortified* includes an outline of the production process:

1. Unearth. You dig up some of your old embarrassing childhood artifacts (old letters, lyrics, journals, cassettes, artwork, plays, videos, even old blogs).
2. Contact. You request a producer's session on the form on this page.
3. Collaborate. We meet up and help you identify excerpts & a backstory that our audience will love.
4. Share. You share the results on stage.
5. Impact. Someone in the audience returns home, inspired to unearth their own stuff! (Fun, eh?)[56]

This outline emphasizes the confessional entrepreneurs' expertise in conceptualizing and producing texts. Contributors are not assumed to be literate in the making of engaging, well-crafted, or appropriate autobiography. In this sense, confessional entrepreneurship is like the digital storytelling movement, which seeks to train everyday people in life narration and the use of digital technologies.[57] There is expertise at work here, and it is expressed through the framing statements that clearly articulate the entrepreneurs' vision for the *kinds* of texts they are seeking and the *effects* these texts will have on the audience. The message of confessional entrepreneurship is that autobiography is a universal practice that we all engage in every day, but that we need the help of the entrepreneur (and those trained in their storytelling method) to tell those stories *properly*. Without the use of the narrative template developed and marketed by the entrepreneur, our storytelling will fail to reach its full potential: as a form of social connection, and as a record of humanity's shared struggle and joy. Crucially, however, the centrality of the entrepreneur's expertise in storytelling to the success of the project is downplayed in the public representation of the entrepreneur's persona, where the emphasis is on their personal experience of the feelings the project addresses, a point I shall return to momentarily.

Even in an example like *Mortified*, which explicitly acknowledges the curatorial process involved in producing the texts, all projects organized by confessional entrepreneurship avoid associating the creation of autobiography with the creation of its meaning. In this sense, they carry on the function of confession articulated by Foucault: the texts they coax are positioned as *representing* a preexisting truth about the self, the articulation of which grants the individual an identity and membership as part of the community. Of course, it also opens that identity up for surveillance and discipline, and one place this is manifest is in the terms of service agreements used in the projects.

But before considering terms of service, it is also worth noting that confessional entrepreneurial sites must negotiate the question of the truthfulness of their contributions. There are two kinds of truth here, one affective, the other legal. As discussed earlier, *PostSecret* uses the aura of the handmade postcard and the discourse of "art" and epiphany to ground the affective truth claims of its content. In the logic of the intimate public, it is important that contributions *feel* authentic to the readers and contributors—and this feeling comes through matter and specific media forms associated with authenticity. This reliance on feeling becomes what Brian Massumi calls an "affective fact"[58]—a self-fulfilling prophecy—once the intimate public reaches a certain level of participation and success. "See! People *love* this project, so what it says about life *must* be true!" We see this in *The Moth*'s claim that it has facilitated the sharing of "over 18,000 stories," with the podcast downloaded "over 30 million times per year,"[59] and Frank Warren's citation of the number of postcards he has received (more than half a million) and

David Isay's claim that "more than 100,000 people . . . have recorded StoryCorps interviews."[60]

The thornier question of the verifiable truth of the individual contributions is dealt with through the inclusion of statements online that attempt to mark out the jurisdictional space in which contributions are made. Most confessional entrepreneurs (with the exception of Frank Warren) find a way to incentivize the use of real names by their contributors. These projects largely solicit material outside the infrastructure of social network platforms that utilize their own protocols for guaranteeing identity, such as Facebook's infamous policing of the use of "real names." Therefore, other means for mandating the use of a "real" identity must be found. For example, the frequently asked questions page of *Six-Word Memoirs* states:

> *If one of my Six-Worders is selected for a book, will I be notified?*
> Yes. We'll send a note to the email you signed up to let you know you're either a finalist or have been chosen to be in a book. Note: *You must include your real name* in your profile to be considered for a book. Your real name won't be visible on Six Words, only to editors. We credit each memoirist by first and last name, and can only consider submissions for which we have this information for our books.[61]

These stipulations—while worded as statements enforcing the jurisdictions of the genre of autobiography—function more as wishes than requirements. They ensure that the confessional entrepreneur has undertaken due diligence in attempting to gather content that approximates what it claims to be: autobiographical fragments from "everyday" lives. This stipulation allows the confessional entrepreneur to market the content of their project as authentic to book publishers, advertisers, the media, and the larger public who might consume the texts but not necessarily become active members of the intimate public. As Julie Rak has shown, the commercial success of memoir brings with it the logics of the market and, as Oprah Winfrey insisted when she realized that she had been "duped" by James Frey's memoir of addiction, it is the publisher's responsibility to ensure that the product it markets is what the publisher says it is: nonfictional, and an accurate representation of the experience of the author.[62] The instruction to contributors that they must follow the logic of the autobiographical pact—for there to be a seamless line between the named author, the narrator and the subject of the narrative—allows the confessional entrepreneur to market the content they solicit as autobiographical, but it says nothing concrete about the authenticity of the content beyond the entrepreneur's hope that people will do what they ask. A more important factor is that in order for the confessional entrepreneur to package the autobiographical content they coax for consumption, they must get people to agree to sign over their ownership of their autobiographies.

Who Is the Author of Affect? Terms of Service Agreements

Terms of service agreements are an important interpellation device in Web 2.0 and are a place where the privacy paradox—discussed in the introduction to this book—is clearly enacted.[63] In the case of confessional entrepreneurial projects, terms of service agreements are checkpoints for participation in the intimate public. When they are encountered, they momentarily situate contributors as legal subjects who sign over the natural right of copyright held on their contribution to the legal body of the project, which is owned by the confessional entrepreneur or the not-for-profit organization they lead. In the second it takes to check the box and click the button (if that is even required), the participant agrees to grant the confessional entrepreneur "perpetual, royalty-free license to use, reproduce, modify, publish, distribute, and otherwise exercise all copyright and publicity rights with respect to that information at its sole discretion."[64] In this gesture, the legal subject position is hailed, and dismissed. In the exchange facilitated by the terms of service agreement we see the core tensions of autobiographical discourse—exceptionalism and universality—negotiated through interpellation and splitting of the autobiographical subject in the online environment. The legal subject is exceptional, an individual who has naturally conferred rights that recognize the uniqueness of the autobiographical fragment they contribute to the project. That subject is linked to the contributor's real name, which they must use to create their profile on *Six-Word Memoirs* or pitch their story to *The Moth* (no such requirement exists for *PostSecret*). However, in agreeing to the terms of service, the uniqueness of the legal and authorial subject is explicitly traded off for universality and entrance to the intimate public. This trade-off is situated and encouraged by the discourse of the framing statements that emphasize how sharing one's story will educate others and confirm social bonds. To participate in the intimate public on offer, participants must enter the circuits of communicative capitalism through the terms of service checkpoint. Thus, the privacy paradox is materialized by statements that indicate that participation equals consent, which are buried in out-of-the-way places in the web presence of the project.

In confessional entrepreneurship, the legal subjectivity that grants permission to the curator to use, edit, and repackage their autobiographical fragment is kept distinct from the subject of universal affect that "seeks expression" through participation in the project. This separation is largely maintained by the lack of physical action the rights-bearing subject undertakes to give consent. There is no box checking to progress here, the kind we are familiar with when terms of service agreements act as gateways to progressing the sign-up or log-in protocol of Facebook, Dropbox, or iTunes. Confessional entrepreneurial sites, instead, posit consent as implicit: "Thanks for coming! Welcome! By the way, this is what you are consenting to." The details of consent are buried deep within the websites' frequently asked questions pages or in other obscure parts of the website away from the landing and promoted pages of exhibition, curation, and framing in order for the legal subject position to remain a secondary (or even tertiary) identity in relation to the autobiographical text that is sought.

We might be tempted to say, then, that consent is immaterial here: that because no boxes are checked, no "Agree" button pressed, that the privacy paradox takes on a different valence in confessional entrepreneurship because people do not have the opportunity to read, and therefore understand, what they consent to. This might be an example of the immateriality of digital space—that the placement of terms of service in the less trafficked parts of the site, but covering all activity on the site, means that for all intents and purposes there is no consent. The privacy paradox, then, becomes an issue of legality—can Frank Warren really claim the copyright over something I mail to him?

A quantitative study might be interested to interview participants in confessional entrepreneurial sites to discover just how many of them engage with the agreements, how, and why. Yet this will most likely reveal another instance of the privacy paradox—that people express the view that Frank Warren should not "own" their secret, but their behavior will not reflect this belief. The power of the intimate public to generate positive affective experiences of collectivity and apprehension overrules a rational investment in one's own rights because collectivity is a fundamental element of our identity. In this sense, choosing to waive one's right to privacy in order to experience the intimate public might indeed be rational. The participants in these projects are not inconsistent dupes, but actors whose practices materialize the fundamental need for apprehension and relationality—confessional entrepreneurship shows us that autobiography is as much about collectivity as it is about individuality, and that forms of mediation that structure the scene of collective apprehension can be experienced by contributors and readers as fulfilling, despite the fact that those scenes are predicated on a violation of their right to claim ownership over the presentation of their lived experience.

But an audience's preparedness to allow one's secret, childhood diary, or anecdote about a meaningful experience to be collected, created, and commodified should not be taken as a given. A key reason contributors are prepared to do this is that the confessional entrepreneur presents themselves as an unwitting, and unprofessional, recipient of their narratives, rather than as a project manager or entrepreneur who seeks to generate cultural, social, and financial capital by collecting and repackaging autobiography. Thus, the circuits of commodification are covered over by an additional layer of self-representation: the persona of the entrepreneur themselves.

The Entrepreneur Is Just Like You: Persona

I knew I had this creative inner-life of private fears and jokes and desires. And I thought if I could create this "place" where others could share their inner-selves honestly, it could really be special. In the end, I don't think the success of *Post-Secret* is so much about the idea. It's a simple idea—mail me your secrets. I think the reason I was able to make it work was because I had crazy faith.

If anyone is looking for the secret for finding that idea that
wakes up the world, my suggestion would be: Find a way to
give voice to the unheard and tell the untold stories.
—Frank Warren

While books have authors who assert their rights as copyright holders, the terms of service agreements I just discussed hail and dismiss
the authorial subject of the project's contributors.[65] As we have already
seen, crowdsourced autobiographical projects have entrepreneurs who
use terms of service agreements to take legal ownership of the content
submitted to their project. These people are not mentioned *in* terms of
service agreements, which instead name the project itself as the legal
entity that holds rights over the content. Instead, the entrepreneurs are
present in the project as the author-narrators of the framing statements
and as the curators of the project's content. Tellingly, their names appear
as authors when anthologies are published from the project, and they
represent the project and its claims to universality in the media.

The confessional entrepreneur's identity is key to the project as its
success increases: they first appear as spokespeople in media coverage,
where their credentials for curating the project are established. This authority is predicated on direct *experience* of the phenomenon that is the
focus of the intimate public, the entrepreneurial willingness to experi-
ment, and the delighted discovery that their experience resonates with
others. For example, Dave Nadelberg and Neil Katcher—the founders of
the spoken word event *Mortified* (which has gone on to produce books
and a film)—appear on the *LA Weekly* blog to promote the documentary
(*Mortified Nation*) that has been released about the project. Nadelberg
and Katcher, both thirty-eight at the time, pose with photographs of
their youthful selves of whom they feel lightly ashamed. The project's
inception is narrated in the story as beginning with Nadelberg's personal
archive: "*Mortified* started 11 years ago when Nadelberg, then an entertainment journalist and TV writer, found a love letter he'd chickened out
on sending to his high school crush. It. Was. Mortifying."[66] Nadelberg's
mortification is quickly eased by the discovery that his experience of
finding the text and feeling embarrassed by it "was not original." Even
more exciting was the realization that "people of all ages, races and de-
mographics had saved the diaries, poems, short stories, songs or even

plays they wrote in their teenage years."[67] Here, then, is the flattening out of individual experience—a strong preference for universality over uniqueness—that stems from the cultural use of commercial memoir that "expose[s] ambivalent desires for a post-racist, democratic, nonhierarchical world that readers aspire to join by consuming certain kinds of narratives,"[68] combined with the two phenomena required for entrepreneurship: a profitable opportunity and someone willing to exploit it.[69] Nadelberg is presented in this piece of journalistic promotion as the person who happily stumbles upon a universal experience and seeks to give access to affect by re-creating it. Nadelberg's expertise, like that of all entrepreneurs, is in recognizing the potential of his experience to be expanded into a project.

Similarly, Warren's persona (often referred to as "America's most trusted stranger") emphasizes his use of personal experience to "wake up the world."[70] Warren is the most adept confessional entrepreneur when it comes to using his persona to reinforce the values of the project. Presenting himself as an "everyday" person—a husband, father, and small-business owner—who has been transformed into a unique person by becoming an accidental confessor for hundreds of thousands of people, Warren's persona is at the center of *PostSecret*'s claim to address a preexisting need. The persona is another medium through which the project regularly operates, and he utilizes it most consistently in the sellout *PostSecret Live* events that have been presented across the United States—mainly at university and college campuses—and in the United Kingdom and Australia. These events are held in large lecture theaters or performing arts spaces such as, in the case of the Melbourne event I attended, Hamer Hall at the state-funded arts center, which seats just over twenty-three hundred people. The description and analysis that follow are based on my attendance at the *PostSecret* event held in Melbourne, Australia, in 2013.

As you enter the venue for a *PostSecret* event, upon each seat sits a postcard—a copy of the original postcard Warren designed to invite people to send him his secrets (shown in figure 3.1). This signals to the audience their role in authoring the project, in responding to Warren's hail, and Warren encourages the audience during the talk to use the card and send a secret to him. When Warren takes the stage, he advises the audience that we cannot take photographs or record the presentation, nor can we send text messages during the event. These regulations are not framed as Warren protecting the copyrighted material in the performance (as is often the case at live music events) but are designed to create and protect a private and intimate space of secret sharing. As outlined earlier, Warren's discourse about secrets is focused on their preciousness, power, and danger, and the stated need for privacy at the event reinforces this.

After a video introduction the presentation is made up of two parts: Warren shows a slide show of his favorite secrets, ones that "didn't make it into the book," and discusses the power of sharing secrets to heal individuals and bind communities. In the second part, he invites people to share their secrets. The first part of the presentation, which is largely autobiographical, works to foster a sense of intimacy between Warren and the audience. He tells the story of the project as being a personal one, lived by him. This is powerfully communicated when Warren emphasizes that the secrets are sent *to his home*, where he lives with his family. This detail strengthens Warren's narrative of being a full-time, yet decidedly amateur, confessor. The narrative implies there is no "professional" distance between Warren and the project; he lives it, the secrets arrive every day at his house, and he has become (he tells the audience) "the most trusted person in the English-speaking world." This information sits in a specific way alongside Warren's appearance. In beige chinos, a plain colored shirt, and sweater, Warren looks like a low-level bureaucrat (he tells us he makes his living running a small business that handles medical records) or a primary school teacher. His everyday mediocrity is vital to his role in curating the intimate public because it reinforces the logic that the feelings it gives voice to preceded its existence. An intimate public consists of products that claim to tap into an existing need in the market. It does not produce that need, nor is it the result of the unique artistry of the literary author. Warren narrates this logic throughout the presentation, stating that he "tapped into something that has been there the whole time," rather than creating a market and set of specific meanings around secrets.

Yet this narrative of happening upon a rich vein of preexisting need in the human condition sits uncomfortably alongside Warren's strident narration of the meaning and power of secrets. Throughout his presentation, Warren reiterates the discourse of secrets seen on the website and in the books, that *not* sharing a secret can be debilitating and danger-ous. Warren has learned that "secrets are like walls but they can become bridges." An unshared secret—a secret not posted to him—shuts us off from the world and from the people in our lives. But if we are brave enough to push those secrets over and share them, we can be connected to each other and the intimate public the project has created. We have a choice, Warren tells us, to "bury" a secret "deep down like a coffin, or share it like a gift."

This powerful discourse full of stark choices and strong images that evoke binaries of experience where one is either cut off or connected, secrets are buried or gifted, echoes Foucault's conceptualization of con-fession as a

> ritual of discourse . . . that unfolds within a power relationship, for one does not confess without the presence (or virtual presence) of a partner who is not simply an interlocutor but the authority who requires the con-fession, prescribes and appreciates it, and intervenes in order to judge, punish, forgive, console, and reconcile.[71]

In previous eras confession occurred in highly structured environments of power, as Foucault outlines. One confessed the truth about oneself to a priest, a master, an interrogator, or a doctor as part of the process of becoming a subject, and becoming subject to the truth that privileged person represented and embodied (the truth of medical or religious dis-course, for example). While *PostSecret* retains the rhetoric and certainty of confession "as one of the main rituals we rely on for the production of truth,"[72] Warren—like all confessional entrepreneurs—occupies a more ambivalent position of power in relation to the confessing subjects that he coaxes. Warren's persona as an everyday person who became an amateur expert in secrets allows him to dictate the meanings of the practices he oversees, but remain *personally* detached from the power of that discourse. Warren is not *instructing* us to confess from a position of power reinforced by traditional structures and discourses of author-ity. He is not like a priest, an analyst, or Oprah Winfrey. Rather, it is our voluminous response to his innocent invitation to confess that has created him as an expert in secrets. His status as the single recipient of all the secrets, the curator of the blog and the books, affords Warren an authoritative position in relation to the intimate public of *PostSecret*, and the autobiographical narrative that structures the presentation works to both articulate his authority and downplay it.[73]

The ritual of confession is staged in a somewhat confused conclusion of the *PostSecret* event. Individuals are invited by Warren to share their secret with him and the audience. Here, Warren acts as a confessor and the audiences as witnesses. At the end of the slide show, Warren asks for the house lights to be turned on, so that he can see the audience. Microphones are placed in the aisles, and lines quickly form. Each person steps up to the microphone and confesses, and Warren looks directly at them, asking what their secret is. After the person shares a secret, the audience applauds them. Warren makes no comment on the secret; he merely thanks them for sharing it and looks to the next person.

What does the experience of speaking a secret to Frank Warren at such a live event offer? If the intimate public confirms that we are all literate in the keeping of secrets, Warren's persona has additional expertise: he is the expert in *hearing* them. In his performance as confessor, Warren is a benign and expert presence for whom each secret is confirmation of the doctrine he has espoused: sharing is always better than hoarding one's secrets. The extension of the project to the live event maintains the connection between secrets and embodiment I traced in my earlier analysis of the connection between the handmade postcard and the confessing body. The importance of this connection became starkly visible when Warren expanded the project to an application for smartphones. When *PostSecret* moved from blog to app, and from the postcard and mail service to the smartphone, Warren inadvertently and unwittingly disconnected the secret from the bodily presence of the confessant and put the logic of the intimate public, and the project itself, at risk.

The Limits of the Intimate Public: *PostSecret* and the Abject

The cautionary tale of Frank Warren's attempt to take the anonymous content that defines the intimate public of *PostSecret* into online production via an app provides a useful case study for considering how confessional entrepreneurship relies on the interplay between material strategies that link the anonymous secret to *some body* as a guarantor of truth in analog forms, and the claim to universality buttressed by networked media forms that make the intimate public widely available. It also opens a different line of inquiry for thinking about the importance of materiality for our understanding of what a life is, which I return to in the conclusion of this chapter. The short-lived *PostSecret* app demonstrates the central role played by analog media in grounding the authenticity of the autobiographies produced. Unlike analog forms of anonymity, digital anonymity creates a means for trolls and other internet pranksters to dilute the focus of the public and undermine the commodity that the confessional entrepreneur creates. More important, however, it reveals how quickly the limits of tolerance can be reached when an intimate public coaxes material that resists the formula of consolation it relies on.

In 2012, Warren released the *PostSecret* app into Apple's App Store. For $1.99, subscribers gained access to specially designed software that allowed them to construct secrets by using photographs in their phone and overlaying them with text. Secrets were contributed anonymously, and the app included affordances for audience feedback—people could "love" a secret by clicking on a heart icon, respond to a secret in text, or post their own secret. Secrets could also be geotagged, using the phone's location, and users could browse maps to find secrets that had been uploaded in specific areas. It quickly became a best-selling app, appearing in the App Store's best-seller list, and being written up in the technology press.

Not long after its release, however, the app was overrun with material that was far from the "spirit" of the successful project. Images of nude bodies, material that threatened or celebrated violence, images of feces and vomit, and "secrets" that were demeaning to minorities appeared in large volumes. With the app, the *PostSecret* intimate public was overrun by the abject. While this might seem ironically fitting for a project dedicated to secret keeping, it threatened to destroy the *PostSecret* project's business model and logic. As Julia Kristeva elucidates, this is the very function of the abject: to destabilize borders, threaten annihilation of the self, and endanger systems of meaning.[74] Institutionalized art forms such as literature and visual art, and the physical locations of the book and the gallery, have long offered encounters with the abject in safe, bounded environments. The book and the gallery are locations that have long-standing cultural associations with encounters with the new, the challenging, and the controversial. Perused on a smartphone, however, the *PostSecret* app brought the abject into the intimate space of the user's pocket, handbag, or home. One could—and often did—encounter the abject secrets during the casual practice of browsing the app while waiting for public transport, before going to sleep, or killing time waiting in line. The technology of the app and its mode of delivery—the smartphone—freed the abject from its usual (contained) cultural sites of the cinema, art gallery and the book and put it in people's hands wherever they were. Understandably, this was distressing for the fans of the project who had been the app's first consumers and users. When the app was released, the repressive function failed, and the abject was let loose.

Attempts to moderate the abject content that was rapidly uploaded were quickly overwhelmed. The app included calls for volunteers to help moderate each upload *after* a secret was shared. In essence, the *Post-Secret* app was undone by the removal of Warren's role as the first *sole* reader of the secrets. The app, instead of "freeing" the community to share their secrets, created an instant audience for trolls who gleefully took up the role of giving voice to the aggressive abject forces of the collective unconscious online.[75] When forced to close the app because of an inability to moderate the content and complaints to the Federal Communications Commission and the Federal Bureau of Investigation (FBI), Warren claimed that "99% of the secrets were created in the spirit of *PostSecret*."[76] Yet the failed app demonstrates the continued importance of gatekeepers in the crowdsourcing space, whose role is to police the adherence of content to the aims of the project and community standards (however defined), and ensure the continued coherence and therefore marketability of the product.

Yet, as Warren himself tells us in his live event, *PostSecret* has always involved the darker, weirder secrets that were unleashed on the app. During the first part of the performance, Warren reveals that the most common secret he receives is the confession "I pee in the shower." This abject moment—violating the line between the spaces and practices of cleanliness and bodily waste—is so banal and common that Warren rarely publishes the postcards on the blog in his weekly updates. We might speculate as to what kind of collectivity *PostSecret* would make possible if Warren published a book solely of the peeing secrets, or at least made the universality of the practice visible on the blog. In curating the project in such a way that the visibility of abject secrets is minimized, Warren created a logic for the intimate public that was unsupportable once the secrets began flowing freely.[77]

Conclusion

While life stories have always had a commercial component—as exemplified by the whore biographies of the seventeenth century—crowdsourced self-life-inscription makes life a potential source of commercial enterprise for the entrepreneur. This is because it confirms and markets *universalizing truths* about the life we are living, rather than providing salacious insight into the lives of others. Life, as seen through the practices and texts of confessional entrepreneurship, produces material that burdens us: secrets, archival material such as teenage diaries or photographs, and everyday experiences themselves. Living, then, requires the logic of confession: we are unburdened from the material, and in return we are promised the feeling of being seen for who we are by others. This confession brings the promise of intimacy, of greater knowledge about others and the potential for stronger or new social bonds. In participating in intimate publics through the creation and witnessing of autobiographical fragments, we contribute to the production of truth about life itself—at least, that is what the confessional entrepreneur would like us to believe. Recognition from the collective, *feeling* included in the intimate public, produces the effect of community, and community is a component of the good life because it offers recognition of "who we *really* are."

On the one hand, then, the version of the social bond and relationality narrated in the intimate publics created by confessional entrepreneurs offers a form of intimacy that Michael Hardt argues cannot lead to a "properly political" account of love or knowledge. According to Hardt, this form of intimacy "generally names either the bond experienced by those who are already the same or the process of unification by which differences are shed or set aside."[78] The coaxing of autobiographical narratives to highly prescriptive templates in order to make a reliable commodity form in confessional entrepreneurship is based on formal unification: the modes of expression that facilitate intimacy must be identical—postcard, interview, live performance with a clear narrative arc. In this sense, then, confessional entrepreneurship claims to produce social bonds, but these bonds are predicated, to quote Hardt again, on "logics of sameness and processes of unification," which are inimical to the reality that "politics requires multiplicity and must function through the encounter and interaction of differences."[79] That confessional entrepreneurs, always American, slip so easily in their discourse between America and the world, between specific communities and humanity, while also finding significant audiences outside of America, demonstrates that the *feeling* of being seen or being included—as Berlant has shown—is, for some people, a genuine experience of the social bond.

This claim to universality is advanced through another strategy common to confessional entrepreneurial projects and demonstrates how crowdsourced life narrative projects have successfully exploited the neoliberal preference for opening up education and community services to nongovernment service providers. Many confessional entrepreneurial projects are registered not-for-profit organizations (*The Moth, Six-Word Memoirs, StoryCorps*) that solicit donations from the community and support from government and philanthropic organizations to expand their work beyond crowdsourcing to specific communities that are often the subject of increased surveillance and forms of biopolitical management by being described as underrepresented or marginalized, such as young people and African American and immigrant communities. *The Moth*, for example, has had enormous success in introducing its narrative and performance template in New York high schools and youth juvenile justice programs.[80] In so doing, the confessional entrepreneur overwrites existing practices of autobiography within those communities with story formats and media forms that adhere to their "proven" model. These "proven" models are also marketed to corporate clients where the confessional entrepreneurial project offers access to their narrative and media expertise through "storytelling workshops" that can enhance a corporation's engagement with their clients, highlighting how self-life-inscription can be adapted to institutional and commercial environments where giving an account of oneself serves the purpose of inscribing individuals into commercialized transactions and corporate identities.[81]

Given all this, what might we say about the social bond that is constructed by crowdsourced autobiography that is collected and remediated by confessional entrepreneurs? It is one that is readily accessible, but which makes few demands on us beyond occasional participation through the production of content and the purchase of merchandise or a ticket to a live performance. The intimate public created offers a lighter mode of experiencing connection and recognition. This mode involves using sentimental narratives and affective encounters to "imagine yourself with someone else's stress, pain, or humiliated identity."[82] The intimate public is spread across media to form a transmedial scene that can be visited—online or through books or events—when needed, or when filling in time. Like the practice of "love locks"—padlocks attached to public architecture such as bridges, that create installations of mass love—confessional entrepreneurship works through accumulation and attracts audiences who "drop in" for some uplifting togetherness and confirmation of truths about life. Crowdsourced autobiography, in the model developed by confessional entrepreneurs, is about creating shared pockets of buoyancy that have fewer demands than permanent structures of belonging. Like love locks, the aim is to adorn the bridge, not build it.

"Affective attachments to media are not in themselves sufficient to produce actual communities," Jodi Dean argues. "Neither does the circulation of affect through multiple, networked media imply stimulus junkies in blank-eyed isolation before their screens. Affective networks produce feelings of community, or what we might call 'community without community.'"[83] While Dean argues that networked attachments are dynamic forms that refuse formalization, confessional entrepreneurship and its most successful projects such as *PostSecret* and *The Moth* demonstrate that affective networks can be profoundly stable and formalized when grounded in analog media forms whose materiality anchors the affective claims of the public. This coherency is organized and mediated by cultural professionals with strong visions and flexible strategies for ensuring coherent contributions to their projects. The central role of the entrepreneur in structuring, policing, and perpetuating the scene confirms that while crowdsourced affective networks *imply* collectivity based on preexisting skills and feelings, they rely on the work and vision of a core group of professionals to be sustained. These are the people who stand to benefit from the insertion of intimacy into the circuits of communicative capitalism through increased cultural, symbolic, and financial capital. But their skills and influence in the project must be carefully negotiated in order to maintain the logic that the intimate public merely expresses and collects what already existed.

There is, of course, a danger in dismissing light and nontraditional modes of feeling community on the basis that they don't look like or function as "traditional" modes of community do (or should). Such traditional modes often involve uneven distribution of emotional and physical labor, as well as uneven forms of recognition. We might think of the communities made by confessional entrepreneurship as the "lighter touch forms of sociality" theorized by Nigel Thrift.[84] Not everyone wants to build the bridge, after all; some just want to walk on it, adorn it, or enjoy the view—at least some of the time. From this perspective, we might think of crowdsourced self-life-inscription as a means of creating and valuing these lighter forms of connection that are not invested with permanence, seriousness, and the weight of life as in a book or archive. Despite the grandiose claims of the entrepreneurs who run the projects, *PostSecret*, *The Moth*, and *StoryCorps* will not change the world, or make one, and they remain embedded in the logics of communicative capitalism. The extent to which the narrative and media templates they developed are integrated into institutional practices of coaxing life stories demonstrates their strong alignment with the role of confession in bringing the subject within the realm of power/knowledge of civic institutions such as the school.

To those who voluntarily participate in these projects, they offer up a collectively authored practice of making life matter that temporarily relieves the individual from the quandary of their own life. Do we call this intimacy? Certainly we can see the logic of the intimate public at work here—attachment to the public is driven by desire and affect, rather than purposive will, and people feel like the logic of the intimate public "gets them" before they *know* why it does.[85] Engaging with a confessional entrepreneurial project could be described as a process of *feeling* communal and feeling the significance of being in common without thinking about it too much. It privileges ambiance over archive.

The distinct forms of mediation and remediation offered by networked media, and the social web in particular, are synchronous with the aims of these intimate publics. Unlike the materially grounded and monumental archive produced by Warhol, confessional entrepreneurship uses the distinctive immediacy, ephemerality, and accessibility of online platforms and live events to offer up a space of belonging that people can integrate into their everyday lives and "dip into" as required. These projects also reorganize and resituate the primary importance of the narrating subject in autobiography, from one who seeks their place "on the record" of history to something more akin to a voice in a choir. This shift in emphasis and use of the voice of the autobiographer is the focus of the next chapter, where I consider how queer autobiographers use collage to remediate popular culture to stage an encounter between audiences and queer lives.

4

Collage

In the previous chapter, I examined how the voices in the choir of crowdsourced autobiography sing a tune of self-life-inscription that is orchestrated by confessional entrepreneurs. This chapter continues an interest in the role of voice in self-life-inscription, but it returns to single-authored autobiographical texts that, while claiming to be about one person's life experience, use the words and voices of others to present it. I explore how the use of collage creates a form of ventriloquized self-life-inscription that destabilizes the unique relationship between author, text, and life many believe is the root of life writing's cultural and political power. The argument being developed across the chapters of *Stories of the Self* is that scholarly approaches to autobiography are particularly good at accounting for the complex ways in which self-life-writing is a narrative, cultural, aesthetic, psychological, and social practice, but are not as good at contending with autobiography as a *mediated* and *material* practice. To this end, this chapter develops a way of reading materiality and mediation in some examples of queer autobiography by expanding on Eve Sedgwick's speculative theory of the periperformative utterance.

Like Sedgwick, I approach the survival and flourishing of queer lives as an issue intrinsically linked to inventive, counterintuitive, and disobedient practices of reading and adaptation. Sedgwick links the lived experience of reading for survival and the academic practice of reading at the center of her theory of queerness in the influential essay "Queer and Now." Under the heading "Promising, Smuggling, Reading, Overreading," she offers a theory of queer reading in the form of an autobiographical vignette:

> I think that for many of us in childhood the ability to attach intently to a few cultural objects, objects of high or popular culture or both, objects whose meaning seemed mysterious, excessive, or oblique in relation to

the codes most readily available to us, became a prime resource for survival. We needed for there to be sites where the meanings didn't line up tidily with each other, and we learned to invest those sites with fascination and love. This can't help coloring the adult relation to cultural text and objects; in fact, it's almost hard for me to imagine another way of coming to care enough about literature to give a lifetime to it. The demands on both the text and the reader from so intent an attachment can be multiple, even paradoxical.[1]

In the work of many scholars of queer culture, we see how aesthetic experiences—which are mediated and material—are resources for living.[2] Indeed, the impact of Sedgwick's influential theory of reparative reading—which offers queer practices of reading and writing as counterexamples to acts of paranoid reading—enshrines the relationship between life and texts, living and reading, into the heart of a reconsideration of critical practice.[3] This chapter extends this strand of Sedgwick's work by focusing explicitly on how some queer autobiographers voice their experiences of reparative reading through a very material form of ventriloquism. The queer collages I explore in this chapter *narrate* the importance of media texts in the lives of queer young people while making complex use of mediation and material strategies. They open out our consideration of self-life-inscription as a mediated practice to the creative reuse of media materialities in the project of valuing queer lives.

Here is an example of the kind of text I am referring to:

> i wanna be like tweet, the kind of person who can call their own body *tantalizing* in just such a tone of voice that you can't help believing it. yeah stare if you want to. feeling kinda twisted. my shirt lifted up over my head, i'm slipping. they got me thinking all kinds of crazy thoughts and touching myself & wanting myself loving myself. that's so nasty. the do it yourself renaissance. what are the politics of living beautifully, intensely—wanting more—wanting everything to be slippery and audacious, forever in glamorous transition—wanting what you can't have—wanting it badly—wanting you to call at the break of dawn—i'll be sure to meet you with no panties on—wanting to be like tweet. the kind of person who says *tantalizing* like they mean it.[4]

This paragraph appears in a personal zine written by an Australian who identifies as a queer person with progressive political views. As I discuss in more detail in *Intimate Ephemera*, *Handpash* is a wonderful example of the vibrant, tactical, and compelling use of autobiography in zine culture.[5] I will return to a close analysis of Sandy's use of Tweet's performance to narrate the possibility of a queer life defined by self-love and self-respect later in the chapter. For now, I want to briefly comment on their use of a song about masturbation and consider how this choice strikes at the heart of a mode of reading autobiography that is deeply invested in the social use value of personal storytelling.

The song in which Tweet so compellingly describes her body as "tantalizing," which Sandy draws on to articulate their desires for a queer life, is "Oops, (Oh My)" (2002). It is sung by a female performer and narrates and celebrates masturbation. This is of critical importance to Sandy's question of how living might be "forever in glamorous transition." Tweet's performance of the masturbating girl,[6] like Sandy's reuse of that performance, opens up a new way of thinking about the relationship between an autobiographer and their audience by directly challenging the genre expectations that structure the production and reception of self-life-inscription.[7] The scholarly emphasis on the interpersonal nature of the truth and the work that autobiographical discourse performs (discussed in more detail later) codifies the requirement that the autobiographer convince the audience that they are not merely a masturbator, interested in the narcissistic self-pleasure of narrating themselves. Masturbation, I would suggest, is *the* pejorative of choice when criticizing autobiography, although we often encounter the charge of self-pleasuring described with the more polite term "narcissism." In contemporary popular debates about the rise of memoir, the term "narcissism" acts as a synonym for onanism. When a columnist or critic writes "narcissism," they are often accusing the autobiographer of making work merely to please themselves; acting out of self-interest, being interested in self-pleasuring, and engaging in unproductive labor (a corollary to the sin of engaging in nonreproductive sex).[8] As Karen Barad remarks of the perverse self-touching habits of electrons discovered through quantum field theory: "Apparently, touching oneself, or being touched by oneself—the ambiguity/undecidability/indeterminacy may itself be the key to the trouble—is not simply troubling, but a *moral* violation, the very source of all the trouble."[9]

We can see this trouble in the subtext of Neil Genzlinger's *New York Times* article "The Problem with Memoirs." In the essay, Genzlinger describes being exhausted by the memoir boom, admonishing authors of memoirs, decrying their mediocrity and the lack of interest their stories and experiences offer others. His opening line—"A moment of silence, please, for the lost art of shutting up"—clearly establishes Genzlinger's opposition to the excessive, unnecessary practice of memoir production. The subtext of Genzlinger's critique is immediately familiar to those working in the field of life writing scholarship: in its performative mode, the narrator of an autobiography must exorcise the masturbator if they are to successfully interpellate an audience to their utterance. In the wake of the rising visibility and commercial success of memoir, autobiographers must increasingly convince a skeptical critical culture not only of the authority of their experience but also of the relevance of that experience to a community beyond the narrator. Thus, for many life writers, "the authority to narrate is hard-won in a constant engagement with readers posited as skeptical, unbelieving, resistant, and even hostile."[10]

The vein of sentiment against memoir and autobiographical discourse in mainstream commentary such as Genzlinger's can be reinforced within scholarship on life writing that relies too heavily on arguments about the performative power of autobiographical discourse in empowering marginalized subjects by making them available for intersubjective encounters with audiences in the social field. Both sites of commentary on autobiography insist that the value of self-life-inscription is founded on a rejection of self-pleasure by the autobiographer and insist on a specific morally valuable form of relationality, which strongly echoes the early negative depiction of masturbation in discourses of sexuality.[11] A categorical rejection of the pleasure of self-life-inscription is a means of policing the insistence on intersubjective truth that scholars and commentators often posit as being the value of life writing in contemporary culture, politics and society.[12]

The Dual Performative Function of Autobiography

Current scholarship on autobiography situates the act of presenting a narrative of one's life as the performative utterance that produces the self and a life, and their value.[13] Autobiography is performative in the sense that it is through the utterance of narration that the subjectivity and the life are brought into being—and the reiteration of this utterance, as Butler argues, involves the continued citation of norms of identity.[14] Thus, self-life-inscription is both a continuation of the requirement to constantly perform identity in relation to preexisting norms, and a chosen creative act that offers a potential reader an encounter with a version of one's lived experience that promises to enhance the reader's understanding of a life and of the social world.[15] Autobiography is a "form of writing that keeps less, gives more . . . the reader, becomes the guest invited in, the unknown, self-selected other whose response matters."[16]

This dominant account of autobiography as a performative utterance conceptualizes self-life-inscription as having three interconnected social, cultural, political, and historical functions: it is a narrative form that makes specific kinds of truth claims (claims about an individual's experience that are made available through the text); it holds a unique status as a nonfictional genre or mode because it make claims about reality; and the claims made in autobiography matter because they offer authors access to the field of social recognition, and readers a means of engaging in an intersubjective exchange in which they learn something new about the world.[17] This way of understanding self-life-inscription has been particularly important for analyzing the use of autobiographical discourse by marginalized subjects, where it is often examined in terms of its ability to make specific identities and lived experiences visible in the social field.[18]

G. Thomas Couser, for example, is deeply committed to thinking about memoir as a genre that is inherently political: uniquely democratic, and important to democracy, because, in narrating their lives in memoir, "previously marginalized or oppressed populations: gays and lesbians, people with various stigmatized illnesses and disabilities, and so on" claim their rights.[19] In such cases, Couser argues, "their very speech is significant work . . . the work has a performative dimension. It *acts out* its message: I'm here and I can speak for myself."[20] Media studies scholar Nick Couldry agrees, arguing that voice has a "*second-order value* that is embodied in the process of mutually recognizing our claims on each as reflective human agents, each with an account to give, an account of our lives that needs to be registered and heard, our stories endlessly entangled in each others' [*sic*] stories."[21] Yet, returning to Sandy's desire for a tantalizing life, we see a problem arise when claims about the performative force of the autobiographical speech act assume a direct correspondence between the body of the speaker, the content of the utterance, and the materialization of the voice (its sound, timbre, and so on). Does Sandy speak for themself when they speak as/with Tweet? And what, exactly, is the truth that is claimed, or the self they give an account of, when they use Tweet's performance to write their desire for a tantalizing queer life?

How people find a voice to speak for and about themselves is important for our understanding of collective politics because, as the scholars I have just been engaging with acknowledge, the social field requires, and is predicated on, our relationality. Thus, the cultural and political value of autobiography lies in the fact that it facilitates relationality through the intersubjective connection that occurs between author and reader when autobiography is created and shared. The important cultural, social, and political work undertaken by autobiography means that textuality, materiality, and aesthetics intersect with social structures of value in unique and pressing ways.[22] To begin with the textual and aesthetic, when autobiographers speak about themselves and their lives, they draw on preexisting genre and rhetorical conventions that mark out personal storytelling as a distinct textual practice that is underpinned by a promise to speak "in a spirit of truth."[23] In the case of formal techniques, the "autobiographical pact" is materialized through a combination of literary techniques and the author's and reader's awareness of preexisting genre expectations.[24] Common techniques associated with the pact in prose include the name of the author corresponding with the name of the narrator, and the use of voice to constitute both the authorial subject (the narrating "I") and the subject of the narrative (the narrated "I").[25] While individual authors make use of other techniques relating to the presentation of evidence, memory, and the role of others in their lives, these autobiographical techniques are largely accepted as the minimum textual requirements for autobiography to be recognized as a nonfictional genre, and are fundamental to its performative power.[26] As I am exploring throughout this book, however, mediation also plays an important role in securing, or problematizing, autobiography's performative power that is rarely given sustained attention.[27]

However, the underlying problem of the relationship between autobiography and the circulation of normative concepts of identity and what constitutes "a life" remains a tension within contemporary cultural studies. As Lauren Berlant observes, after her attendance at the largest biennial academic conference dedicated to life writing:[28]

> To my ear, the genre of the "life" is a most destructive conventionalized form of normativity: when norms feel like laws, they constitute a social pedagogy of the rules for belonging and intelligibility whose narrowness threatens people's capacity to invent ways to attach to the world.[29]

"Get a life!" is perhaps the most easily recognizable phrase that articulates the structuring power of the genre of the "life" Berlant evokes, and which haunts any attempt to characterize self-life-inscription as "giving voice" to lived experience and in so doing establish one's identity in the social field.[30] The injunction to "get a life" passes judgment not on the subject but on their actions, orientations, investments, and attachments. "A life" in this sense—indeed, as evoked by early modes of autobiography and biography—is an achievement not of subjectivity but of action. It is the *doing* that counts in *having* "a life." As a significant thread in recent queer theory argues—Sara Ahmed's critique of happiness, Berlant's theorizing of intimate publics and cruel optimism, Halberstam's rethinking of failure, Edelman's critique of hopeful futurism, and Flatley's exploration of Warholian liking—the objects and goals we attach to and pursue as the things that give life meaning are fundamental to how we find a place in the social field, and what opportunities for survival and thriving are open to us. This other way of thinking about the life in self-life-inscription—not as a subject made visible or precarious through the citation of discourses of identity but as an ongoing process of being in the world made up of activities, fantasies, attachments, and orientations—raises a challenge for how we read and understand the performative function of autobiography.

Taken together, scholarship on queer cultures that demonstrates the importance of reading to queer lives, and queer theory that argues that what constitutes "a life" is as much about orientations and objects as it is about identity, productively challenge an overinvestment in autobiography as a narrative of identity intended to be encountered in a generalizable mode of reading that can be summarized as an "intersubjective exchange" between two fixed subjects (narrator or writer, and reader). In queer accounts, reading and living are far more complicated, involving inventive strategies of (to return to Sedgwick) "promising, smuggling, reading and overreading." An account of autobiography that insists on the social and political use value of autobiography to marginalized subjects and those who wish to encounter them can promote instrumentalized reading that prioritizes autobiography as a social good rather than a complex, aesthetic, creative practice. This chapter develops a way of reading queer collaged autobiographies that maintains a critical investment in the importance of presenting and encountering queer lived experience, but which recognizes that how an individual text achieves this may queer our understanding of what self-life-inscription is and does (or could be).

In order to advance this line of inquiry, in this chapter I propose a method for reading periperformative autobiography, extending a speculative concept outlined by Eve Sedgwick. The chapter reads for examples of queer self-life-writing that cluster around autobiography as a performative mode and identifies how they attempt to respond to the consensus assumed by its forms, aesthetics, and ideologies. Sedgwick's theory of the periperformative makes possible an alternative way of reading the relationship between marginalized subjects and the practice of autobiography, which redirects our understanding of the citational power of the performative toward a reconsideration of the primacy given to the original voice of the autobiographer in our understanding of what autobiography is,[31] and the importance of media to finding ways to materialize and inscribe queer configurations of *auto*, *bios*, and *zoē*.

Periperformativity: Voice and Response

The term "periperformative" describes a particular kind of utterance that seeks to respond to the normative claims and subject positions that are enabled by the performative utterance theorized by J. L. Austin. Extending the poststructuralist interest in linguistic performativity, Sedgwick argues that in spatial proximity to Austin's performative statement—an elite class of statement that does not describe an action in the world but constitutes one—exists the *possibility* for another kind of statement. This other statement seeks to disentangle *its* speaker from the assumed consensus that emanates from the performative utterance and its speaker.[32] Rather than pay attention to the speaker of the performative and the speech act they undertake, Sedgwick draws our attention to the reliance of the performative on a consenting audience or witness, crucially returning critical attention to the interconnectedness of production and reception. Sedgwick illustrates this point with two examples. One is the seemingly innocuous performative utterance of "I dare you." The other is the highly charged and ideological utterance "I do" in the marriage vow.[33] In both cases, her focus is not on the relationship between addressor and addressee, but on the interpellating power these statements have on those who witness them being uttered, and how the performative utterance is a material, spatialized act. In the case of "I dare you," Sedgwick demonstrates how the statement—made by an addressor and directed at an addressee—interpellates an audience of people *in front of* whom the statement is made. When "I dare you," I interpellate an audience of people whom I hail to bear witness to both your having been dared and your reaction to that dare. This interpellation of an audience is the source of the power of the utterance to function as an act, and is a materialization of discourse. The witnesses to my speech act are interpellated—made *material witnesses* to the dare—because the force of my statement implies that they side with me in being interested in your capacity to do whatever you have been dared to do, or be branded a "wuss."[34] Witnesses are presumed to share the value of defending one's honor and the problem posed by the possibility of dishonor or wussiness by virtue of being physically or materially present when the dare is presented. "Thus," Sedgwick suggests, "'I dare you' invokes a presumption, but only the presumption, of a consensus between speaker and witness, and to some extent between all of them and the addressee."[35]

It is in the *assumption* of consensus—the speaker's ability to *assume* that the addressee and the audience agree with the values that underpin the utterance, and in doing so interpellate them as subjects who hold those normative values—that the performative statement is normative. Eschewing negotiation or the possibility of disagreement about the value of wussiness or the privileged legal and social status of the married couple, the performative utterance shores up and is a materialization of the values it assumes preexist it and which are consensus.[36] As Judith Butler argues, it is in the act of citation and reiteration that discourse materializes power.[37] Thus performatives are themselves localized, material instances of discourse that draw on a range of media forms and material conditions to enact power.

The periperformative utterance—or at least the idea of its possibility—responds to this localized moment of the materialization of discourse by attempting to describe how things might be otherwise. In drawing our attention to the interpellating and materializing power of the performative statement, Sedgwick highlights the problem one faces in disentangling oneself from the normative, consensus view presumed by it. There is no formulaic negative response to witnessing a performative (one cannot immediately chime in from the sidelines with "I undare you"): "To disinterpellate from a performative scene will usually require, not another explicit performance nor simply the negative of one, but the nonce, referential act of a periperformative."[38] In the case of the wedding vow, the most realistic strategy may be to not show up to the moment when the performative will be uttered in the ceremony.[39] Periperformative statements, then, "are *about* performatives and, more properly, . . . cluster *around* performatives";[40] they are attempts by individuals interpellated by being the witness of a performative utterance to destabilize the consensus values or ideologies that are materialized by the performative utterance and to contest its power to *do* some specific *thing* in the world (create obligation, sanction specific forms of attachment, make an experience intelligible) and presume the witness's agreement with the values that underpin that thing.

Sedgwick herself wondered whether positing the concept of the periperformative could produce any critical insight. When she revisited the concept in her final work, *The Weather in Proust*, in a discussion of the poetry of C. P. Cavafy, she tells us:

> I've long puzzled over the status of the idea of the periperformative utterance. Given that there logically has to be such a thing, as long as there is a class (however uncircumscribable) of explicit performative utterance—given that, does the new classification have any more than a nominal substance; is it of any *use?*[41]

In trying to read for the periperformative in a field that already has a strong reliance on the concept of the performative, this chapter attempts to answer Sedgwick's question. The possibility of the autobiographical periperformative draws the critic's attention to those artists who may wish to critique the terms, genres, and *media forms* through which an "I" is constituted, under what medial conditions it can speak, is materialized, and considered trustworthy. To recognize the possibility that such texts might exist, and to go in search of them, we must first acknowledge the "high threshold of initiative"[42] required by the periperformative and to think differently about the role of formalist readings that aim to further our understanding of why and how making nonfictional claims about selves and lives matters.

There is some urgency for this intervention, to my mind, given the kinds of conclusions that can be produced by the intersection in current scholarship of the privileged role given to autobiographical discourse in making visible trustworthy subjects, and statements regarding aesthetic techniques that materialize that discourse. One example of this is Couser's proposition that, in thinking about how memoir makes previously unheard voices legible "we," as readers, don't need to read for meaning.[43] The straightforwardness associated with the performative, the agreement that we all know what underpins both the authority of the speaker and our consensus with the values their utterance implies, leads Couser to suggest that interpretation is not what "we" do when "we" read "memoir." Instead, he suggests, we must ask, "what is its purpose?"[44] The suggestion that we no longer need to read for meaning, but only for purpose, is central to Couser's theory of the distinction between memoir and fiction: memoir has a more specific, and limited, function in order to exert "*leverage* (force) on reality."[45] This leads Couser to conclude that the performative function of memoir means its materialization in media and style must be less ambiguous (and ambitious?) than in fiction. In what follows I propose that the periperformative is a way of expanding our critical purview to attend to autobiographies that seek to tell other kinds of truths about living while not evoking the normative values and techniques that materialize and authorize the performative power of autobiography. Inventive and disruptive remediation of existing media texts is a primary aesthetic technique used in this process, and thus the concept of the periperformative can also contribute to the project of reading for the variety of ways mediation contributes to the process of making lives matter.

Homemade Queer Life

Homemade autobiographical texts by queer subjects made using collage present a compelling counterexample to the prioritizing of intelligibility and recognition promised by adherence to the aesthetic and generic expectations of giving an account of oneself.[46] In what follows, I read some examples of these texts as attempts to make a periperformative response to the normative discourses and media forms associated with autobiography. They are periperformative because they do not conform to the expectation that one must use one's own voice when speaking a truth about one's life or lived experience. These texts invite us to reconsider the centrality of a unique voice as a guarantor of the truth of autobiography.

In the examples I explore here, the use of collage produces autobiography characterized by ventriloquism and remediation. One of the texts, a documentary film, uses split screen and montage in order to speak back to the power of life narrative to exert leverage on reality. The other, as we have already seen, is a personal zine that uses ventriloquism as a means of narrating the importance of other people's voices in speaking the truth about the desire to live a tantalizing queer existence. In both cases, the autobiographers speak as and with figures from popular culture to tell the story of trying to develop an understanding of what having a life might mean. They evidence the importance of media forms—popular music, television, film, rock opera—and remediation to the process of making queer life matter. They depict the role of media in the author's search for hope, identification, possibility, and experimentation. The authors, like numerous authors of personal zines, blogs, and Tumblrs, tell a story of "the emergence of the first person, of the singular, of the active, and of the indicative" which insists that such positions "are all questions rather than presumptions for queer performativity."[47]

The first case study, the documentary *Tarnation* (2003), gives numerous examples of how aesthetics and media are fundamental resources for making a life through self-life-inscription and demonstrates how the voices of others can become resources for giving an account of queer life.

Tarnation: Assembling a Way to Live

In *Tarnation*, Jonathan Caouette uses the associative logic of collage to tell a number of interconnected stories. One narrative follows the story of Caouette's family and their poverty, his mother's severe and ongoing mental health problems, and the inadequate care and treatment she has received. Another prominent narrative in the film details Caouette's childhood, adolescence, and young adulthood in this context, and is a relational narrative that explores the influence of his mother, grandmother, and grandfather on his early life. The third narrative is about Caouette's practices of reparative reading: his relationship with popular culture as a resource for living and making sense of his family environment.[48] Like *Stories We Tell*, discussed in chapter 2, *Tarnation* makes use of an existing archive of home movie footage. The film is made up of such footage taken from Caouette's family archive (most of it shot by Caouette when he was an adolescent); material shot on a digital video camera explicitly for inclusion in the documentary, including observational footage, interviews with family members, and reenactments; and numerous clips taken from television and cinema texts. While *Tarnation* exposes the impact of his mother's illness on Caouette's life, the film also shows the variety of ways Caouette found to hope, dream, and live in and around his changing family situation. *Tarnation* is a digitally assembled collage (made using the consumer grade editing program iMovie) that uses techniques such as split screen, intertitles, and montage. These techniques of mediation and remediation both mimic Caouette's impression of his mother's dissociative cognition and proffer ways of living alongside it. As I discuss in further detail later, these formal techniques for assembling the film from a variety of media materials mirror the strategies for living that Jonathan developed in his childhood and which are also the subject of the film.[49]

One example of how the techniques of montage and subtitles are used for periperformative ends is a sequence that describes the media fantasies of the fourteen-year-old Jonathan. The narration is placed as subtitles below a montage of short audiovisual clips from television and cinema that mimic the quick movement across content achieved by channel surfing. The text reads:

At 14, Jonathan began having this recurring dream. / The dream was about a tall blonde boy. / Who resembled a grown-up version of "The Little Prince" / Jonathan also began to have a fantasy / of being in rock musicals like "Hair." / Jonathan thought that if one day / He met producer Roger Stigwood / They could collaborate / on a rock opera about Jonathan's life / Zero Mostel could play Adolph [Jonathan's grandfather] / Louise Lasser could play Rosemary [Jonathan's grandmother] / Robbie Benson could play Jonathan / Joni Mitchell could play Renee [Jonathan's mother] / Mavis Staples could play the social worker / Nina Hagen and Klaus Nomi could play the foster parents [who Jonathan was sent to live with as a child] / and the cast of "Zoom" could serve as a chorus / of troubled kids in foster care. / There would be nothing like it.

In this montage sequence, Caouette stages an encounter between his audience and an important strategy he used as a child and adolescent to maintain belief in a future that might be different from the present. Importantly, this strategy involves remediating his experience, but the genre and media form the child turns to is not one associated with print autobiography—the canonical material on which most claims about the performative power of autobiography are based—but the melodramatic hybrid genre of the rock opera. The rock opera, with its visceral embodied power of physical performance, sidesteps the rhetorical requirements for narration in "a spirit of truth" in favor of a melodramatic transmission of truthful feeling in performance. For Jonathan, it is rock opera, not autobiography, whose genre traits and materiality offer the aesthetic strategies needed to represent his childhood experience.[50] The montage enacts the channel-surfing strategy the child Jonathan used to seek out narratives and media forms he could draw on to make sense of his experience.

In narrating his fantasy of telling the story of his life *as* rock opera, Caouette demonstrates that this strategy moved beyond consumption to the performance and reenactment of popular culture in a way commonly associated with camp. Caouette's use of camp is defined by "prizing the form away from its content" and valuing style, and the "playing" of various roles.[51] Caouette presents the audience with an example of his belief in the transformative potential of the style and materiality of the rock opera using the technique of montage.

His childhood coping strategies of remediation *are* the life narrative, rather than the subject of a confession that would confirm the causal relationship between poverty, parental mental illness, and unhappiness that would establish his identity as a survivor. In his recurring dream, the child resists the paranoid position that sees in the future only a confirmation of his fears (in this case the determining and monolithic power of mental illness and poverty).[52] He also refuses to believe that these material conditions determine what his life is or what it means. Caouette narrates the dream itself as a technique to distance his autobiographical storytelling from the normative conditions of autobiography and "its almost legalistic definition of truth telling, its anxiety about invention, and its preference for the literal and the verifiable."[53] The dream *is* the reality Caouette wishes to present with fidelity, rather than the *need* for the dream being the focus of his narrative. Jonathan's passionate attachment to the rock opera form and its various figures critiques the powerful association between testimony (as a form of speaking about one's life) and the trustworthy subject that is constructed by the performative utterance of the memoir of traumatic childhood that rose to prominence in the 1990s and 2000s.[54] By representing his use of melodramatic forms and subjects from popular culture to make sense of his experience, Caouette creates a periperformative autobiography to tell the story of his life that queers the relationship between the narrating "I" and the narrated "I."

Sedgwick speculates on the relationship between the periperformative and camp when she revisits the periperformative in *The Weather in Proust*. After wondering about the usefulness of the concept, she notes:

> My particular range of reading being what it is—or indeed probably for a more substantive reason—such moments of art have seemed to me to cluster around recognizably queer authors and cultural values. Queer, I might even say, verging on camp. But that's supposing we managed to think of camp, as I believe we need to, not in terms of parody or even wit, but with more of an eye for its visceral, operatic power: the startling outcrops of overinvested erudition; the prodigal production of alternative histories; the "over"-attachment to fragmentary, marginal, waste, lost, or leftover cultural products; the richness of affective variety; and the irrepressible, cathartic fascination with ventriloquist forms of relation.[55]

It is the "cathartic fascination with ventriloquist forms of relation" that Caouette uses in the sequence described earlier to critique autobiography as a performative, specifically its citation and materialization of the discourse of identity through the autobiographical pact. The genre of the rock opera, the fourteen-year-old Jonathan feels, is a far more effective medium for seeking recognition of his experiences, for materializing their importance, than crafting a narrative that can be easily believed by the audience to be true by avoiding aesthetic strategies that destabilize the truth claims of the text.

In the next sequence in the documentary, Caouette furthers his use of camp to critique the formal requirement of the autobiographical pact and the use of voice to constitute both the authorial subject (the narrating "I") and the subject of the narrative (the narrated "I") as constitutive of the performative power of autobiography. Here, Caouette replaces the montage with the technique of the split screen; first three screens, then four, are visible. Each screen cycles through a collage of home video footage showing Jonathan, his mother and grandparents, films (such as *The Little Prince* [1974], *Come Back to the 5 & Dime Jimmy Dean, Jimmy Dean* [1982], and *Rosemary's Baby* [1968]), and television programs (such as the 1970s children's program *Zoom!*). The soundtrack is also a collage: the sequence is accompanied by Shelley Plimpton singing the song "Frank Mills" from *Hair*, with the audio from the other screens audible, and intelligible, in the mix. Recurring footage in the right-hand bottom corner shows a head shot of Jonathan as a teenager, lip-synching the song "Frank Mills" along with the soundtrack (figure 4.1).

One of the things we see in this sequence is that, for the young Jonathan, camp performance is a means of creating and sustaining a reparative position in relation to the *possibility* of his life.[56] He achieves this by drawing on the power of the performer's agency in popular culture. Jonathan's youthful performances are perhaps a precursor to the reworkings of camp studied by Aymar Jean Christian, where lip-synching performers on YouTube are "infusing sincerity, emotion and deeper meanings of selfhood in 'camp,'" heralding a shift away from previous uses of camp for ironic distancing.[57] In borrowing the voices and agency of others, Caouette disregards the primacy of the autobiographical pact that secures the relationship between subject, narrator, and author. Instead, he

Figure 4.1. Split-screen sequence to the soundtrack of "Frank Mills," from Caouette, *Tarnation*.

speaks as and with Plimpton through the character Crissy, the fictional narrator of "Frank Mills." But this is not impetuous rule breaking for its own sake. This technique of remediation and ventriloquism is adopted to materialize something vitally important to Caouette's life and way of living, namely, his experience of growing up queer in Texas in a family shaped by his mother's mental illness. Rather than adopt the established techniques of truth telling that insist on an indexical relationship between author, narrator, and subject—unified by voice—Caouette deploys ventriloquism, a technique associated with camp and postmodernism. In so doing, he does not adhere to the aesthetic requirements of autobiography that secure its status as a performative utterance that brings a subject and a life into being. Yet his documentary is still clearly an act of self-life-inscription.

We can better appreciate Caouette's film as an example of a periperformative autobiography by considering Couser's discussion of the (im)possibility of postmodern memoir, where he suggests that postmodern techniques fundamentally risk the performative power of autobiographical discourse:

> There is a danger to the memoir in flaunting this notion [of the work as a construction] as postmodernism does: the more the creator insists on its artificiality, the less force the narrative may have, the weaker its "purchase" on the world. . . . to flaunt the artificiality of memoir is to go against the grain; to contradict its essence.[58]

Couser's concern returns us to Sedgwick's idea that periperformative statements are attempts by individuals (in this case, Caouette) interpellated by being the witness of a performative utterance (autobiographical discourse in specific media forms) to destabilize the consensus values or ideologies (the formal techniques for narrating a life that construct a trustworthy subject) that give the performative utterance its power to *do* something in the world, what Couser refers to as the "work that memoir does" and its "essence." Couser's belief in the essential (and essentialized) value and function of memoir returns us to the dominance of the view among life writing scholars that the power of autobiography often resides in its role as a discourse that is cited to gain access to culturally dominant modes of subjectivity and the recognition that flows from them. Here we see how this investment can misrecognize when autobiographers challenge genre conventions through specific aesthetic techniques and uses of mediation. Couser dismisses the aesthetic techniques of postmodernism *because* they risk the ideological function of autobiography as a discourse through which marginalized subjects can access recognition in the social field. What is at stake in such a dismissal?

One thing that distinguishes periperformative autobiography from postmodern memoir is that periperformative autobiography does not take up the postmodern critique of the impossibility of truth or a relationship between text and reality. Periperformative autobiography, rather, *wants* to make truth claims about the author's life experiences. The media and aesthetic used for these ends critique the terms and material conditions under which those claims can be made, and the consensus views about what makes a life meaningful that they assume, what Berlant refers to as "the presumed self-evident value of the bionarrative" and the idea of "the good life."[59] When Sedgwick revisited the concept of periperformativity in her discussion of the poetry of C. P. Cavafy, she further clarified the terms under which periperformatives respond to performatives by emphasizing that "the periperformative . . . is the grammar in which affect and subjectivity can be explicitly brought into relation with issues of performative force."[60] By describing the periperformative as grammar, Sedgwick highlights that speaking back to the force of performatives requires innovation not just in the content of what is said but in its very structure and materiality. Caouette gives us one example of a periperformative response to print forms of autobiography through his use of home video footage of his childhood self lip-synching to Shelley Plimpton's rendition of "Frank Mills." But to fully account for Caouette's use of Plimpton's voice as a means of narrating his life and putting the performative force of autobiographical discourse into a relation with affect and subjectivity, we must slow our reading down and take some time to contend with Jonathan's use of Plimpton's performative agency.[61]

The process of utilizing popular culture forms and genres as a means of building a queer identity is described by José Esteban Muñoz as a tactic of disidentification: "to read oneself and one's own life narrative in a moment, object or subject that is not culturally coded to 'connect' with the disidentifying subject."[62] This appropriation of an already powerful voice, or performative agency, has different valences for different critics. For Edward O'Neill "*performative agency* itself, the very power to perform," is central to camp not as an ironic form of distancing or paranoid lens but as a reparative position that responds to the experience of being interpellated as straight by mainstream culture.[63] In identifying with the power of the diva to bring *her* style to the character and the camera, "the very moment of stylization within the text becomes a point of identification as labor and as style and taste . . . and it is this *process*—not a static image, not an object for a subject—that beckons."[64] For Muñoz, it points to the melancholia that attends the lives of queers and people of color in white supremacist heteronormative culture.

In Jonathan's reparative reading, it is the pathos in the style and the mastery in Plimpton's performance that are marshaled as a resource for not only surviving, but seeking to thrive, in a family environment characterized by disassociation, disruption, and poverty—a context represented in the archival footage and narration that depict his family. In remediating the child's use of Plimpton into the split-screen sequence in *Tarnation*, Caouette demonstrates the importance of performative agency as a means of affectively registering—materializing—his own potential, and the potential latent in his life. Jonathan speaks in the voice of Plimpton in a melancholic tone about loss and longing (*I met a boy called Frank Mills on December 12 right here . . . but unfortunately, I lost his address*) and more complex feelings of ambivalence (*I love him, but it embarrasses me to walk down the street with him*). The sequence that precedes this, discussed earlier, uses the practice of channel surfing to structure the narration of Jonathan's fantasies of turning his life into a rock opera. In this sequence the everyday practice of media consumption and Jonathan's strong relationship with popular culture are presented as a resource for giving his experience of family dysfunction greater meaning ("There would be nothing like it"). As a document of his childhood strategies for staying attached to a belief in his life, the inclusion of the footage *is* the story of *Tarnation*. Accessing the style and labor of Plimpton's performance, by identifying with her performative agency, was a strategy Jonathan used to stay attached to life in the face of family dysfunction, poverty, and his own mental health challenges.

This desire to *show* how performative agency can be a resource for living is not limited to *Tarnation*. It is a strategy common in personal zines, where collage is also a primary technique,[65] and in feminist visual art, where, as Jack Halberstam has argued, the violence of cutting and reformatting blurs the boundary between self and other and explores the materially transformative and pleasurable potential of destruction and remaking.[66] Let's return to Sandy's narration as/with Tweet. This time I have underlined the words and turns of phrase taken directly from Tweet's song, her performance, and the rap interlude in the track performed by influential hip-hop artist Missy Elliott.[67]

i wanna be like tweet, the kind of person who can call their own <u>body tantalizing</u> in just such a tone of voice that you can't help believing it. yeah stare if you want to. feeling kinda twisted. <u>my shirt</u> lifted <u>up over my head</u>, i'm slipping. they got me thinking all kinds of crazy thoughts and <u>touching myself</u> & wanting <u>myself</u> loving <u>myself</u>. that's so nasty. the do it yourself renaissance. what are the politics of living beautifully, intensely—

wanting more—wanting everything to be slippery and audacious, forever in glamorous transition—wanting what you can't have—wanting it badly—wanting you to call at the break of dawn—i'll be sure to meet you with no panties on—wanting to be like tweet. the kind of person who says *tantalizing* like they mean it.[68]

The first thing to note when rereading this extract is that the passage *describes* a performance; the narrator invites us to "stare if you want to" as they perform the actions described in Tweet's song. The sensuous materiality of the embodied performance is remediated through the powerful rhythm of meter: the repetition of "myself" and "wanting" and the short sentences enacting the beat of desire.[69] At the same time the text is an example of performative identification. The narrator wants to be like Tweet in order to access the sensual authenticity of her performance of the word "tantalizing." Tweet's agency as a performer—her power to use embodied performance to make an undeniably true statement about herself—becomes a resource for nurturing a queer self who is not freely offered adequate sustenance from the culture surrounding them,[70] just as Jonathan uses the transformative potential of rock opera's style and the pathos of Plimpton's performance to believe in his own agency.

In *Tarnation* and *Handpash*, ventriloquism and remediation are the techniques used to materially stage an encounter with Jonathan's and Sandy's use of performative identification. Speaking as and in the voice of professional performers and the characters they create is presented in both texts as a resource for making a queer life. While there are important differences between the two texts, their collaged aesthetic and deployment of performative agency points to the importance of media forms (television, film, popular music) and their actors in enabling autobiographical works. These periperformative autobiographical texts do seek an intersubjective exchange between reader and text, but that exchange travels in a different direction than the one most commonly associated with reading autobiographical texts. It also uses vastly different material strategies to construct the scene of that exchange. Rather than locating the intersubjective exchange in the encounter between the narrating I of the autobiography and the implied reader, *Handpash* and

Tarnation perform the intersubjective exchange between performer and audience as generating affect, strategies, modes of embodiment, and ways of speaking that can form an important part of a life.

Autobiographies read as collage respond to the consensus view that the truth claims that underpin autobiography's unique status as a genre are dependent on the text being materialized through the voice of the person whose lived experience it claims to narrate. As a strategy for "putting into question," collage is a compelling means of making a periperformative intervention, as a collaged text never speaks in a single voice but always in at least two. By exposing its construction and influences, collaged autobiography becomes periperformative when it is not a means of representation, but is rather a construction, a way of materially restaging fantasies and attachments, a mode of temporarily bringing into being the possibility *of* a certain kind life through assemblage. As Gregory Ulmer suggests of the closely related screen technique of montage, "Montage does not reproduce the real, but constructs an object . . . or rather, mounts a process . . . in order to intervene in the world, not to reflect but to change reality."[71] In her work on lesbian archives of feelings, Ann Cvetkovich encourages us to read "the archive as a practice of fantasy made material" and identifies in the documentaries of Jean Carlomusto the use of popular culture texts as "the document of emotions."[72] In the case of Caouette and Sandy, popular culture texts are resources for producing an autobiographical text that documents responses to the normative genre of a life. In doing so, the texts critique the performative utterance of autobiography by insisting that fantasy, hope, and attachment *are* life—a way of living—rather than an attempt to escape or survive it. Using the process of collage, they demonstrate the importance of speaking in a "spirit of truth" about what one hopes might be possible, as well as what has been and is possible. These fantasies are presented not so that we can evaluate their capacity to change the material existence of the author's lives or to reify the entrepreneurial self of neoconfession.[73] Rather, they materialize a way of living in itself. In this sense, collage becomes a means of making a periperformative utterance regarding the normative genre of "a life" that remains focused on achievement and acquisitiveness, on what Berlant describes as "the presumed self-evident value of the bionarrative."[74] These texts insist on the possibility of an account of one's life that emphasizes the aesthetics and attachments that are formed during the process of figuring out what having a life might mean. This process is fundamentally material and active, and involves remediation. Reading these texts as periperformative allows us to recognize that they do not seek to occupy the performative speaking position that authorizes autobiographical discourse, but rather that they respond to the normative claims made by and for autobiography by being proximate to it.

In following Sedgwick's suggestion and going in search of the periperformative responses to the performative utterance of autobiography, I have found my way to queer life narratives produced largely outside the commercial cultural industry. In using such texts as cases, it is not my intention to imply that only works created in the spirit of DIY culture, or that use collage as a primary technique, are *the* exemplars of periperformative autobiography. There are no doubt other methods and other responses to the performative utterance of autobiography.[75] *Tarnation* is undeniably a documentary that is in conversation with the complex histories of film, television, and documentary, yet in reading a documentary as a response to autobiography's performative power and cultural force, I have indicated the potential of the periperformative to illuminate the formal qualities of autobiography across media. This links Sedgwick's theory to N. Katherine Hayles's call for a "medium-specific analysis" that derives its power as an interpretive approach from "holding a term constant across media . . . and then varying the media to explore how medium-specific constraints and possibilities shape texts."[76] In this case, I have held autobiography as a performative act constant and looked across media for periperformative responses to it.

It is worth remembering, too, Sedgwick's warning that there is nothing "inherently antinormative about the highlighting of periperformative utterances."[77] In the case of *Tarnation*, the periperformative makes possible a way of classifying and reading the film's use of collage and ventriloquism that recognizes these material strategies are "in complex dynamic interplay with content, coming into focus or fading into the background, depending on what performances the work enacts."[78] Periperformative autobiographies such as *Tarnation* and *Handpash* are *about* collage as a material practice—about cobbling together ways of attaching to the world that cannot be subsumed into existing formats of identity or bionarrative—as much as they are products of collage as a technique. Their creative reuse of the power of existing forms of media and the voices of other performers asks us to reconsider the importance accorded to uniqueness of voice as grounding autobiography as a cultural and political practice vital to the relationality and recognition that defines the social field.

5

Dossiers

I began *Stories of the Self* by reflecting on the information shared by Edward Snowden in 2013, framing this project as an attempt to understand the role of media and materiality in how we value who we are and what we do. Looking at the news that Snowden brought us from the end of the decade, the arguments appear to be the beginning—rather than the culmination—of revelations that require a cultural, legal, political, and social response to the role of "data doubles" in social life, democratic politics, markets of communicative capitalism, and social welfare.[1] The Cambridge Analytica scandal, where academic research into social media was used as a front to gain access to data that were then used as the basis for a political campaigning business, is but one recent example that demonstrates how the primary use of autobiography for generating and maintaining social bonds leaves a medial trace that, when it reaches a usable scale, becomes a potentially meaningful commodity and tool for political influence. On March 30, 2018, technology commentator Dylan Curran published an article in the *Guardian* in which he examined the enormous amount of data about his everyday life held by Google and Facebook. In his report he demonstrates that the dossiers held by each company are extensive: they record where he went and who he communicated with, and include his photographs; his e-mails, instant messages, and chats; the contents of his cloud storage (even deleted files); and his web search history. Throughout the article, Curran emphasizes the *size* of the dossier: Google has been collecting some data since 2009, while Curran's Facebook dossier "was roughly 600MB, which is roughly 400,000 Word documents." The size matters because, as David Golumbia has argued, the more information these companies hold on us the more detailed their potential insight into the population's habits, preoccupations, and fears.[2] Curran ends his article by observing:

> This is one of the craziest things about the modern age. We would never let the government or a corporation put cameras/microphones in our

homes or location trackers on us. But we just went ahead and did it ourselves because—to hell with it!—I want to watch cute dog videos.[3]

This observation reinforces a hypothesis that sparked the work of *Stories
of the Self*: that perhaps everyday users of networked digital technology have not collectively rebelled against the mass collection, sale,
and exploitation of their digital data because our ideas about who we
are and what matters in our lives are largely still given structure and
meaning by objects and the rich tangibility of media materialities. The
cameras and microphones have not been installed in our homes; we
have brought them in—in the form of networked mobile devices and
smart appliances—because of the benefits that flow from being constantly connected to the network (cute dog videos) and because they
come in the guise of objects (devices) that we interact with in intimate,
embodied assemblages of use. We handle our phones constantly,[4] and
we "personalize" them with ring tones, apps, images on the lock screen,
and protective covers.[5] Perhaps the enormous digital dossiers that are
amassed from that connection don't bother many of us because, like
the excessive scale of Warhol's *Time Capsules* discussed in chapter 1, we
imagine they are just too large to render any meaningful information
about us, and we find it hard to imagine an audience interested in the
minutiae of our digital lives.[6] But the size of our data doubles also marks
the point where identity intersects with informatics: where we no longer
craft the story of our lives, but multiple narratives are suggested by the
data points that accumulate from our activities. The "story" that results
is largely assembled by algorithms or humans seeking patterns, and it
is constantly changing in response to the informational needs of the
organizations collecting, parsing, selling, and sharing the data. This is
a posthuman form of life-inscription—texts are generated and read by
humans and machines—and it raises new questions about the intersection between the practices of self-life-inscription that are inherent to the
social field, on the one hand, and technology, state and nonstate forms
of surveillance, security regimes, and corporate interests, on the other.

Many commentators argue that if we are to grapple with the ramifications of the increased data collection and aggregation powers held
by government and corporations such as Google, we must learn to care
more about being under surveillance. To do that, they argue, we must

grasp the importance of informatic forms of biopower that capture life in a surveillant assemblage. However, the lack of change in consumer habits indicates that to begin to contend with our data doubles, we need to come to more than a technical understanding of who (or what) the repositories of data *are*. We need to incorporate them into our sense of our social world. Who are our data doubles?[7] How do they relate to others of their kind, and to us? At the moment, this problem is often understood as an issue of technological literacy: the problem is that most people can't fathom the extent to which their devices are logging their activity, or how those individual bits of information are put together to produce extensive and unprecedented insights into the psychology of the population, as demonstrated by Curran's article.

As well as posing challenges for law and policy, data doubles also present us with a social and cultural challenge: the urgency we face is to incorporate the data double into our understanding of our cultural practices of self-life-inscription, given the importance of autobiography to our experience of the social field—given, that is, that we must give an account of ourselves that others find intelligible in order to be recognized as a member of the community.[8] Media as well as language underpin the preexisting norms that structure how a life becomes recognizable as a life.[9] Mark Andrejevic has argued that this is the triumph of surveillance capitalism: activities previously outside the realm of profit extraction, such as leisure time, are brought into mediated spaces where they can be collected and monitored and become a resource for profit generation.[10] John Cheney-Lippold has explained how these practices produce a new predictive space, which feeds off the dossiers of data that are collected and stored. So, one question we face is: How do these dossiers inform the scene of apprehension in which we are vulnerable to each other in our collective living? Is my data double a trace I leave, and therefore a part of me that can be protected by extending my right to privacy? Is my data double its own entity, a "new type of individual, one comprised of pure information"?[11] If so, what is its relationship to me and to the forms of social engagement that take me—an embodied and therefore singularly located individual—as their primary focus? Scholarship on privacy in law and policy is working to develop institutional answers to these questions within legal discourse. But legal, institutional responses to the status of the data double do not, and cannot, answer the larger question of the cultural and social challenge these entities present. This work falls to us, and to the artists and activists who take up the question of the data double to explore its aesthetics, affordances, impacts, and limits. Thinking about the materiality and textuality of the data double might provide us with one way of answering the broader questions about who the data double is and how it figures in the cultural, social, and political field. It can point to how we incorporate it into our understanding of the centrality of self-presentation to social and political life. In this chapter I explore some recent projects that read the dossier as the location of the data double and explore the ways of thinking about these new entities and our entanglement with them that they suggest.

Turning to the Dossier

The artistic remediation of surveillance dossiers from the mid-twentieth century, before networked information technologies revolutionized surveillance practices and capacities, has become a recurring strategy in the wider "archival turn" of contemporary art.[12] In the new millennium, a number of projects have engaged with the material legacy of twentieth-century surveillance: such as *The FBI Files* (2002) series of paintings and collages by American artist Arnold Mesches;[13] Sadie Barnette's *Do Not Destroy* series, which remediates the FBI file kept on her father, who founded a branch of the Black Panther Party in 1968;[14] and *The Watchers File Project*, by Garrick Imatani and Kaia Sand, which originated in an artist residency at the City of Portland Archives and Records Center and worked with police surveillance files.[15] I will focus on two recent projects in this vein: an episode of the Australian documentary series *Persons of Interest*, in which Aboriginal activist Gary Foley gains access to the files the Australian Security Intelligence Organisation (ASIO) kept on him between the 1950s and 1970s; and the durational screen-based work *End Credits* (2012) by visual artist and filmmaker Steve McQueen, which remediates the extensive file kept by the FBI on performer and civil rights activist Paul Robeson, which began in 1941 and continued for two years after Robeson's death in 1976. Works such as these return to an earlier period when various projects for social justice—around race, gender, environmentalism, and sexuality—were reaching levels of publicity and political efficacy that threatened the status quo, and in which surveillance was rampant. At the height of the Cold War, politically progressive individuals and organizations drew the attention of a particularly paranoid state apparatus. A leftover of these surveillance practices is an enormous material legacy in archives of security and state organizations.[16]

In these works, artists, filmmakers, and activists reanimate seemingly dormant archives of the data double in order to interrogate its outsized materiality and informatics. They probe and activate its expansive and strange preoccupations, subjecting it to a range of reading approaches. In doing so, they explore the legacies of enclosing dissident racialized subjects within the disciplinary regime of the security services and demonstrate its importance for contemporary debates about surveillance. These public readings of dossiers respond to the contemporary moment in which we must come to grips with our data doubles. Thus, as well as their historical and political importance, they offer contemporary audiences perspectives that can be extended to the challenge of thinking about our surveilled state and how "our datafied histories remain rewritable, partially erasable, and fully modulatory."[17]

In considering artistic engagements with analog dossiers, this chapter expands the perspective on the question of the data double beyond the digital. Contemporary artists are looking behind the current moment of dataveillance to an earlier moment characterized by heightened information collection and interpretation, providing a historical perspective on what we largely think of as an issue unique to the digital present. Let me be clear: I am not suggesting that we think of the mid-twentieth-century paper- and film-based dossier and the networked digital data double as identical entities. Rather, artistic engagements with the materiality of the analog dossiers provide us with a potentially useful way of thinking more precisely about "the constitution of an additional self, one that may be acted upon to the detriment of the 'real' self without that 'real' self ever being aware of what is happening."[18] These public readings of dossiers offer us some insights into how we might incorporate the data double into our understanding of the cultural and social uses of life-inscription.

Reconsidering the Self in Self-Life-Inscription

You may have noticed that I am no longer using the term "self-life-inscription" when referring to dossiers as autobiographical texts. Clearly, the dossier that is constructed by placing someone under observation without their consent or knowledge cannot count as self-life-inscription in the sense that the self is the active, conscious participant in inscribing the life. Nor can we think of our data doubles—whose existence we consent to by accepting terms of service agreements—as accounts of ourselves we willingly provide. Yet, cleaving to the idea that we are always consciously and willfully engaged in self-life-inscription ignores the importance of others reading us in the scene of apprehension. It also underplays the extent to which we are bound by existing norms and codes (including those that stipulate appropriate media forms) when we give an account of ourselves or respond to the accounts of others, as Butler's and Berlant's work demonstrates. However, the current problem we face regarding digital surveillance is partly constituted by the tension produced by the fact that our data doubles are largely the result of our voluntary use of networked technologies and software. They are the residue left by other acts of self-life-inscription, and they are a form of digital materiality built into the platforms whose audience is entirely different than the people we imagine might be interested in our Tweets, our Facebook posts, or our Instagram stories. The digital platforms have two intended audiences—one public, the other surveillant—and this has raised the question of whether or not we are all knowingly, or at least unwittingly, consenting to the tracking of our behavior. Do we merely accept this duality—this second, shadow audience—as a trade-off, as Curran suggests, for cute dog videos and networked sociality? As surveillance studies scholar David Lyon notes, in conversation with Zygmunt Bauman, this question can lead to a tendency in surveillance studies and public commentary to treat "Facebook users (or anyone else for that matter) as cultural dupes" who just don't care that their data is commercialized and weaponized by contemporary politics and communicative capitalism.[19] In this negative view, we have put our "selves" aside, failing to prioritize their privacy and protect them, in the search for the shallow pleasures of online living.

At the same time, theorists of contemporary surveillance regularly argue that a critical account of surveillance and its impact dislodges the "self" as a focus of analysis. This line of argument reasons that we can no longer critically understand contemporary society and politics with the "self"—understood as a rights-bearing subject—as the assumed basic unit of social and political agency. For these scholars, examining populations, bodies, and affect in the context of surveillance and the data double sidelines the question of the subject and its representation entirely.[20] In this line of thinking, the self becomes less important not because of our alleged complacency but because the aggregating powers of algorithms and security protocols parse individuals into populations that are in turn sorted into identifiable categories and groups that can then be subjected to differing styles of attention at a large scale: from more expensive airfares to political advertising.

In this view, the account of oneself enabled and materialized by the dossier is not fixed—and not a representation—because it is constantly categorized and recategorized by the algorithms and institutional protocols that read it in search of specific understandings of who the user or subject is in relation to preestablished categories. Thus the data double is constantly changing as it is read in relation to those categories, and is not in any representational sense related to "what makes you *you*."[21] The difference between the data double and *you* lies in the space between our embodied lived experience of the world, materially grounded by the perceiving singularly located body (*you* who are reading this now, me who sits at my desk in Utrecht writing it), and the digital network—wired and wireless networks, servers, millions of lines of code that run protocols and applications that keep the cute dog videos streaming. The digital infrastructural network exceeds and reconfigures the significance we attach to located individuals and their interactions (through the figure of the user profile) by assigning new meaning to millions of crumbs of information left by our online interactions.[22] How significance is assigned to these aggregated crumbs is of fundamental importance: as many critics working on surveillance argue, surveillance is a practice of *reading* (by humans and machines), and it is in the scene of reading the dossier that specific epistemological, ontological, and ethical relations are materialized through relationships of power underpinned by categories such as race, ethnicity, class, gender, able-bodiedness, and sexuality.[23] These are the "infrastructural conditions and legacies of discourses that precede and condition our existence,"[24] reapplied to the informational traces left by our online lives.

In staging public readings of dossiers, *Persons of Interest* and *End Credits* remediate surveillance records in order to expose the dossier as the material ground for modes of categorization that serve the distribution of social and political power, that carve up the community into distinct populations that can then be subjected to varying degrees of institutional attention and management. Foley's and Robeson's dossiers evidence the centrality of race and gender discourse to the power that structures and authorizes the archive, particularly the inclination by white supremacist discourses to frame black men as threats to social and political order. In Foley's episode of *Persons of Interest*, what is made available to the viewer is the knowledge and perspectives held by a member of the community subject to race-based surveillance and the race-based management of Aboriginal life mandated in Australia's colonial system. This is offered with the hope that it will educate the audience about the history, practice, and effects of racialized surveillance in the colonial context. In this sense it is a powerful historical document in its own right. Yet Foley's reaction to and reading of his ASIO file also enacts a mode of reading that mocks the omnipotent fantasy that the making of the dossier enacts. Foley's renarration of his file is characterized by the great pleasure he takes in observing where the surveillance assemblage failed in its ability to extrapolate from its rudimentary observation of his activities (his being in certain places, meeting certain people at specific times) to a meaningful understanding of his intentions and capabilities as a committed political actor for Indigenous sovereignty. One important element of Foley's reading of his dossier and his contestation of the version of his life it represents is that it highlights how the dossier functions, and fails, as a text that captures and reads the present in order to predict the future.

The Future Is Now: Reading the Preemptive Capacity of the Dossier

In its proactive and preemptive logic, the dossier is a mode of life-inscription that addresses a reader concerned with gaining an advantage by knowing the future. In this sense, twentieth-century forms of surveillance by security services anticipate the disruption of time Wendy Hui Kyong Chun argues typifies our habitual use of new media, which "reduces the future to the past, or more precisely, a past anticipation of the future."[25] *Persons of Interest* and *End Credits* probe the logic of this past anticipation by reading dossiers whose future is now past. One project (*Persons of Interest*) mocks the dossier as a futile attempt to enclose the desire for Indigenous self-determination within the existing political structures, and by so doing negate it. The other (*End Credits*) emphasizes that the materiality of the data double can act as a substitute means of containment that satisfies the state's need to control and suppress minority populations.

Gary Foley's surveillance dossier depicts the early period of his lifelong commitment to Indigenous sovereignty in Australia. An important figure in Australian Aboriginal politics, Foley is an activist, scholar, writer, and actor who has been centrally involved in several key moments in the long struggle for self-determination for Aboriginal Australians. Born in 1950, he was a founding member of the Australian Black Power movement—inspired by the African American Black Panthers—and was one of the three core members of the Black Caucus, an activist group based in the Sydney suburb of Redfern, a center of the Aboriginal community in Australia, in the Eora nation.[26] As well as instigating a range of protest actions, Foley was involved in the founding of Australia's first "self-help and survival" organizations for Indigenous people,[27] such as the Aboriginal Legal Service in Redfern, which provided support to the local community who were subject to police harassment, and the Aboriginal Health Service in Melbourne, in the Kulin nation. Foley was also involved in the establishment of the Aboriginal Tent Embassy, a protest camp established in 1972 in Australia's capital city—on land shared by the Ngambri, Ngambri-Guumaal, and Ngunnawal people—that contests the lack of recognition of Aboriginal land rights. Foley's involvement in race politics in Australia also includes being an active and visible participant in the landmark protests against the 1971 Australian tour of the Springboks rugby team from apartheid South Africa. Many of these activities coincided with Foley's surveillance by ASIO and are discussed in the fifty-two-minute episode of the documentary series *Persons of Interest* in which Foley reads and narrates his file and his memory of Aboriginal activism in the 1970s and 1980s.

In Foley's account, he drew the attention of ASIO not because of his fundamental commitment to Aboriginal nationalism and self-determination but because of the politically necessary relationship he and other Indigenous activists had with Australia's Communist Party.[28]

But it was also his willingness to use his sharp sense of humor for the purposes of activism that led to his becoming a key person of interest for ASIO. This is established early in the episode, when Foley explains how he and other members of the Black Caucus ended up on the front page of a newspaper as the representative subjects of the rise of Black Power in Australia (figure 5.1). The group had been approached by a

Figure 5.1. Gary Foley (center bottom) with other members of the Australian Black Power movement on the front page of a newspaper, as shown in the documentary series *Persons of Interest*, season 1, episode 3, directed by Haydn Keenan.

white journalist and had agreed to talk about their interest in expanding the US model of Black Power to Aboriginal activism in Australia. Yet the journalist failed to adequately respond to the group's sophisticated use of humor to defuse mainstream white Australia's interest in the new black politics; as Foley narrates the event "We spun him this story," he tells us, irony inflecting his voice, "[which is] where the headline came from, 'We only have a small amount of explosives at the moment, so we thought we'd save them for something useful.' Little did we realize, the following Sunday, was splattered this headline."

Despite having access to the newspaper headline, recorded in his ASIO file, Foley misquotes the headline he credits with provoking heightened interest in his activities from ASIO. What does misquoting this suggest? From the perspective of 2015, when Foley is reflecting on this event in the documentary, it seems a stretch that he and the other members of the Black Caucus thought this inflated claim would not attract attention, given the group's success in using performance and humor to advance the cause of racial justice in Australia. Indeed, Foley tells us something very important about the public reading of his dossier he is undertaking when he tells the story of the interview as a triumph of the black activists over a naive reporter while misquoting the headline: the tenacity required to found the Black Caucus and devise new strategies for bringing attention to the issues affecting Aboriginal Australians is not a feature of his past self, recorded in the dossier that bears his name. Rather, it is an ongoing strategy and use of temperament in his activism, and it shapes his speech to a broader public about the struggle for Aboriginal sovereignty in the present moment. When the activists invited the reporter to Bondi to buy them a beer and hear all about their plans for Black Power in Australia, they exploited the journalist's self-belief that because he was a representative of the fourth estate, they would tell him the truth. Foley's ironic telling of the story exposes the naïveté of a representative of white mainstream Australia in thinking that Indigenous activists will honestly report on their next steps in the long and much-resisted fight for self-determination. Crucially, Foley's misquoting of the line suggests that viewers of the documentary themselves might be having a story "spun" for them. This spinning speaks directly to the preemptive function of surveillance; saying outlandish things becomes a means of gaining, but also directing, attention toward a future you have no intention of bringing about.

Throughout the episode, Foley's public reading of his dossier retains this somewhat gleeful appreciation for the misdirections and mis-understandings evidenced in his file. A telephone call to a woman in Queensland recorded in the file is noted, as is the subject of their con-versation: a possible meeting in the town of Gympie, in the country of the Gubbi Gubbi people. The notes indicate that an ASIO agent suspects this may be evidence of Foley's attempts to expand his collaborations with the Communist Party outside of his home state. "The purpose of the Gympie trip is still unknown," Foley reads from his ASIO file. "In fact, when I looked at this and I saw this woman's name, I thought, I remember *her* . . . then I realized this wasn't about politics at all folks; this was about sex," Foley says with a laugh. Foley identifies a similar misreading when he finds his visits to the Communist Party headquar-ters in Sydney to receive lessons in developing photographic film were recorded. Foley sought knowledge of photography as a means of hold-ing police accountable for their use of force against Aboriginal activists; however, the visit to the headquarters to take lessons in its darkroom is documented in his file as potential evidence that he has communist sympathies.

Foley takes great pleasure in pointing out these failures of the preemp-tive logic of the dossier. The dossier is read as a material reminder of the failure of the state to accurately understand the aims of the Black Cau-cus, whose focus was Aboriginal self-determination (and flourishing), not communism. In narrating these failures, Foley reads the data double as a materialization not of his containment within the white-dominated political structures but of that system's inability to understand or contain the commitment to self-determination that drives his life's work as an activist. Foley's activism forces the Australian state and its white citizens to confront the logic of unseeing Indigenous sovereignty that is at the heart of settler colonial logic and which justifies the occupation of the Indigenous people's land.[29] As Aileen Moreton-Robinson has argued in regard to the biopolitics of Australian colonialism, the white Australian sense of secure ownership over the country is "tormented by its patho-logical relationship to Indigenous sovereignty."[30] In Foley's public read-ing of his dossier, this pathology manifests as a comic farce in which the

white state fails to see that Aboriginal nationalism is a political program
that is independent of the white Communist Party.

While Foley's ASIO file focuses on his individual actions, his public
reading of his data double is also inevitably linked to the pervasive and
destructive history of the use of surveillance and records in the colonial
program of white rule in Australia. Australian colonialism is enacted
through a racialized logic that encloses Aboriginal people within a population category that has always been, and continues to be, subjected to
increased attention, and whose identity and opportunity have always
been inaccurately *constructed* and managed within systems of record
keeping. In the documentary, this is acknowledged by a second narrative thread, which puts Foley in conversation with the white bureaucrat
Barrie Dexter, who led the federal government's Department of Aboriginal Affairs. In a telling exchange between the two men recorded for the
documentary, they discuss their ASIO files: Dexter reveals that when he
requested access to his file recently, it had been destroyed. The fact that
Foley's remains—rife with what he frames as unfounded accusations
regarding his potential to commit acts of political violence—evidences
the materialization of Aboriginality as an identity category subject to
heightened surveillance and management. Without taking note of this
evidence, we cannot come to a critical understanding of surveillance.
This moment in the documentary highlights the fundamental role of
surveillance in establishing political systems in settler colonial countries
such as the United States, Canada, and Australia.[31] In the Australian
case, Indigenous people continue to be subjected to levels of observation
and management that exceed and are of an entirely different order to the
attention given to other members of the community—seen in policies
such as income management which restricts people's financial auton-
omy, government interventions in remote Indigenous communities, and
intrusive observation of family and social life through health and social
services.[32] Aboriginal Australians have extensive and intergenerational
knowledge of surveillance, but this is marginalized in contemporary discussions about the topic. This bracketing of the long history of racial
surveillance maintains a racial hierarchy in thinking about contemporary culture and politics that posits the experiences of white members
of the community as the standard-bearer. Foley's public reading of his
dossier, including his discussion of shared yet very different experiences

of surveillance with Barrie Dexter, demonstrates that mainstream Australia's denial of the long history of surveillance in the service of colonialism hampers our ability to adequately account for the surveillant assemblage as a process of materializing social categories. Surveillance is not new in Australia, Foley's reading reminds us; it is just a new experience for some members of the population. The challenge that faces us in thinking about our surveilled state will not be met by assuming the surveillance of individuals and the aggregation of their data into populations in order to manage their access to the infrastructures that support life is an entirely new occurrence brought about by networked technology.

Gary Foley's public reading of his ASIO file is an opportunity to engage in self-life-inscription in response to the persistent strategies of inscription of colonial discourse. Embedding his autobiography within a documentary that addresses a wide audience, Foley "spins" the story of his data double to show its weakness but also to protest against the ease with which his investment in Indigenous sovereignty is framed as a physical threat to the white Australian community. While the joke that became a headline deliberately sought to provoke the association between black masculinity and the threat of violence that the young members of the Black Caucus knew was an inescapable logic that would frame their work, Foley's ASIO file also shows the extent to which the dossier acts as a means of justifying preexisting positions, rather than providing objectively gathered evidence that could be interpreted without prejudice in order to determine the validity of positioning Foley as a threat requiring surveillance. In his narration, Foley highlights that ASIO was unable to penetrate the small, tight-knit group of the Black Caucus, and so was forced to rely on reports about what the group might plan overheard in spaces where informers were active, namely, the Australian Communist Party. Foley's data double is inscribed through hearsay, rumor, and speculation in conversations and meetings held by Communist Party members that are reported by informers. Foley's sense of humor about this aspect of the data double quickly turns to a piercing anger when he tells us that, despite his commitment to nonviolent political action, to this day his ASIO file records speculation that he was involved in plans to bomb buildings and a naval ship. Clearly angry that these unfounded accusations remain on the record, Foley's reading also highlights the troubling permanence of the paranoid state's interest in him (juxtaposed with Dexter, who ASIO is happy to forget), while also pointedly highlighting that Indigenous sovereignty is still largely framed as an issue that threatens the security and safety of white Australia. The framing of racial equality as a threat to social and political structures, rather than an enhancement of them, is a common thread between the two cases I consider here.

End Credits: The Data Double as Proxy

Nearly thirty years before Gary Foley was placed under surveillance in Australia, African American activist, public intellectual, and performer Paul Robeson had been subject to persistent and pervasive surveillance by the FBI during the Cold War. As with Foley, attention to Robeson's activities as an antiracist campaigner by the paranoid state apparatus framed him as a proponent of communism, and therefore a threat to national security. According to the declassified files now available via the FBI Vault, Robeson's FBI file began in 1941, and, according to Tony Perucci's research, active surveillance of his activities concluded in 1974,[33] while the publicly available file ends in 1967. Unlike Foley's data double, which resides in a dossier dedicated to a short period of his life, Robeson's file tracks more than thirty years. It began when he was well established internationally as an actor and singer, and several years before the blacklisting that prevented him performing (which took effect in 1949) and the suspension of his passport (in 1950), which saw him confined to the United States for almost a decade.[34]

In 2012, British visual artist and filmmaker Steve McQueen debuted a video work titled *End Credits* at the Art Institute in Chicago.[35] The aim of the work is to display every one of the thousands of pages from Robeson's heavily redacted FBI file, in a continuous scrolling projection. Each time the work is exhibited, McQueen adds to it by remediating additional pages into the audiovisual presentation. The work is presented as a two-screen projection, with each screen projecting different parts of the file. The pages are accompanied by a soundtrack of American voices reading the text that is on the screen. The scrolling and reading aloud of the pages are presented asynchronously: the visual track of the work moves faster than the audio.

End Credits enacts an entirely different form of public reading of the dossier than Foley's agentic, humorous reading of his ASIO file in *Persons of Interest*. In its durational approach—played on continuous loop, the work is without beginning or end—*End Credits* stages an encounter with the materiality of the obsessive paranoid gaze of the surveillant assemblage. It uses scans of the individual pages—and their often-striking levels of redaction—to demonstrate the outsized materiality that results from the FBI's attention: page after page passes us by (each page visible for twenty seconds), an endless collection of notes, observations, names, dates, places, and speculations. The data double of Paul Robeson, as rendered in *End Credits*, is endless—an identity inscribed in thousands of pages of documents by innumerable typists, agents holding annotating pens and stamps, and then still more agents wielding black markers in the service of redaction.

Watching *End Credits* in Chicago in 2012, and again in Amsterdam in 2018, I was struck by how it makes visible the amount of time and work the FBI had invested into constructing the dossier: the thousands of hours of writing memos, the careful management of each sheet of paper, the attention to order and detail required to keep the dossier in a manageable format. The data double, *End Credits* makes clear, is a proxy subject totally available and determinable by the organization that initiates and controls it. The file itself—its many pages and folders—satisfies the paranoid state's desire for total control over the body of the activist. Unlike Robeson the man, the data double can always be found, is always available for interrogation, can always be handled and seen.[36]

An analog file that can be called upon at will, added to, continuously interpreted, and physically contained in folders and files is an object in the psychoanalytic sense—"a thing in respect of which and through which *the instinct seeks to attain its aim*."[37] The object relation here is specific and structural, not generalized; the FBI is a physical entity whose aims include "the spatial means of organizing scribal labor."[38] The white supremacist desire for control over racialized populations finds its most direct route to satisfaction by the creation of a proxy body over which it has material dominion.[39] The dossier is a kind of fetish object that stands in for the autonomous, agential body of the man the state wishes to control.[40]

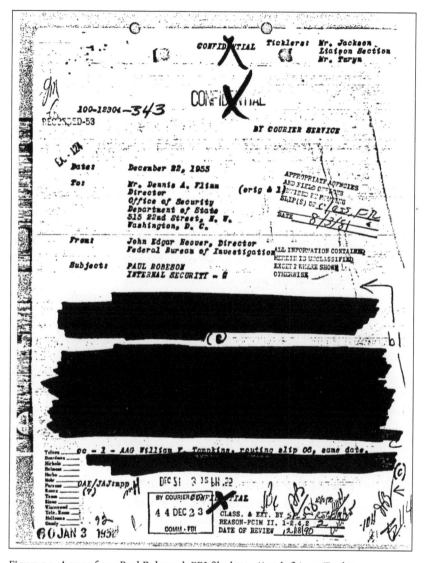

Figure 5.2. A page from Paul Robeson's FBI file. https://vault.fbi.gov/Paul%20 Robeson%2C%20Sr.

The fetishistic, constant labor and attention that produce the expansive materiality of Robeson's dossier are exposed in the public reading staged by *End Credits*. All that writing, all that paper; as the projection runs—its conclusion only brought about by the daily closing of the gallery in which it is exhibited[41]—the possibility of knowing anything about Robeson recedes (if it was ever considered a possibility by the viewer) and is replaced by an insight into the file itself as an object created to provide satisfaction for the bureau's need for information. The problem of scale here is similar to the one explored in chapter 1, where I examined how Andy Warhol refused to organize one's life and self into an edited and concise statement of identity. In the case of Warhol's *Time Capsules*, he ignored the injunction that the self be edited down to a manageable size in order to be apprehended. With surveillance, the inverse logic is at play: the more material and information that is collected, the greater the belief and investment in the assembling organization that some truth about the subject and their intentions will be revealed. This obsessive attention and writing of a version of Robeson is a materialization of the government's instinct to possess and manage the racialized subject.

However, satisfying the need to know the intentions of Robeson (and Foley) by surveilling and writing them covers over a relationship of interdependence between the bureau and the subjects it surveils. These subjects are central to the bureau's identity and its aims. This constant writing in order not to forget Robeson is not an expression of a preceding power relation (between individual and state); it is the material, mediated practice that forms and maintains it. Without subjects to surveil, threats to manage, the bureau has no purpose. I will return to this element of active production and prediction in the logic of surveillance that the dossier materializes later in the chapter. For now, I will consider how the paper-based memo is the material, mediated form that inscribes the surveilled subject into the sense of purpose and identity of the surveilling agency.

The memos that make up Robeson's file demonstrate what John Guillory argues is, summarizing the work of business historian JoAnne Yates, the informational and memory function of the memo.[42] In Guillory's account, the memo is a genre of writing that abandons the emphasis on persuasion through rhetoric in favor of an investment in the importance of recording and transmitting information with as little "noise" as possible.[43] Used in the service of surveillance, the memo is life-inscription of an idealized kind: one invested in extracting value from information by inscribing it and making it available for transmission.[44] The value ascribed to the memo as a single unit of information in the dossier is always in reference to some immediate future moment: it "aspires only to a moment of interest," a moment in which the value of its information can be extracted by being read.[45] This anticipated short transactional reading is a foundation of the surveillance dossier in both its analog and digital forms.

Read publicly forty years after Robeson's death in 1976, the information available in his dossier is no longer that which is inscribed—and often redacted—in its pages. Rather, *End Credits* aims to read the dossier's excessive materiality in its entirety, and the video work inscribes a new insight into the rise of the surveillance assemblage as a means of satisfying a desire to control and organize the flow of life and living into systems of control and categorization. McQueen's work underscores the complex materiality of this process. The use of voice-over to remediate the memo recasts it as a medium of noise, rather than of information transmission.

McQueen's intention to draw attention to the inherent noisiness of media and materiality is also evident in his use of the redacted page as a light source in the work. In a conversation about the work in Amsterdam in 2018, McQueen explained that he came across the dossier on Robeson while browsing on his laptop computer in his darkened kitchen.[46] Scrolling through the pages—an encounter he restages in the scrolling projection of *End Credits*—McQueen was struck by the effect of the large sections of redaction on the light emanating from his laptop screen. In McQueen's account of his kitchen reading, the redactions "eclipsed the light," and this underscored the threat and fear McQueen associates with surveillance. In the large backlit projections of *End Credits* this effect is heightened: as the only light source in the room, the projected pages throw varying amounts of illumination depending on the level of censorship applied to the information they contain. Frequently whole paragraphs, and indeed almost entire pages, are blackened by the ink of marker pens. This visual rendering of the materiality of surveillance is accompanied by a complex linguistic rendering of the file that emphasizes the multilayered materiality of surveillance. McQueen's direction of the voice-over emphasizes the linked activities of writing and reading the memos, the constant return to the fetish object of the dossier in the bureau's object relation. We can see on the screen that the original typewritten memos and their confidential stamps are overwritten and rewritten when the documents are prepared for release to the public: confidential stamps are crossed out, handwritten annotations classify pieces of information with shorthand identifiers (see figure 5.2). All of these annotations are described (or is it read?) in the voice-over, and so the information on each page—the narrative (if it can be called that) that unfolds through the chronological reading of the file—is interspersed with long sections of voice-over that narrate the processes of information categorization and classification. These parts of the reading—including the naming of redacted sections of the document—dramatize the rhythm of reading for information and categorization that underpins surveillance. The reading of a section of the file that includes a list of the informants—and thus is almost entirely redacted—foregrounds this (algo)rhythmic reading process. Here is a transcription of the soundtrack to a section of the work, as it was exhibited in Amsterdam in 2018:

NY one zero zero dash five six six eight zero
Administrative page
Informant
Identity of source
Date of activity and or description of information
Date received
Agent to whom furnished
File number where located

T one
Redacted
SA
Redacted
Instant report

T two
Redacted

SA
Redacted
one zero zero dash five six six eight zero SA
Redacted

T three
Redacted
SA
Redacted
Instant report
US Post Office, one four nine, East Twenty-Third Street, New York City

T four
Redacted
T five
Redacted
SA
Redacted
one zero zero dash five six six eight zero dash nine zero
Redacted
SE
Redacted

T six
Redacted
SA
Redacted
one zero zero dash five six six eight zero dash three six

T seven
Redacted
T eight
Redacted
T nine
Redacted
Handwritten: of unknown reliability
Redacted

SA
Redacted
one zero zero dash five six six eight zero dash one one two
Redacted

T ten
Redacted
SA
Redacted
one zero zero dash five six six eight zero dash one one seven

This sequence of informatics is read in an informational tone by professional voice-over artists who McQueen intends to sound like they are "from the East Coast" and "WASPISH."[47] The word "redacted" is performed by a differently gendered voice than the one performing the reading of the text on a given sequence of pages; in the case just quoted, a female voice reads the informatic content, while a male voice renders the redactions in the reading. Thus, in the public reading and screening McQueen intercuts the visual representation and reading of all the marks on the paper—regardless of their potential to signify— with an audible rendering of the black marks that frequently travel past on the screens. Presenting a soundtrack that moves between linguistic information and code and redaction in an art gallery in the age of digital surveillance creates a powerful connection between analog forms of surveillance and digital surveillance. This parallel highlights both as systems that produce data doubles who are largely constituted in lines of code, and subjected to algorithmic mechanized forms of reading. The affectless reading of marks and language is the place where the public reading can connect the analog dossier and the digital dossier through aesthetic strategies that highlight scale, repetition, and the constitution of the data double in a language its subject may not speak, and a form of reading that is instrumentalized and instrumentalizing of both the reader and the read.

Both *End Credits* and Foley's reading of his data double in *Persons of Interest* offer an alternative view of the problem of the data double that can be extended into the contemporary moment. By focusing our attention on surveillance as a record-keeping practice that has long been embedded in processes of racial hierarchization, they productively disrupt a tendency to see data doubles as a "new" social and political problem. The newness of the problem—and the anxiety it produces—stems from the extension of invasive surveillance to sections of the population that have previously had the privilege of claiming a right to privacy based on how their gender, race, sexuality, class, and bodily ability have been assigned in the surveillant assemblage. The public readings also, then, do important work of advancing a cultural account of the dossier that builds on the knowledge of those populations that have a long and intimate knowledge of its power and potential uses. One thing we learn from these readings is that the dossier is a textual and material form that enacts a desire for unimpeded access to the subject who is perceived as a threat by the paranoid state. The data double is the thing that can be handled and consulted, developed and managed, while the subject themself remain outside the systems of control. From this perspective, the digital data doubles compiled for commercial and security purposes can be understood as coping strategies by the structures of late capitalism and state sovereignty to confront the anxiety produced by all the *zoē* that exceeds, by definition, their purview.

But this optimistic view is tempered by a recognition that materialization of the desire for control that produces the data double can have lasting effects. This is because of the power of the apparatus of inscription to fix a version of life and make it transmissible beyond the original scene of its production. Gary Foley's outrage that rumors suggesting he may have intended to commit terrorist violence, and McQueen's screening of the dossier in acknowledgment of its role in blacklisting Paul Robeson from performance and therefore limiting his connection to community and activism also point us to the agency of the data double itself.

Both of these projects explore the variety of ways the individual is both the center and the periphery of the surveillant assemblage. They also demonstrate the continued utility of thinking about the self when attempting to understand the cultural, political, and social implications of contemporary surveillance. We see a similar attempt to advance the urgency of thinking about the data double in a widely publicized interview between John Oliver and Edward Snowden, conducted in Russia in June 2015. The interview was occasioned by the upcoming reauthorization by the US government of the Patriot Act, the law that granted the intelligence community sweeping data collection powers. As the political debate that would inform the renewal of the bill got under way, comedian and journalist John Oliver flew to Russia to interview Edward Snowden. Oliver's news satire program *Last Week Tonight* has become a successful vehicle for progressive political frustration, in which Oliver plays the part of an outraged, plain-speaking critic of contemporary political discourse and practices. Oliver's performance in hosting the show works in the now-familiar affective register of outrage that is paired with the journalist's role as a presenter of information governed by a commitment to rational assessment of the facts. With this performance of combined affect and rationality, Oliver offers cathartic expression for the audience's assumed feelings about democratic politics—exhaustion, frustration, panic, and disillusionment—while also holding out the promise of the possibility of a way out through a better-informed public debate. Using the ancient privilege of the court jester, the news satire comedian is authorized by the community to ask questions of the powerful and the famous that would otherwise be taboo. Oliver's interview with Snowden is framed in this way and is introduced with Oliver's concerns about technical literary: a 2015 Pew study, Oliver tells us, found that 46 percent of Americans were not concerned, or not very concerned, about government surveillance. How an informed public debate about the Patriot Act can be advanced in this climate of widespread low concern was Oliver's key motivator for undertaking the interview.

The crux of Oliver's interview with Snowden combines the two roles of jester and journalist and posits Snowden as a technical expert who has failed in his democratic duty to educate the public. A key point in the interview begins with Oliver berating Snowden for his inability to make the extremely technical issue of *how* mass digital surveillance is conducted comprehensible for everyday citizens, a charge to which Snowden meekly submits. The informational section of the interview centers on Oliver's proposal for how Snowden *could* have framed the revelations so that an "average" citizen could grasp the seriousness of the situation and more fully comprehend the extent to which their right to privacy had been eroded. Oliver diagnoses this problem as a failure by Snowden to identify the limit case that would allow the everyday person to grasp the issue of mass digital surveillance. For Oliver, the much-needed missing example is obvious: the fact that the data collection programs authorized by the Patriot Act approved the collection of naked pictures that people might share with lovers or, crucially for the predictive logic of the dossier, potential lovers. "This is the most visible line in the sand for people," Oliver tells Snowden. "Can they see my dick?"[48]

Leading up to this point, Oliver demonstrates the force of framing digital surveillance with the issue of dick pics by turning to the vox pop. He shows Snowden, and us, snippets from interviews with people (all of whom present clearly as either male or female) on the streets of New York who were asked whether or not they think the government should be able to access dick pics. They all agreed that they would be outraged if the government was collecting dick pics. In between this vox pop footage, we see Snowden watching, a slightly defeated look on his face. After this framing, Oliver asks Snowden about each of the specific data-gathering programs authorized in the Patriot Act and whether or not it exposes a dick pic to collection, storage, and viewing by the government or other agencies. At the time of the writing of this chapter, the video of this interview available on YouTube had been watched more than twenty million times.

In presenting the dick pic as the fulcrum for anxiety over the data double, and using that anxiety to anchor an "informed debate," Oliver reinscribes the sovereign male sexual subject as a stand-in for the citizen whose privacy and desire must be protected. Yet, as Rachel E. Dubrofsky and Shoshanna A. Magnet argue, "Many communities—including prisoners, those receiving certain forms of welfare from the state, people with disabilities living in institutional care, as well as immigrants and refugees—have historically had, and continue to have, their bodily privacy invaded, but there is almost no public discussion about the infringement of their rights to privacy."[49] How useful is it to conflate the citizen with a male subject who has the right to determine when and how his dick becomes visible to others? Oliver's reframing of the issue of surveillance in terms of the dick pic successfully reinserts the body and desire into thinking about surveillance as a form of biopower, but it is also a poorly chosen example given the large numbers of people (women, men, and nonbinary identified) who receive unwanted dick pics through social media, dating apps, and other forms of digital communication. It reveals the problem of appeals to subjectivity that assume commonality in terms of bodies and media use. Turning the visual depiction of male genitals into the standard-bearer for thinking about data doubles reinstates the male body as the norm and overwrites the complications that arise from our differing access to the "intersubjective and infrastructural conditions of a livable life."[50] Putting aside the question of whether or not I have a dick to photograph, being outraged about the possibility of "my" dick pics becoming visible to others will not motivate me to care more about surveillance if I am regularly engaged in the labor of deleting and blocking unsolicited dick pics from apps that are part of the infrastructure of my social life.

By offering the dick pic as symbol of the data double in the service of technical education, Oliver mischaracterizes the issue as one solely about collection and unintended audiences, rather than addressing the more central problem of surveillance as a practice that stores material traces of social interactions that then shape future scenes of apprehension.[51] As Puar notes, surveillance after September 11, 2001, is dominated by the temporal logic of intelligence and its focus on proactivity. This results in a "profound sway in the tenor of temporality: the realignment from reactive to preemptive conversion from past-tense subject formation to future-tense subject anticipation."[52] This is precisely the logic we see articulated and critiqued by Foley in his reading of his ASIO file. Framing surveillance as an issue concerned with the collection and storage of media texts generated by past events—dick pics that have been sent—doesn't help us think about how our data doubles shape the scenes of engagement we are moving into. Rather, it retains an association between surveillance and law enforcement, "a reactive activity" designed to gather evidence of an event.[53] Given contemporary surveillance is preemptive, how do we come to grips with the decreased importance of the past self, and the increased importance of possible future selves that is materialized in surveillant practices?

Our past and present selves are intelligible because they are mediated and materialized along preexisting vectors of power by being sorted into categories that shape what is normal, what is possible, and what is desirable or interesting, both socially and commercially.[54] The identity created by surveillance does not represent our individual achievement in finding ways to adapt our way of living to those norms. Rather, the predictive power ascribed to the data double in social and commercial spaces where surveillance is utilized alters our understanding of the centrality of giving an account of oneself to sociality. First, we must remember that it is not cute dog videos that keep us on social media; it is that for many people the social field is now partly constituted online and is therefore unavoidable. Sociality requires mediation. As the chapters in this book have demonstrated, life-inscription occurs within prescribed, but not determining, discourses and infrastructures that influence the ways of speaking about oneself and the media forms that are seen as suitable material foundations for that speaking. One justification for thinking about surveillance dossiers through their artistic remediations, then, is that unlike journalistic attempts to respond to the data double, they read dossiers with a critical eye to the processes of categorization that the dossier serves and materializes, and how those categories come into being through the textuality and materiality of the data double.

As I have shown, this materialization is future focused. The formation and interpretation of data doubles is largely predictive: their purpose is to provide a detailed picture of us so that our *future* behavior and desires can be anticipated. However, this focus on the future is not a characteristic that has come with the rise of digital dossiers, even if its possible ramifications are more widely and keenly felt in the present moment or in the possible future moments we imagine the data double might help materialize. In a study of the role of records in American culture in 1969, Stanton Wheeler draws on reports on the use of records in education, insurance, criminal justice, and legal contexts to construct a generalized picture of the dossier.[55] Many of the key characteristics he identifies provide a useful way of thinking about the textuality and materiality of digital data doubles. Dossiers are institutional documents that have power because of their institutional setting and their use as reference material to inform decision making.[56] Because they use media of inscription (such as paper and film, or code) in an institutional setting, they have long material lives: they can be sent in advance of the person to establish their identity, and outlast an individual's engagement with the institution and thus be retained in the institutional memory.[57] But what this means will vary widely depending on how we are positioned by the discourse of the institution and the categories used to generate and interpret the dossier. The data double materializes the modes of categorization that shape our interactions with institutions, and which, in turn, can shape our position within the social field.

Because they materialize categories through media of inscription, dossiers often ground decision making within organizations that utilize them. Wheeler notes they are used to make decisions about individuals and (crucially) to *"justify* decisions already made."[58] In this sense, dossiers are bound up with the troubled status of all records and archives, outlined extensively in archival science and critical theories of the archive; they are formed, stored, circulated, and accessed through institutional forms of power, yet invite the reader to consider them as objective material products of observation and recording.[59]

So, where does this leave us in terms of the current challenge of integrating our data doubles into our understanding of the social field?

End Credits and *Persons of Interest* offer public readings of dossiers that suggest a radical, and possibly productive, inversion of the power relation assumed to be materialized in the surveillant assemblage. These public readings suggest that the surveillant assemblage needs us more than we need it, and the desire to know us and our future intentions is constitutive of institutional identity—our data doubles are the object in the object relation that allows the commercial or security organization to satisfy its instinct for knowledge and power which underpins its identity and its fantasies of control.

It is this desire for control, coupled with the predictive logic and temporality of the dossier that should (and does) concern us. Across a range of scholarly fields and disciplines and in public discussion, we must continue to debate and decide, collectively, how we respond to this desire and the very real impacts it has on the scenes of apprehension that extend beyond our individual social worlds, such as democracy, legal and institutional contexts, and sites of social justice. But that worry must be tempered by a recognition that our data doubles can shape certain textual and physical scenes of apprehension, but never fully determine them. There is always the unfolding of life, beyond its scenes of inscription and the conditions they denote, and thus the possible futures our data double may help inscribe remain a *possible* future, rather than fate.

While the version of Gary Foley inscribed in his dossier went to Gympie to further develop the program of communism in Australia, the zoē was moving in another direction: toward intimacy through sexuality. The joy Foley takes in reinserting the zoē into the autobiography he tells through a public reading of his data double points us to the importance of thinking self-life-inscription as a relational practice pluralistically and holistically: using media of inscription to inscribe ourselves into the scene of apprehension is important, but it is not all we do.

Nor does the reality that our data double is, by design and use, trapped in circuits of control automatically mean that we are too. The quickness and dynamism of zoē as a counterbalance to the fantasies of control enacted in the preemptive logic of surveillance can also be seen in Barbara Beeching's account of an interaction between Robeson and the FBI:

> In late July of 1950, acting on orders from J. Edgar Hoover, FBI agents in New York City set out to find Paul Robeson, ordinarily a highly visible figure. After searching for several days they managed to contact him by phone, and he agreed to meet them at a St. Nicholas Avenue apartment. When they arrived, Robeson was there along with his lawyer, who established a formal tone by asking to see their identification. The agents then told Robeson what he already knew—that the State Department had cancelled his passport and they had come to pick it up. The actor replied that he did not have it with him, but offered to meet them the following morning to turn it over—something he had no intention of doing.[60]

In this account, we see how Robeson's public profile and the status of the dossier as a supplement for the body of the surveilled subject produce a narrative expectation that Robeson should be easily found. Yet the man does not behave like the data double materialized in the file: his location cannot be assumed, his ability to be reached *eventually* might be a given, but the effect of the time it takes for that search to succeed remains open. As we have seen when law enforcement has attempted to track the flight of terrorist suspects across continental Europe, the presence of a data double does not directly correspond to the ability to find the person to whom the data double refers in the physical world; while institutions may seek to continually close that gap between the *you* and the data double, life itself will always exceed the forms of inscription that produce the data double.

This leads me to a central point that this book has been developing: we are never totally inscribed in a single media, and this is precisely because each form of media inscribes us differently. This difference is the result of the specific affordances and ideologies that each media form materializes, and how these intersect with the forms of power, knowledge, and ethics that inform what we value about a life, and how. Rather than thinking of the individual as *solely* inscribed in a single form of media—most often these days, we think of this as digital, social media—we must think about the variety of media forms in which each life comes to matter: from the cardboard box of mementos in the cupboard, to the contribution to collective autobiographical projects, to the selfies sent via WhatsApp to friends or lovers, to the posts on Twitter or Facebook. It is through a broad range of analog and digital forms that each of us responds to the requirement to give an account of ourselves, and thinking about autobiography and media requires that we attend to these practices comparatively, rather than individually.

Conclusion

Life Matters

Throughout this book I have explored autobiography as an activity that draws on a range of media forms and their material properties to materialize the significance we attach to lived experience. Drawing on Judith Butler's theory of ethics as being founded in a shared relationality and vulnerability, and performativity as practice that materializes and authorizes discourses through their citation, media studies approaches to mediation and materiality, and Karen Barad's extension of this insight to the level of matter itself as an agential property in that citation, I have offered a range of examples that demonstrate how we might pay attention to the role of media and materiality in cultural practices that utilize self-life-inscription in order to make lived experience consequential. Along the way, I have proposed that assigning significance to lived experience is a process shaped by regimes of value that extend beyond language as a vehicle for ideas about proper identities, forms of relationality and attachment, life courses, and behavior. Although it is important for us to keep the linguistic and symbolic component of giving an account of oneself in view, my larger point has been that significance itself is materialized through media forms and the kinds of reading encounters they enable or suggest or foreclose. I make this argument in order to make a claim for a stronger recognition of media forms and their material properties as agential forces in the process of citation through which ideas about why life matters are made tangible, available, and portable into other scenes.

In thinking of autobiography as self-life-inscription, then, I have been trying to demonstrate that while autobiography clearly plays an important role in the process of subject formation and representation, it is also a cultural practice in which the inherent relationality of our shared reality—our exposure to, reliance on, and vulnerability to each other—is made tangible. This tangibility is variable and produces a range of effects. These effects make the issue of the ethical responsibilities that stem from our unavoidable entanglement with each other available for critical reflection, discussion, debate, and extension.

To think through some of these issues, and to underscore the importance of a comparative media studies approach to thinking about self-life-inscription as occurring across media, I will offer one final example. I will track one thread in the diverse cross-media practice of Chinese artist Ai Weiwei, focusing on his use of the selfie in both Instagram and art galleries. In tracking Ai's use of the selfie in analog and digital forms, I emphasize the importance of thinking of life as multiply mediated—as being inscribed across digital and analog forms—and propose how we can read transmedial self-life-inscription as both an aesthetic strategy and a component of everyday life. I focus on Ai's use of the selfie in some of his recent works that respond to the issue of migration and the human right to seek refuge from violence, war, and persecution. I read his strategies of remediation of the selfie in the work *iPhone Wallpaper* (2016) alongside Ai's extensive use of Instagram. In discussing *iPhone Wallpaper*, I will be referring to its manner of display in the context of an exhibition of work by Ai Weiwei titled *#SafePassage* at the Foam photography gallery in Amsterdam in 2016.[1]

In taking selfies with people arriving in Europe seeking "safe passage" from war-torn countries, Ai critically engages with the selfie as a degraded aesthetic form negatively associated with the role of networked digital technologies in propagating discourses of celebrity and narcissism. At the same time, he presents a critique of European governments' selective approach to whose lives are worthy of protection, and who will be the recipient of hospitality and welcome. By exhibiting selfies taken with the adults, youths, and children seeking sanctuary from political and religious persecution and safety from civil war in the art galleries of Europe, Ai Weiwei refuses to allow his own status as a political refugee in Europe to be interpreted as inherently *different* from the request for refuge issued by the hundreds of thousands of people arriving on Europe's shores. As I argue in what follows, Ai's use of the selfie uses his status in Europe to create safe passage into the social field of Europe by deploying the affordances of digital and analog forms.[2] In *iPhone Wallpaper*, Ai deploys the individualizing logic of the selfie to insist upon the recognition of people arriving in Europe as requiring an ethical response. Ai's work and its reception in Europe sit at a complex intersection between the adoption of self-life-inscription as a primary means for making arguments regarding human rights in the West, and what Christian Sorace has shown to be Ai Weiwei's use of life narrative within the tradition of public criticism and self-criticism in Chinese communism.[3]

Like the Colombian installation artist Doris Salcedo, who creates installations that respond to the survivors and victims of political and drug violence in Colombia, Ai uses the physical space of the art gallery to materialize moments of testimony and witness. Salcedo and Ai Weiwei have had significant success in using visual art and its institutions as a means of generating acts of witnessing to political violence that cannot be, or are not, widely discussed within the local communities affected by them.[4] Ai's use of multiple forms for self-life-inscription—installation, video, photography, sculpture, social media—for testimony and witnessing combines the traditions of autobiography with the strategies and self-reflexivity regarding medium that characterizes avant-garde conceptual art. His practice explores the space of the gallery as an analog site of inscription that will make the memory of political violence available in the future.

At the same time, Ai Weiwei's blog, Twitter, and Instagram accounts are (or were) used to extend the impact of "the artist" beyond the circumscribed field of visual art, and insert acts of witness and testimony into the global digital networked publicity enabled by these platforms. As the 2016 exhibition organized by the Andy Warhol Museum and the National Gallery of Victoria demonstrated, Ai has been strongly influenced by Andy Warhol's interest in extending the distinctive subject position of the artist beyond the gallery through the production of mainstream media. Warhol worked with the dominant popular forms of his time, the magazine (*Interview*) and film, and Ai has likewise become a prolific user of social media, such as the blog, Twitter, and Instagram.[5] A cross-media practice combined with self-life-inscription is a recurring characteristic of Ai's conceptual approach to art making.

Like Warhol's use of the popular media forms of his time, Ai Weiwei's use of social media allows him to "reach new and diverse audiences, and to expand the influence of contemporary art."[6] His tweets and his Instagram feed are available to audiences directly on the social media platforms he uses, creating scenes for the circulation and reception of life-inscription beyond the locatedness of specific gallery environments. He also consistently brings this work *into* the gallery through remediation. His works of digital autobiography are remediated into other material forms. For example, his blog, which was written in Mandarin and ran between 2006 and 2009 before being closed by the Chinese government, is now available as a book published, in translation, by MIT Press.[7] His use of online forms has increased with the demise of this blog. Ai's Twitter feed has a significant amount of English-language content, and his Instagram account—being dominated by photographs—includes content that often crosses language (if not cultural) barriers. The ephemeral status of online forms of self-life-inscription—susceptible as they are to the sale or closure of service providers, political interference, and the problems presented by software and hardware obsolescence—is a subject of Ai's use of social media.[8] *#SafePassage* is one recent example of how he creates work that uses remediation across the gallery and the screen, the analog and the digital, in order to critically engage the different capacities of media to materialize—and challenge—ideas about whose lived experience matters in political debates regarding migration.

#SafePassage is an exhibition made up largely of photographic works shot by Ai Weiwei using his smartphone. The works have three distinct, but related, subjects and are grouped in three sequences in the gallery. The first group of images documents Ai's reaction to the subject of his persistent surveillance by the Chinese authorities. In October 2015, during renovations to his Beijing studio, listening devices were discovered in the power sockets in several rooms.[9] Images of these devices taken by Ai Weiwei and posted to his Instagram feed are included in the exhibition. This most recent act of surveillance is contextualized through images and short text works that document the longer history of Ai's responses to being under surveillance by the Chinese government. *#SafePassage* presents several photographs of people Ai Weiwei suspects are conducting surveillance of him: they are snapped eating at nearby tables at restaurants, drinking tea in cafés, and sitting in parked cars. Ai's strategy of self-surveillance as a response is also documented in photographs and text from the internet-based work *Weiwei cam* (2012), a short-lived work that used a digital camera in his home to broadcast directly to the

internet (the website was shut down by the Chinese government within two days of going live).

The second component of the exhibition consists of the remediation and exhibition of photographs from Ai Weiwei's Instagram account, which he began posting in December 2015 when he established a studio on the Greek island of Lesbos. Since December 2015, Ai has traveled to other sites where people fleeing war have congregated, including refugee camps "all around the Mediterranean, including in Syria, Turkey, Italy, Israel and France" and released the widely screened documentary film *Human Flow*.[10] For *#SafePassage*, large sections of Ai's Instagram feed have been printed as wallpaper and cover the walls of two rooms in the gallery in a work titled *iPhone Wallpaper* (2016). In the center of each room, on the floor, lies a one-to-one scale reproduction of a personal flotation device, rendered in marble. The third component of the exhibition consists of short video works also shot along the Mediterranean coast.

In its layout, *#SafePassage* positions the autobiographical work documenting Ai's harassment by Chinese secret police at the beginning of the exhibition. In doing this, the exhibition explicitly reminds, or informs, the viewer that Ai Weiwei has been subjected to political violence, intimidation, and ongoing surveillance in China. Ai responds to his position as a surveilled subject by using his iPhone to document—and expose— the people sent to observe him. By exhibiting these photographs, Ai testifies to the reality of political oppression in China, situating the viewer as a witness to these events. In the opening of the exhibition, taking and exhibiting the photographs is positioned as a means of speaking back to the power of the Chinese government to inscribe and assign meaning to Ai's lived experience. Ai refuses to submit to, or ignore, his surveillance and uses his iPhone and the gallery walls of Foam to refuse the subordinate position that surveillance and imprisonment create. This part of the exhibition establishes an important personal story that the viewer then associates with the figure of Ai Weiwei they see repeated in *iPhone Wallpaper* in the next two rooms.[11]

In many ways, the selfie exemplifies the undeniable force of self-life-inscription in contemporary culture and politics that has motivated this book, and the need for scholars of contemporary culture to develop responsive, sensitive frames for reading the importance of everyday acts of mediated self-representation. As a seemingly ubiquitous mode of self-representation, the selfie is a divisive and degraded form.[12] The polarized response to the selfie in contemporary media—where it is decried as both the symptom and the cause of widespread narcissism, or celebrated as a form of empowerment—is the most recent example of the long history of contestation regarding the role of media forms in the sedimentation of values and perspectives in modern culture.[13]

Media and communications scholars approach the selfie through histories of celebrity,[14] ethnographies of everyday media use,[15] and the history of photography.[16] Although their approaches vary, scholars working on the selfie agree that the term "selfie" refers to three distinct elements of self-representation that highlight the processes of production, circulation, and reception I have been tracking across this book: the practice of using a smartphone to produce self-portrait photography, the visual text that is produced by that practice, and the circulation of the image through digital social networks.[17] While selfies are taken by a wide variety of people in a range of situations for very different purposes, scholars agree that we can refer to something called "the selfie," which is commonly practiced and has established a level of coherence and function as a form of mediated communication. The selfie has grown in popularity and become of interest to media studies scholars because it exemplifies three defining characteristics of the mediated nature of cultural, social, and political life in the twenty-first century: the ubiquitous placement of humans and nonhumans in assemblages,[18] the democratization of media production that has seen everyday people producing media objects for circulation,[19] and the centrality of self-life-inscription in the media that is produced by everyday people.[20] These are the very things I noted in the introduction that demand the amalgamation of media and autobiography scholarship. As Paul Frosh notes, the selfie always calls attention to its mediated status at the level of action (the act of taking a selfie is always what is recorded in the selfie), and the selfie is a "genre of *personal* reflexivity" through which we inscribe the self in order to consider it.[21]

Given the selfie's status as a ubiquitous form of everyday self-representation and its self-reflexivity, it is not surprising that Ai Weiwei has become one of the key proponents of the selfie in the field of visual art. That the selfie is a genre of photography is important here, given the role photography has played in undermining the aura of the individual art object.[22] Working across a wide variety of media, Ai's practice exemplifies what art critic Rosalind Krauss has described as a turn in conceptual art toward the "reinvention of the medium."[23] This reinvention, Krauss argues, is the response offered by the avant-garde to the changing status of the art object in what Walter Benjamin famously described as "the age of mechanical reproduction."[24] The change in the treatment of medium Krauss identifies in conceptual and avant-garde art "does not imply the restoration of any of those earlier forms [oil on canvas, sculpture] . . . that the 'age of mechanical reproduction' had rendered so thoroughly dysfunctional through their . . . assimilation to the commodity form."[25] Rather than try to reinstate the aura of the object, Krauss argues that "post-medium" artists redefine "a medium as a set of conventions derived from (but not identical with) the material conditions of a given technical support, conventions out of which to develop a form of expressiveness that can be both projective and mnemonic."[26] It is as a medium in this sense, rather than as photography, that Ai Weiwei uses the selfie in *iPhone Wallpaper* and in his Instagram feed.

One the one hand, then, Ai's use of the selfie can be understood as a continuation of "the general avant-garde practice of mimicry, of assuming the guise of whole ranges of non- or anti-art experience in order to critique the unexamined pretensions of high art."[27] In his enthusiastic use of online platforms such as Twitter and Instagram, and of consumer grade hardware such as the iPhone camera, Ai takes up the role of provocateur in the gallery inaugurated by Duchamp/von Freytag-Loringhoven and continued by Warhol with his box sculptures. Ai's remediated selfies are a deliberate insertion of an out-of-place, nonaesthetic object into the rarefied space of the gallery. The use of wallpaper—famously also produced by Andy Warhol—strengthens the alignment of the work with the avant-garde tradition.[28] The selfie is a common—rather than a rarefied—self-reflexive technical support for materializing self-life-inscription, while also commenting on the process of construction and projection it enables.[29] By remediating the selfie into wallpaper in the gallery, Ai Weiwei maintains the avant-garde tradition of refusing an appeal to the distinctiveness of the art object by critically working the different ways in which digital and analog forms materialize values and ethics.

Yet Ai Weiwei's work does not flow solely into the field of visual art: he takes the perspectives of the conceptual, avant-garde artist into the larger cultural field by publishing his work in online forums. We must, then, consider Ai's reinvention of medium as working in two directions: bringing the practices and aesthetics of social media into the field of visual art, and bringing the point of view of the conceptual artist to the broader media culture through platforms such as Instagram. Unlike the artists considered by Krauss, such as Sophie Calle and Jeff Wall, Ai Weiwei continuously uses public media spaces as sites of exhibition. It is in accounting for the flow of images and aesthetic strategies between the gallery and the screen that his reinvention of medium draws our attention to the diversity of mediation in contemporary life. His recurring use of the selfie—that ubiquitous and maligned photographic genre—enacts a dual reinvention of medium to demand that Europeans act ethically toward the people arriving on the shores of the continent.

In going to Lesbos in December 2015 and explicitly stating that he was setting up a "studio" on the beaches where people are, today, still arriving by boat, Ai Weiwei refused to recognize a barrier that might see the beaches at such a moment as "off limits" to those not directly engaged in the provision of material assistance to the people arriving, or journalists reporting on the situation. Although Ai and his team did, reportedly, contribute to addressing the immediate physical needs of the people arriving, his presence on the beach was not solely directed at the immediate requirement for physical warmth, hydration, and food. Instead, his Instagram feed, and the later exhibition of the remediated images in analog works in galleries in Europe, addressed an ethical need beyond helping people from the boats and providing them with food and water. He used analog and digital media to create scenes of encounter in which the meaning of a life, and of lives, could be addressed. Ai Weiwei's studio on Lesbos was attempting to offer a safe passage into European culture and media. Standing on the beach with his iPhone, Ai offered the new arrivals an immediate opportunity to begin the work of entering the social field of Europe.[30]

Part of the critical work of *iPhone Wallpaper*, then, is to examine the selfie as a norm—an established technical support for the convention of self-inscription that is embedded in everyday life. The selfie in *#SafePassage* is both a nonaesthetic object inserted in the gallery through the logic of conceptualism, and an attempt to extend our understanding of whose lives are grievable in the social field of Europe by creating embodied, located encounters with the people arriving that are grounded by the familiar media form of the selfie. On at least two levels, then, the very everydayness of the selfie—its use of technical supports available to most people (the smartphone, the digital network, the free Instagram app) and its status as a norm (a convention) for self-life-inscription—is vital to the work of self-life-inscription #SafePassage undertakes.

But what kind of norm is the selfie? If, following Butler, we understand norms as both discourses and practices that constitute the field in which we are intelligible as subjects, and standards that are maintained through their iteration, then we could suggest the following paradigm: that the selfie is a practice which has range of functions, some quite similar to the diary, in terms of the recording of everyday life and the documentation of what Virginia Woolf famously called "small lives."[31] Making selfies is now an established means of making oneself intelligible as a subject to oneself (an act of self-assessment, for example), to one's community (through the posing together and sharing of selfies), and within the broader social field (as a kind of public statement of one's existence, for example).[32] Ai Weiwei's use of Instagram is important in this regard because Instagram is a platform—a mode of exhibition—that is the selfie's indigenous habitat.[33] By posting his selfies with people arriving in Lesbos to Instagram, Ai inserts them into the media environment which is a primary locus of the selfie's power as a norm. Instagram both evidences and materializes the ubiquity of the selfie; it is a technical support for the selfie as a norm that frames the subject. In his use of the selfie, Ai Weiwei explores all these elements of the form and process and, vitally, uses himself and his reputation within Europe as a framing device.

Over the course of four years, between 2011 and 2015, Ai became a potent symbol in Europe of the continued struggle for human rights in China, and of Europe's role as a champion for global human rights.[34] This position is the product of many factors: Ai's consistent use of autobiography as a convention in his work, his status as a privileged subject of empathy in the eyes of influential cultural workers in Europe, and his subsequent role as a symbol of Europe's preparedness to stand up for human rights. Ai critically deploys his identity as an exiled Chinese artist as a frame within the selfies. As Ai Weiwei routinely points out, he is not alone in suffering imprisonment, loss of liberty, torture, and intimidation. Standing on the beaches of Lesbos with his iPhone turned toward himself and the people seeking refuge, he challenges the people and institutions that so readily accept—and valorize—his status as a political refugee in Europe to extend that apprehension to those who continue to arrive at Europe's borders. Ai's presence in the frame materializes a direct challenge to a selective view of whose flourishing should be fostered (the artist's) and whose life is grievable (that of the nameless person arriving by boat).

These individual selfies are circulated in two directions, and reading these two together helps us consider how the diversity of media forms allows for differing forms of valuing lived experience and enables different kinds of claims about that value. When they appear in the context of Ai's Instagram feed (which is a constant stream of images of his meals; his son; exhibitions being installed; selfies with friends, colleagues, and fans; and photographic works themselves), they appear within the context of a serial autobiographical work in its own right. And, as he reminds us in the first section of *#SafePassage*, this autobiographical work sits in relation to the shadow biography that is created by Ai's ongoing surveillance by the Chinese authorities. Digital life narrative forms are, in Ai's oeuvre, a powerful means of exposing surveillance as a form of intimidation in China, and his widespread and voracious use of digital media is a strategy for staging a public reading of his life that acts as a contemporaneous data double to the one nurtured by the Chinese authorities.

In the gallery environment, printed on wallpaper that is pasted from the floor to ceiling on every wall in the room, *iPhone Wallpaper* materially registers the number of people seeking refuge in Europe and stages a form of embodied looking that asks the viewer to continually move between the collective and the individual. It is precisely in this movement, between crowd and individuals, that the demand for an ethical response to the flow of people arriving in Europe must occur. While an individual selfie in Ai's feed focuses the viewer's attention onto a single face or a small group of faces through the phone they hold in their hands as they scroll the feed, *iPhone Wallpaper* puts the viewer in front of scale. Yet it is the body of the viewer that looms large in this scene, not the bodies of the people in the photographs—who stand before us as tiny thumbnails. The material remediation of the selfie at a small scale asks the viewer to adopt a position of literally close reading—standing close to the wall, peering at the faces, moving across them. Or we can stand in the center of the room, registering the scale of the issue but choosing not to engage in the close attention that may engender relationality and occasion a scene of apprehension.

Accounting for how media materialities play a role in making life significant, then, requires that we learn to read each assemblage of self-life-inscription as a scene of possibility, the outcomes of which are not predetermined. Rather than producing a weak argument regarding the inherent subjectivity of any text or act of reading, accounting for media materialities means accounting for the dynamism of cultural production at the level of the linguistic, symbolic, and material.

ACKNOWLEDGMENTS

This book has emerged from conversations, invitations, walks, meals, car trips, train journeys, and visits to galleries in Australia, Canada, Europe, the United Kingdom, and the United States. As a result of my peripatetic life, it has been sustained by Facebook posts and comments, Skype calls, instant messaging chats, and e-mails. *Stories of the Self* has always been strung across time zones, and I am particularly grateful to all the people listed here who have been prepared to get up early, or stay up late, to talk with me. My work on this book has been made possible by collegiality, openness, friendship, inquisitiveness, and generosity. The final product has its feet in the scholarly argument for the importance of thinking life relationally, and the years working on this project have been a constant reminder that we become who we might be, think what we might think, and write what we hope we might write through our interactions with others. In what follows I acknowledge a diverse array of connections: some ephemeral, some structured by the temporal logics of conferences and employment contracts, and those that have their own timeline. Some names appear more than once because some people are deep in the web.

For twenty years, Samantha Arnull has been teaching me about objects and materials, and this book is (I hope) a testament to some of what I have learned—thank you.

Since they acted as external assessors of my doctoral thesis more than a decade ago, I have had the benefit of the mentoring and conversation of Julie Rak and Gillian Whitlock. I am indebted to them for their ongoing support for my work, for their scholarship that continues to shape my approach to the study of life writing, and for their intellectual friendship.

Julie and Gillian are part of a strong and generous scholarly community anchored by the International Auto/Biography Association (IABA) that sustains and challenges me. Within that community I have benefited greatly from listening and talking to Tully Barnett, Sarah Brophy, Kylie Cardell, Hillary Chute, Kate Douglas, Cynthia Franklin, Leigh Gilmore, Pamela Graham, Elizabeth Hanscombe, Emily Hipchen, Alfred Hornung, Craig Howes, Margaretta Jolly, Eva C. Karpinski, Emma Maguire, Nicole Matthews, Laurie McNeill, Nancy K. Miller, Aimée Morrison, Jay Prosser, Sidonie Smith, Julia Watson, and John David Zuern, as well as the wide range of scholars whose work I have heard at various events associated with IABA.

Most of the writing and research for this book was undertaken on the land of the Kulin nation, and I acknowledge the Traditional Owners and recognize Aboriginal sovereignty of land, waters, and culture. I pay my respects to elders of the Boon Wurrung and Woiwurrung (Wurundjeri) peoples—past, present, and emerging.

This book was developed during my time at Monash University. My colleagues Ali Alizadeh, Robin Gerster, Melinda Harvey, Sue Kossew, and Simone Murray provided support, humor, and camaraderie—thank you! At Monash, I was also very lucky to supervise the doctoral work of Oscar Schwartz and Nicola Rodger, and this has had a lasting impact on *Stories of the Self*. I also want to thank the Faculty of Arts at Monash for a period of sabbatical leave, and research funding, that supported primary research at the Andy Warhol Museum in Pittsburgh.

My archival research at the Andy Warhol Museum was in many ways defined by the knowledge, enthusiasm, patience, and humor of Matt Wrbican, Cindy Lisica, and Erin Byrne.

Over the years that I have been thinking about lives and objects, various people have invited me to write, speak, and think along with them. I am grateful to Lauren Berlant, Max Delany, Zara Dinnen, Kate Douglas, Margaretta Jolly, Sam McBean, and Kiene Brillenburg Wurth for their interest and for their generous engagement with my ideas when they were in nascent form.

Thank you to the following groups and projects for inviting me to present work from the project: the Back to the Book: Analog Literature in the Digital Age 1990–2010 project funded by the Netherlands Research Council; the IABA Students and New Scholars Network; the Flinders Life Narrative Research Group; the Australian Council for the Humanities, Arts and Social Sciences; the Center for the Study of Gender and Sexuality, University of Chicago; the IABA biannual conference

"Life Writing and Intimate Publics," University of Sussex; "Charismas of the Book" hosted by New York University Abu Dhabi; "Life Writing and European Identities," organized by Praemium Erasmianum (the Erasmus Prize), the Huizinga Instituut, and the Netherlands Research School for Literary Studies (OSL); the "Mediating Contemporary Literature" project, funded by the British Academy and Leverhulme; and the Institute for Information Law, University of Amsterdam.

Henry Jenkins and Karen Tongson showed great enthusiasm for this project, and I am indebted to them for their willingness to support a book that sits at the intersection of a range of fields. Their contributions always came at the right time to steady me for the work ahead. Lisa Gitelman provided sage advice at a key moment. Eric C. Zinner has been an unfailing supportive editor, and Dolma Ombadykow has shown me considerable hospitality as a new author in the Press's stable. The anonymous reviewers of the proposal and manuscript provided me with much-needed clarity and guidance about how to negotiate the diverse investments of the project; I am grateful to them for the insights, advice, and encouragement. I am also thankful for Susan Ecklund's keen eye for detail.

Ali Alizadeh, Balázs Bodó, Erin Byrne, Michelle Dicinoski, Melinda Harvey, Rosanne Kennedy, Johannes Klabbers, Anne Kustritz, Emma Maguire, Kathrin Thiele, Julie Rak, and Gillian Whitlock read early versions of some of the work presented here. I am very grateful to them for their criticism and enthusiasm, which sharpened my thinking and dulled my defensiveness.

Since arriving at Utrecht University in mid-2016, I have been thankful every day for the warm welcome and support from Debbie Cole, Kári Driscoll, Johanna Hoorenman, Birgit Kaiser, Susanne Knittel, Anne Kustritz, David Pascoe, Ann Rigney, Ted Sanders, Kathrin Thiele, and Kiene Brillenburg Wurth. I have been surprised at how quickly the other side of the world can feel like home, and it is thanks to my colleagues at Utrecht, as well as Balázs Bodó, Babs Boter, Erin La Cour, Marijke Huisman, Paul Koopman, Marleen Rensen, and Mia You that I have found intellectual community after leaving Melbourne. Thank you to my research assistant Eamonn Connor for help finalizing the project and to the Institute for Cultural Inquiry at UU for funding his work.

Thanks to my parents, Virginia and Carl, for their support, their anchoring, and for adopting my beloved cat Stripe.

I have been sustained by the conversation, laughter, empathy, cooking skills, and creativity of Samantha Arnull, Sapphira Arnull, Paul Byron, Jon Dale, Michelle Dicinoski, Quinn Eades, Danielle Fuller, Melinda Harvey, Johannes Klabbers, Anne Kustritz, Julie Rak, Catherine Strong, Kathrin Thiele, Petra Watson, and Kiene Brillenburg Wurth.

An element of the introduction was first published as:

"What's Next? Mediation," in *a/b: Auto/Biography Studies* 32, no. 2 (2017): 263–266.

Chapter 3 is an expanded and revised version of an article first published as:

"Intimate Economies: *PostSecret* and the Affect of Confession," in "Life Writing and Intimate Publics," ed. Margaret Jolly, special issue, *Biography: An Interdisciplinary Quarterly* 31, no. 4 (2011): 25–36.

Chapter 4 is an expanded and revised version of an article first published as:

"Periperformative Life Narrative: Queer Collages," *GLQ: A Journal of Lesbian and Gay Studies* 22, no. 3 (2016): 359–379.

Some of the material included in the conclusion first appeared in:

"The Selfie on Europe's Shores: Ai Weiwei and the Selfie as a Means of Safe Passage," *International Journal for History, Culture and Modernity* 6, no. 1 (2018): 1–13. http://doi.org/10.18352/hcm.546.

NOTES

INTRODUCTION

1   D'Onofrio, "2013 Year in Review." In recognition of the fact that Aboriginal sovereignty was never ceded in Australia, when Australian locations are referred to in *Stories of the Self*, their colonial-geographic name, along with the name of the people associated with the location or the name given to the location by its Traditional Owners, is used.

2   Shanklin, "2013 Smartphone Comparison Guide."

3   *Oxford English Dictionary Online*, "Word of the Year 2013."

4   Ewer, "14 Surprising Statistics about WordPress Usage."

5   Poitras, *Citizenfour*.

6   Greenwald, "NSA Collecting Phone Records of Millions of Verizon Customers Daily."

7   Popper, "Google Announces over 2 Billion Monthly Active Devices on Android"; Leswing, "Apple Says People Send as Many as 200,000 iMessages per Second"; Lincoln Park Strategies and Rad Campaign, "The State of Social Media and Online Privacy."

8   Ha, "Edward Snowden's Privacy Tips."

9   See Barnes, "A Privacy Paradox"; Barthe and de Jong, "The Privacy Paradox."

10 See Brown, *Studying the Internet Experience*; Kokolakis, "Privacy Attitudes and Privacy Behaviour."

11 Kozinski, "The Dead Past."

12 Rachel E. Dubrofsky and Shoshana A. Magnet, "Introduction: Feminist Surveillance Studies: Critical Interventions," in Dubrofsky and Magnet, *Feminist Surveillance Studies*, 3–5; Puar, *Terrorist Assemblages*, 151–165.

13 See Dubrofsky and Magnet, *Feminist Surveillance Studies*; Puar, *Terrorist Assemblages*; Zuboff, "Big Other."

14 Zuboff, "Big Other," 75.

15 Dubrofsky and Magnet, *Feminist Surveillance Studies*; Cheney-Lippold, *We Are Data*; Chun, *Updating to Remain the Same*; Lovink, *Sad by Design*.

16 For a discussion of communicative capitalism, see Dean, *Blog Theory*. For an influential discussion of surveillance capitalism, see Zuboff, "Big Other."

17 Butler, *Frames of War*, 7.

18 Butler, 2–13. See also Tsing, *The Mushroom at the End of the World*.

19 See, for example, James Olney's characterization of his interest in autobiography as being "focused in one direction on the relation traceable between lived experience and its *written record* and in the other direction on what that written

experience offers to us as readers and as human beings" (Olney, *Metaphors of Self*, x–xi [emphasis added]). Leigh Gilmore's argument that "the recurring mark in the women's autobiographies I study is that a *written record*, a testimonial, or a confessional document can represent a person, can stand in her absence for her truth, can re-member her life. Indeed, even in the narrowest and most ambivalent sense, writing an autobiography can be a political act because it asserts a right to speak rather than to be spoken for" (Gilmore, *Autobiographics*, 40 [emphasis added]). And see G. Thomas Couser's discussion of the role of memoir in democracy where he comments that memoir "often puts *on the record* lives that would otherwise be transient, evanescent" (Couser, *Memoir*, 181 [emphasis added]). See Poletti, "Putting Lives on the Record," for further discussion of the importance of "the record" for thinking about life writing as a socially and politically consequential act.

20 See, for example, Kathleen Stewart's influential work of anthropology and affect theory, *Ordinary Affects*.

21 Gilmore, "American Neoconfessional," 657–679.

22 Fernandes, *The Uses and Misuses of Storytelling*, epilogue; Whitlock, *Soft Weapons*.

23 Tumarkin, "This Narrated Life."

24 Strawson, "The Unstoried Life," 284–301.

25 See, for example, Kozinski, "The Dead Past."

26 Tsing, *The Mushroom at the End of the World*, 28.

27 "Assemblages cannot hide from capital and the state; they are sites for watching how political economy works" (Tsing, 24).

28 Puar, *Terrorist Assemblages*.

29 Cheney-Lippold, *We Are Data*, chap. 3.

30 For a discussion of how digital technologies and big data are potentially changing the formation of trust between individuals and institutions, see Bodó, "Mediated Trust."

31 Noble, *Algorithms of Oppression*.

32 See Dean, *Blog Theory*; Chun, *Updating to Remain the Same*.

33 *Oxford English Dictionary Online*, "privacy (noun)."

34 Berlant, "Intimacy," 283.

35 Butler, *Giving an Account of Oneself*.

36 Butler, *Frames of War*, 51.

37 Frow, *Genre*, 102–103.

38 See Warner, "Publics and Counterpublics," 49–50; Berlant, *The Female Complaint*, viii.

39 Gitelman, *Always Already New*, 6. Gitelman explains: "Inscriptions don't disappear into the air the way broadcasts do (though radio and television can of course be taped—that is, inscribed). The difference seems obvious, but it is important to note that the stability and savability of inscriptions are qualities that arise socially as well as perceptually" (6).

40 Hayles, *Writing Machines*, 24.

41 See Kadar, "Coming to Terms," 3–16; Smith and Watson, *Reading Autobiography*; Rak, "Life Writing versus Automedia," 155–180; and Rak, "Are Memoirs Autobiography?," 483–504.

42 See Rak, "Life Writing versus Automedia"; Couser, *Memoir*, 24; Poletti and Rak, *Identity Technologies*, 7–11.

43 Smith and Watson, *Reading Autobiography*, 2; Whitlock, *Postcolonial Life Narratives*, 2–3; Rak, "Are Memoirs Autobiography?," 307. There has also been a tendency to augment the term "autobiography" with a slash ("auto/biography") as seen in the title of the journal *a/b: Auto/Biography Studies*. The slash represents two key elements of life writing scholarship: (1) the commitment to extending analysis of life writing beyond the literary genre of the autobiography, conceived of as a linear narrative of the sovereign self to include other forms of life writing and life narrative, and (2) the theorizing of life writing, presented by influential critics such as Nancy K. Miller, as inherently relational (that all stories of the self must involve telling the story of our relation with others). The slash also gestures toward the field's recognition that biography is a distinct life writing practice and, in this sense, "auto/biography" is an inclusive term; the other version of this inclusiveness is represented by the term "AutoBiography" in the name of the field's largest association, the International AutoBiography Association (IABA), which is also sometimes written as the International Auto/Biography Association.

44 Heddon, *Autobiography and Performance*.

45 Brophy and Hladki, *Embodied Politics in Visual Autobiography*.

46 Renov, *The Subject of Documentary*.

47 van Dijck, *Mediated Memories in the Digital Age*, 3–4.

48 Smith and Watson, *Reading Autobiography*, 63–102.

49 van Dijck, *Mediating Memories*. See also Strawson, "The Unstoried Life," 284–301.

50 Eakin, *How Our Lives Become Stories*, 11–42.

51 Butler, *Giving an Account of Oneself*, 3–40.

52 Pascal, *Design and Truth in Autobiography*, 9; Sayre, *The Examined Self*, 4.

53 Agamben, *Homo Sacer*, 9. Marlene Kadar offers a different definition of *bios*, "quick, vital" (Kadar, "Coming to Terms," 6).

54 Agamben, *Homo Sacer*, 105.

55 Rak, "Life Writing versus Automedia," 156. For discussions of indeterminacy as the basis of relationality, see also Barad, *Meeting the Universe Halfway*, and Tsing, *The Mushroom at the End of the World*.

56 Bolter and Gruisin, *Remediation*, 55.

57 Foucault, *The Will to Knowledge*, 135–159. See also van den Hengel. "Zoegraphy," 2–4.

58 van den Hengel, "Zoegraphy," 4.

59 Hayles, *Writing Machines*, 30.

60 For an alternative account of the relationship between the linguistic and material turn in comparative literature, see Wurth, "The Material Turn in Comparative Literature," 247–263.

61 Smith and Watson, *Reading Autobiography*, 193–21.

62 Such as Plummer, *Telling Sexual Stories.*

63 See also the two issues of the journal *Biography: An Interdisciplinary Quarterly* on the subject of "Online Lives," the first in 2003 (edited by John David Zuern), the second in 2015 (edited by Laurie McNeill and John David Zuern), for how rapidly the relationship between life writing and media studies has changed. Julie Rak and I also consider the lack of integration of media studies perspectives in life writing studies in the introduction to *Identity Technologies.*

64 Horton and Wohl, "Mass Communication and Parasocial Interaction," 41–48.

65 Williams, *Keywords,* 204–205.

66 Williams, 206.

67 See, for example, Turkle, *Alone Together.*

68 Williams, *Keywords,* 206. "All 'objects,'" Williams further explains, "and in this context notably works of art, are mediated by specific social relations but cannot be reduced to an abstraction of that relationship; the mediation is positive and in a sense autonomous" (206). *Stories of the Self* seeks to understand how we can account for, without abstracting, the discursive and material mediation of autobiography.

69 van Dijck, *Mediated Memories,* 21 (emphasis in original).

70 van Dijck, 21.

71 Williams, *Keywords,* 206–207.

72 Gitelman, *Always Already New,* 6.

73 See Wendy Hui Kyong Chun's discussion of "habitual new media" in *Updating to Remain the Same* for a different account of the disappearance of media and what it means for our understanding of the mediation of subjectivity and community.

74 Gitelman, *Always Already New,* 6.

75 Gitelman, 6–7.

76 van Dijck, *Mediated Memories,* 19.

77 Kember and Zylinksa, *Life after New Media,* 18 (emphasis in original).

78 Kember and Zylinska, 23.

79 Kember and Zylinksa, 12.

80 Hayles, *Writing Machines,* 30–33.

81 Tilley, "Materializing Identities," 348. See also Tsing, *The Mushroom at the End of the World.*

82 Miller, *Materiality,* 3.

83 Coole and Frost, *New Materialisms,* 2.

84 Gitelman, *Always Already New,* 6.

85 Gitelman, 7.

86 Whitlock, "Testimony of Things," 20.

87 Whitlock, 17.

88 Couldry, "Mediatization or Mediation?," 380.

89 Chun, "Somebody Said New Media," 3.

90 Tsing, *The Mushroom at the End of the World,* 36.

1. CARDBOARD BOXES

1 Other containers used in the work include several two-drawer filing cabinets (forty drawers in total) and one large steamer trunk.

2 The *Time Capsules* are not the only work of Warhol's that challenge the would-be audience. His diary, for example, runs to 20,000 pages in manuscript and 807 pages in its published form. His "experimental novel," *a: a novel*, is described by his longtime amanuensis and collaborator Pat Hackett as consisting of "transcripts of conversations that he'd taped of his superstars and friends as they operated in the amphetamine and pansexual subculture of New York . . . 'transcribed' by amateur typists who, guessing at words and phrases when they couldn't be certain, perpetrated technical and conceptual mistakes galore that Andy then made sure were reproduced, typo for typo, as the published text" (Pat Hackett, "Introduction," in Warhol, *The Diaries of Andy Warhol*, xxi). *Empire*, a film work that runs continuously for eight hours and five minutes, is also evidence of Warhol's interest in duration; see Gopnik, "Monumental Case, but Not Much Plot." Wayne Koestenbaum opens his biography of Warhol by observing, "Every effort in his career as an artist and whirlwind, as impresario and irritant, was to give the public too much, more than it wanted" (Koestenbaum, *Andy Warhol*, 1–2). See also Jonathan Flatley's theory of Warhol's use of liking as a process of maximization through mediation (Flatley, *Like Andy Warhol*, 69).

3 Of course, there are differing accounts of what that mode of seeing is. See Danto, "The Artworld," 571–584; Danto, *Andy Warhol*, 55; Flatley, *Like Andy Warhol*; and Foster, *The First Pop Age*, 109–171.

4 Hal Foster argues that the punctum in Warhol's silk screens "arises less through content than through technique, especially through the 'floating flashes' of the silk-screen process, the engineered accidents (the slipping of the register, the streaking of the image, and so forth) that appear as the ink is squeezed onto the canvas and the screen is repositioned" (Foster, *The First Pop Age*, 115).

5 See Judith A. Peraino's discussion of a cassette tape of songs by Lou Reed recorded for Andy Warhol and of cassette tape as a medium of inscription that can serve "the revelation of self to an intimate other" (Peraino, "I'll Be Your Mixtape," 402–403).

6 This audaciousness is performed in his diary, when, in one of only three instances where the work is mentioned, Warhol says of the *Time Capsules* on September 30, 1986 (twelve years into the project): "Took a few time capsule boxes to the office. They are fun—when you go through them there's things you really don't want to give up. Some day I'll sell them for $4,000 or $5,000 apiece. I used to think $100, but now I think that's my new price" (Warhol, *Diaries*, 762).

7 Robert Rauschenberg, for example, made *Dirt Painting (for John Cage)*, which consisted of dirt and mold in a wooden box, in 1953. Hal Foster's posits that Rauschenberg's work of this period can be thought of as an exploration of Bataille's "base materialism" (Foster, "'Made Out of the Real World,'" 91).

8 Koestenbaum, *Andy Warhol*, 167. Koestenbaum is not alone in drawing on the imagery of a tomb when describing the *Time Capsules*; Bourdon describes the storage of the boxes in The Factory (in preparation for the move to The Office) as "an entire wall . . . lined with neatly stacked containers of miscellaneous memorabilia, eerily evoking the funerary goods that Egyptian pharaohs stashed in their tombs to comfort them in their afterlives" (Bourdon, *Warhol*, 348).

9 Butler, *Giving an Account of Oneself*.

10 Butler, *Gender Trouble*, 2–3. For a discussion of Warhol and identity, see, for example, Wolf, "Introduction through the Looking-Glass," xi–xxxi.

11 "For the most part, the attempts to find stable ground from which to determine the real Warhol obscure his actual practices, whose queer appeal and queer effects vanish under this identificatory gaze" (Flatley, *Like Andy Warhol*, 34).

12 Hackett, "Introduction," xvii.

13 Bockris, *Warhol*, 380.

14 The then chief archivist at the Andy Warhol Museum told me during my visit that researchers working on Warhol regularly make appointments to see the *Time Capsules* but often find the experience yields little "new" information. This is, as this chapter argues, the nature of the work in my opinion.

15 Foster, *The First Pop Age*, 110.

16 Wrbican. *A Guide to the Exhibition*.

17 Wrbican, Matt, e-mail messages to the author, August 26, 2013–August 8, 2014.

18 Frank, "Corrugated Box Compression," 105.

19 Twede, "The Birth of Modern Packaging," 245–246.

20 Twede, 245–272; Cross and Proctor, *Packaged Pleasures*, 15–17.

21 Deutsch, *Building A Housewife's Parade*, 43–72.

22 Danto, *Andy Warhol*, 66.

23 Frei and Printz, *The Andy Warhol Catalogue Raisonne*, 53.

24 Danto, *Andy Warhol*, 66.

25 Bockris, *Warhol*, 199.

26 Danto, *Andy Warhol*, 48.

27 See Hustvedt, "A Woman in the Men's Room," for a discussion of the authorship of Duchamp's fountain.

28 Danto, *Andy Warhol*, 51–58. See also Frei and Prinz, *The Andy Warhol Catalogue Raisonne*, 54.

29 See also the description of the exhibition in the *Catalogue Raisonne*: "The exhibition consisted of several hundred individual boxes. . . . It would have been impossible for visitors to enter the south gallery where the *Brillo* boxes were shown. . . . His sense of sculpture as a spatial obstruction is striking" (Frei and Printz, *The Andy Warhol Catalogue Raisonne*, 55).

30 Danto, *Andy Warhol*, 68.

31 Frei and Printz, *The Andy Warhol Catalogue Raisonne*, 55.

32 See Flatley's discussion of the *Time Capsules* in the context of his analysis of Warhol's collecting: "By establishing a protocol for his mode of perceiving and

encountering the world, Warhol's perfumes, cassette tapes, photographs, and Time Capsules all keep him connected to and caring about—*liking*—the world" (Flatley, *Like Andy Warhol*, 69).

33 Flatley, 69.

34 Frank, "Corrugated Box Compression," 120.

35 Frank, 120.

36 Koestenbaum, *Andy Warhol*, 152.

37 Erin Byrne, archivist at the Warhol Museum, advises me that "this was a promotion for Man Ray, Inventor/Painter/Poet, December 20 Through March 2, The New York Cultural Center—Man Ray famously has a work titled Pain peint [Blue bread: favourite food for bluebirds]" (personal communication, May 6, 2019).

38 Frank, "Corrugated Box Compression," 107.

39 Frank, 109.

40 "The story of Andy Warhol is the story of his friends, surrogates, and associates. It would be easy to narrate his life without saying much about him at all, for he tried to fade into his entourage" (Koestenbaum, *Andy Warhol*, 2).

41 I suggested earlier that in their use of scale, the *Time Capsules* can be read as a means of intervening in the biographical impulse by creating privacy through excessive materiality. When I visited the archive, I was surprised to be told that many Warhol scholars and biographers had visited the work and found the experience of exploring the *Time Capsules* largely unhelpful. One biographer who was in the archives at the same time as I was confessed that he had never found the *Time Capsules* very useful. He just didn't know what to do with them. This could be interpreted as a great victory for Warhol; he has succeeded in leaving behind a work made up entirely of objects he came into contact with in his everyday life that are seemingly unable to tell us anything about him. See Bockris's introduction to his biography of Warhol for his account of Warhol's reaction to the biographical project (Bockris, *Warhol*, 1–7).

42 See, for example, Bockris's account of attempts to keep Jean-Michel Basquiat out of the Warhol circle (*Warhol*, 449–451). The initial assessment of Basquiat as an undesirable person who should be kept at a distance by Warhol and members of his entourage evidences the racism of the New York social scene and the more conservative approach to membership of the entourage after Warhol was shot.

43 See Ubuweb, *The Andy Warhol Tapes (1994)*, accessed September 12, 2014, www.ubu.com/sound/warhol_tapes.html.

44 One compelling example of Warhol's curation of the *Time Capsules* relates to the trace of Valerie Solanas. There are photocopies of some of the letters she wrote Warhol from jail following her attack on him. The originals are kept in the Warhol archive.

45 *Oxford English Dictionary Online*, "rummage, v."

46 David Bourdon, in his biography of Warhol, repeatedly describes Johnson as Warhol's "housemate" (*Warhol*, 292, 308). The anemic label indicates a disinclination to name the relationship as intimate, despite Bourdon noting the closeness

of Warhol and Johnson's relationship, and Johnson's role as co-carer for Julia Warhola: he accompanied her to her weekly doctor's appointment and cooked her meals during the last year she lived with Warhol and Johnson (Bourdon, *Warhol*, 292, 308). This is indicative of what Doyle, Flatley, and Muñoz refer to as the "degaying of Warhol" (Jennifer Doyle, Jonathan Flatley, and José Esteban Muñoz, "Introduction," in Doyle, Flatley, and Muñoz, *Pop Out: Queer Warhol*, 2).

47 The cause of the explosion remains unknown.

48 Doyle, Flatley, and Muñoz, *Pop Out*.

49 Berlant, "Intimacy," 286.

50 Berlant, 282.

51 See David M. Henkin's overview of the history of the evolution of the US Postal Service from a news delivery service to a conveyer of personal writing. In regard to the shift from the collection of the mail at centralized offices to delivery to the home, see his discussion of the gendered nature of the arguments for postal delivery to the home in the United States in the 1850s. Henkin, *The Postal Age*, 87–90.

52 Henkin, 11.

53 Henkin, 9.

54 Henkin, 103–104.

55 I thank Erin Byrne for this suggestion.

56 In the chapter of Bockris's biography detailing Warhol and Johnson's move to the townhouse on 57 East Sixty-Sixth Street in 1975 (after an extensive renovation overseen by Johnson), in which an interview with Johnson is quoted, Johnson describes how their new house—immaculately furnished by him—became a private space for Warhol. The couple rarely entertained guests at home: "It was always a disaster, so it just wasn't fair [for Johnson to entertain]. He didn't enjoy it, I think he was embarrassed by it. Andy saw so many people all day long, and the Factory was so accessible and pretty much of an open house, and then he was out so much . . . he did lunches at the Factory, he entertained in restaurants. I think he just needed a place to be alone" (Bockris, *Warhol*, 394).

57 Most accounts of how the *Time Capsules* were assembled refer to Warhol's use of boxes in the professional site of The Office, but the mail and the diaries (see note 5) suggest that Warhol was also compiling them at home.

58 Hal Foster, in reviewing Koestenbaum's *Andy Warhol*, gives a clear restatement of this view of Warhol's persona: "Especially after his shooting by the paranoid Factory fade-out Valerie Solanas, he countered his vulnerability with psychological defenses and physical trusses of different sorts: buffering entourages, opaque looks (big glasses, silver wigs), protective gadgets (the omnipresent Polaroid and tape recorder), plus a weird ability to pass as his own double or simulacrum (even when he was right there in front of you he seemed somehow disembodied)" (Foster, "Andy Paperbag"). Jonathan Flatley offers an alternative view of Warhol's praxis, arguing that it was "disintrumentalized affective labor, which aimed to engage and transform the world in a context where (as Warhol put it) 'it would be so much easier not to care'" (Flatley, *Like Andy Warhol*, 4).

59 Flatley, 4.

60 See the 1996 edited collection *Pop Out*, Wayne Koestenbaum's *Andy Warhol*, and Jonathan Flatley's *Like Andy Warhol*.

61 Lisa Duggan defines homonormativity as "a politics that does not contest dominant heteronormative assumptions and institutions but upholds and sustains them while promising the possibility of a demobilized gay constituency and a privatized, depoliticized gay culture anchored in domesticity and consumption" (Duggan, "The New Homonormativity," 179).

62 See Berlant, "Love, a Queer Feeling," 423–451; and Berlant, "Intimacy," for elaborations of the formalism of love. An example of how Johnson and Warhol engaged in more open forms of intimacy can be found in *Time Capsule* 166, which includes "large brown envelope with recto labeled to A.W.—F.H.—J.J.—V.F. [Andy Warhol, Fred Hughes, Jed Johnson, Vincent Freemont] Andy Warhol Enterprises and verso labeled as B.A.D. Ltd. c/o J. Johnson + Nana and containing Correspondence envelope labeled to B.A.D. Ltd c/o A. [Andy] Warhol & J. [Jed] Johnson containing a two page handwritten letter from [illegible] and with four Polaroid photographs of unidentified men and male genitals and having handwritten notations on versos, one Polaroid photo negative, and one piece of Polaroid photo ephemera with handwritten note." Flatley argues that Warhol worked against the logic of the couple form as the dominant narrative of intimacy (Flatley, *Like Andy Warhol*, 44–47, 76). I think Flatley's argument is convincing, and indeed it could be said to heighten the need for an account of Johnson and Warhol's cohabitation.

63 Flatley argues that Warhol's affective labor of liking was inherently disruptive of the logic of the couple: "In composing and promoting an affect theory that does not privilege the normative, monogamous couple as the organizing hub for sociality or the primary site of affective affiliation, comfort or pleasure . . . Warhol's is an effort to create an opening where nonmiserable, even joyous, plural queer singularity could come into being" (Flatley, *Like Andy Warhol*, 47). How we do this without erasing Jed Johnson from readings of Warhol's life and practice is a challenge this chapter attempts to grapple with.

64 The numbering system was not introduced by Warhol but is a feature of the cataloguing of the boxes after Warhol's death.

65 Berlant, "Love, a Queer Feeling," 435.

66 In the process of opening and cataloguing every *Time Capsule*, the boxes have been repacked and paper folders introduced into many of the boxes to keep items together. The order that things come out of the box reflects the repacking by the archivists, not Warhol's original packing.

67 Koestenbaum, *Andy Warhol*, 133.

68 See Derrida, *Archive Fever*, 1–5. Archivists themselves have written extensively on the status of archiving as a science, and how its practices and protocols are enmeshed in and materialize discourses of knowledge and evidence. See, for example, Schwartz and Cook, "Archives, Records, and Power," 1–19; Caswell,

Punzalan, and Sangwand, "Critical Archive Studies," 1–8; Yeo, "Concepts of Record (1)," 315–343.

69 Warhol, *The Philosophy of Andy Warhol*, 103.

70 Koestenbaum, *Andy Warhol*, 2.

71 "We are saying the *Freudian signature* so as not to have to decide yet between Sigmund Freud, the proper name, on the one hand, and on the other, the invention of psychoanalysis: project of knowledge, of practice and of institution, community, family, domiciliation, consignation, 'house' or 'museum,' in the present state of archivization" (Derrida, *Archive Fever*, 5 [emphasis in original]).

72 Not long after Warhol exhibited his box sculptures, Arthur C. Danto used them as a primary example in his attempt to articulate the importance of preexisting knowledge of art theory in contemporary art; see Danto, "The Artworld."

73 Koestenbaum, *Andy Warhol*, 1.

74 Derrida, *Archive Fever*, 5.

75 Benjamin, "The Work of Art in the Age of Mechanical Reproduction," 217.

76 Benjamin, 218.

77 Benjamin, 218–219.

78 For a few years, an alternative was to watch one of the videos, made by the Andy Warhol Museum, of a *Time Capsule* being opened. These "one-time-only" performances were presented during the six-year period in which the work of opening all the boxes was being undertaken. They were staged in the theater at the museum, or in the archives department, and included guests such as Benjamin Liu (Warhol's assistant) and John Waters. At the time of writing, however, the videos were no longer available online; there is only a trace of their having been posted, with YouTube explaining that the "video [is] unavailable."

79 Turner, *Understanding Celebrity*, 8–9.

80 Steedman, *Dust*, 77.

81 See Hal Foster's overview of these approaches to Warhol's work, *The Return of the Real*, 127–130.

82 Flatley, *Like Andy Warhol*, 7.

83 Flatley, 5.

84 Berlant, *Desire/Love*, 88–90.

85 Flatley, *Like Andy Warhol*, 6–8.

86 Berlant, *Desire/Love*, 95.

87 There appears to be little material in the *Time Capsules* that stems from Warhol and Johnson getting to know each other. Similarly, the *Diaries* begin in 1976, when Warhol and Johnson are already together; the end of their relationship is recorded (Johnson moves out). In *Popism*, Warhol's autobiography of the 1960s, cowritten with Pat Hackett, Johnson's arrival in Warhol's life is recorded as follows: "One morning when [Paul Morrissey] was down at 33 [Union Square West, the location of Warhol's second studio], a young kid delivered a Western Union telegram there, at just about the time Paul was realizing that there were just too many painted surfaces for one person to do alone. When he noticed that the mes-

senger was well mannered, he started up a conversation and found out his name was Jed Johnson, that he had just arrived in New York from Sacramento, and that he and his twin brother, Jay, were living right across the park in a fifth-floor walk up on 17th Street. Paul hired him to help get the place in shape" (Warhol and Hackett, *POPism*, 264). While there is no discussion of the closeness of their relationship, Johnson's role as a witness to Warhol's shooting in 1968 is also included in Warhol and Hackett, *POPism*, 270–281.

88 Derrida, *Archive Fever*, 36.

89 Warhol and Hackett, *POPism*.

90 Flatley, *Like Andy Warhol*, 6.

91 Koestenbaum, *Andy Warhol*, 134.

92 Derrida, *Archive Fever*, 11–12.

93 Thank you to Erin Byrne for identifying this portrait (personal communication, May 6, 2019).

94 One possible narrative is evoked in Koestenbaum's synthesis of key preoccupations in Warhol's work: "Eight hours. Nine months. Three minutes. All of Warhol's work condenses—or sublimes—into one preoccupation: time, and what time feels like when you are turned on. His art ponders what it feels like to wait for sex; to wait, during sex, for it to end; to wait, during sex's prelude, for the 'real' sex to begin; to desire a man you are looking at; to endure postponement, perhaps for a lifetime, as you wait for the man to turn around and look back at you" (Koestenbaum, *Andy Warhol*, 14).

95 "During this period I took thousands of Polaroids of genitals. Whenever somebody came up to the Factory, no matter how straight-looking he was, I'd ask him to take his pants off so I could photograph his cock and balls. It was surprising who'd let me and who wouldn't" (Warhol and Hackett, *POPism*, 294). The location of these Polaroids is unknown. Thank you to Jonathan Flatley for a conversation that clarified the mythological status of these photographs.

96 See Bockris's account of Warhol and Basquiat's friendship (*Warhol*, 460–469). See also Muñoz, "Famous and Dandy," 143–179.

97 Bockris, *Warhol*, 461–462.

98 Kadar, "Coming to Terms," 3; Agamben, *Homo Sacer*, 9.

99 Flatley, *Like Andy Warhol*, 58.

100 Flatley, 58.

101 For Flatley, a crucial element of Warhol's collecting as a form of liking is that "the collector initiates something or someone into a new existence as a like-being among other like-beings, in a collective space defined by the mutual, nonhierarchical relations of resemblance" (Flatley, *Like Andy Warhol*, 58).

102 I trace a different line, examining the *Time Capsule* dedicated to Julia Warhol and the prehistory of sexting that might be traced in the *Time Capsules*, in "'The Implied Rummager: Reading Intimate Interiors in Andy Warhol's *Time Capsules*," forthcoming in the journal *Life Writing*.

103 Koestenbaum, *Andy Warhol*, 134.

2. CAMERAS

1 Kember and Zylinska, *Life after New Media*, 434.

2 Kember and Zylinksa, 434.

3 I am drawing on Karen Barad's rigorous retheorizing of the role of the apparatus in the scene of making meaning developed in *Meeting the Universe Halfway* (see, for example, 132–153), while also thinking about Hayles's discussion of the apparatus (*Writing Machines*, 22) and theories of the apparatus developed in film theory (Baudry and Williams, "Ideological Effects of the Basic Cinematographic Apparatus," 39–47; Metz, "The Imaginary Signifier," 14–76).

4 Polley, *Stories We Tell*.

5 Joost and Schulman, *Catfish*.

6 Barad, "Posthumanist Performativity," 816. See Jean-Louis Baudry's discussion of the cinematographic apparatus as constituted, at the level of technology, by camera, sound recording, screen, and projector in Baudry and Williams, "Ideological Effects of the Basic Cinematographic Apparatus." I limit my discussion to the apparatus of textual production, thus excluding screen and projector from my analysis until the conclusion. The media of reception of autobiographical documentary requires more consideration, especially as the screen and projector are now augmented (or replaced) by a variety of personal and public digital screens of diverse sizes (from the screen of the smartphone, to the large screens installed in public squares and streets), and the dynamic between projector and screen has been altered in many of the technologies through their amalgamation and the decreasing use of film and film projectors. See also Hayles's discussion of the apparatus in relation to the concept of the material metaphor in *Writing Machines*, 22.

7 Barad, "Posthumanist Performativity," 815.

8 Puar, "'I Would Rather Be a Cyborg Than a Goddess,'" 49–66. Barad explicitly rejects the concept of assemblage for understanding the intra-action between matter and apparatuses (see Barad, *Meeting the Universe Halfway*, 142, 171). However, to my mind there is conceptual clarity to be gained from using the idea of the assemblage rather than Barad's preferred concept of "phenomena" to denote the moment that is created when an apparatus is introduced into a scene. See Barad's definition of phenomena in *Meeting*, 118–121. See also Anna Tsing's conceptualization of an assemblage in *The Mushroom at the End of the World*, 24.

9 In using the term "scene" here, I am drawing on Lauren Berlant's thinking about the scene as an event or moment in which one is aware that something is happening, but the meaning of the event is unclear. See Anna Poletti and Julie Rak, "The Blog as Experimental Setting: An Interview with Lauren Berlant," in Poletti and Rak, *Identity Technologies*, 268–269. There are some correspondences between Berlant's formulation of the scene and Barad's theorizing of the inherent indeterminacy of intra-action involving apparatuses and matter that I am trying to tease out in this discussion (see Barad, *Meeting the Universe Halfway*, 170–171).

10 Puar, "I Would Rather Be a Cyborg Than a Goddess," 57.

11 Puar, 50.

12 Barad, "Posthumanist Performativity," 814. Barad's theory of the agency and relationality of all matter is an extension of quantum theorist Niels Bohr's insights into complementarity. Bohr was a leading physicist who advanced a quantum theory of measurement that Barad argues has wide-reaching implications for our understanding of ontology and epistemology (see Barad, *Meeting the Universe Halfway*, 97–125). Bohr developed a new theory of observation that takes into account the mutually constituting role of observer and observed in the scene of observation. In Barad's account of it, Bohr's theory can be extended to advance our understanding of discourse. Barad develops a theory of performative materiality that extends Judith Butler's theory of performativity to recognize that "materiality plays an *active* role in the workings of power" (see Barad, "Posthumanist Performativity," 65). Barad's materialist theory involves a complex vocabulary through which the relationship between materials in a situation are conceptualized. I will not be adopting all of this language; rather, I present an interpretation of the films in question informed by Barad's theory of agential realism in order to test its usefulness for understanding the role of media forms in determining what a life is and how lives comes to matter.

13 Barad, *Meeting the Universe Halfway*, 184.

14 Barad, 135. This is the primary way that Barad extends Butler's theory of performativity beyond what Barad argues is its residual anthropocentrism: Barad's theory repositions the subject as one agent among many. See Barad, *Meeting the Universe Halfway*, 151.

15 Barad, 135. See Reichert and Richterich, "Introduction," 5–17, for a discussion of three strands of media theory that require this kind of approach. They focus on the importance of these insights for the study of digital media; however, I take the view that the use of digital media can only be understood by thinking of it alongside our relationship to analog media forms such as the cardboard box, the postcard, and the book.

16 Chute, "An Interview with Alison Bechdel," 1006.

17 See Bechdel's description of the "magical" effects of the assemblage from which *Fun Home* emerged, which includes tracing paper, Google image search, family photographs, and her computer (Bechdel, "Alison Bechdel's *Fun Home*").

18 Chute, "An Interview with Alison Bechdel," 1005.

19 Bechdel, *Fun Home*, 100–101. See Cvetkovich, "Drawing the Archive in Alison Bechdel's *Fun Home*," 111–128; Chute, *Graphic Women*, 183.

20 Agamben, *Homo Sacer*, 9. Marlene Kadar offers a different definition of *bios*: "quick, vital" (Kadar, "Coming to Terms," 6).

21 It is not incidental that the media that dominated the lives of the Bechdel family—books (Alison and her father Bruce) and performance (her mother's long career as an amateur actor)—have been mirrored in the writing, and afterlife, of *Fun Home*, which was first a book and then a successful musical. There is a continuity of media forms between the media environment narrated in the autobiography

and the forms the autobiography itself takes. We see this also in *Tarnation*, in which Jonathan's fascination with television and film is amplified by his receipt of a video camera as a gift when he was a small boy, and the subsequent production of two autobiographical documentaries.

22 Chute, "An Interview with Alison Bechdel," 1006.

23 Barad, "Posthumanist Performativity," 816.

24 Barad, 822.

25 Barad, 816–817, 820.

26 For an analysis of *Catfish* as a documentary about the impact of social media on subjectivity and sociality, see Dinnen, *The Digital Banal*, 73–82. Dinnen reads the documentary, and the spin-off TV show, as being concerned with, but ultimately unable to critique, the invisibility of digital media *as* mediator of social life, and how this ultimately blocks "the experience of novelty" (75).

27 See, for example, Polley's description of her role in the film "as the character of the filmmaker, the investigator, the person who was trying to get to the bottom of things" (Lussier, "Film Interview").

28 Barad, *Meeting the Universe Halfway*, 97–106.

29 Barad, "Posthumanist Performativity," 817n21.

30 While I agree that we can speak about autobiographical discourse as being, to a degree, transmedial, for the reasons outlined here I disagree with Kate J. Waites's categorization of *Stories We Tell* as a "memoir" (Waites, "Sarah Polley's Documemoir *Stories We Tell*," 543–555). I would argue, following Julie Rak, that memoir is a print genre and is therefore embedded in the ontologies, metaphysics, and epistemologies of print and, by association, literature. See Rak, "Are Memoirs Autobiography?"; Rak, *Boom!*; Egan, "Encounters in Camera," 593–616.

31 See Nichols, *Representing Reality*, 3–6. See also Belinda Smaill's discussion of documentary and affect, using object relations theory, and documentary as an object of knowledge production for filmmakers and audiences (Smaill, *The Documentary*, 8–19).

32 Barad, *Meeting the Universe Halfway*, 128–129.

33 Nichols, *Representing Reality*, 26–28.

34 See, for example, the essays in Renov, *Theorizing Documentary*.

35 Nichols, *Representing Reality*, 153.

36 Lejeune, "The Autobiographical Pact" 3–30.

37 Forrester, "If *p*, Then What?," 1–25.

38 Herzog, "Crime Stories," 40.

39 Berlant, "On the Case," 665.

40 Forrester, "If *p*, Then What?," 4–7.

41 Brian Winston, "The Documentary Film as Scientific Inscription," in Renov, *Theorizing Documentary*, 37.

42 In an interview conducted after the film's release, Henry credits Rel with having the "instinct" to begin filming so early in Nev's relationship with Abby and her family. When the documentary was released in 2010 and the filmmakers and Nev

began to do publicity for the film, they recorded their interactions with the press (see Gilbey, "Trust Me, I'm a Film-maker"): Nev explains the logic behind the continual recording: "Our lives are undefined. For all we know, our next movie could involve this process somehow . . . if we hadn't filmed the past few years, we wouldn't have that movie, so if we don't record this, we won't have whatever's next. Better to have it than to not have it" (Gilbey, "Trust Me, I'm a Film-maker," n.p.).

43 Barad, *Meeting the Universe Halfway*, 163.

44 Noble, *Algorithms of Oppression*; Chun, *Updating to Remain the Same.*

45 Barad, *Meeting the Universe Halfway*, 114.

46 Barad, 393.

47 Agamben, *Homo Sacer*, 9.

48 In an interview Nev demurs when asked if he and Angela are friends. Instead he responds: "We're eternally connected" (Gilbey, "Trust Me, I'm a Film-maker," n.p.). This observation appears to fit well with the quantum view of matter advanced by Barad.

49 Gilbey, n.p.

50 Barad, *Meeting the Universe Halfway*, 394.

51 Dinnen, *The Digital Banal*, 79.

52 Barad, *Meeting the Universe Halfway*, 148.

53 Barad, 393.

54 See, for example, the discussion of the screen and projector in Metz, "The Imaginary Signifier," 48–53.

55 I would like to thank one of the anonymous reviewers of the manuscript for the phrase "merely social force" and the provocation to articulate how apparatuses of observation materialize discourses while also opening discourses of epistemology and ontology to the inherent agency of matter.

3. CROWDSOURCING

1 Warren, *PostSecret*, 1.

2 Warren, 1.

3 Warren, "Half a Million Secrets."

4 The books from the series are *PostSecret: Extraordinary Confessions from Ordinary Lives* (2005), *My Secret: A PostSecret Book* (2006), *A Lifetime of Secrets: A PostSecret Book* (2007), *The Secret Lives of Men and Women: A PostSecret Book* (2007), *PostSecret: Confessions on Life, Death and God* (2009), and *The World of PostSecret* (2014).

5 Hesmondhalgh, "User-Generated Content, Free Labour and the Cultural Industries," 267–281; Jenkins, Ford, and Green, *Spreadable Media*, 153–194.

6 See Johns, *The Nature of the Book*; Hall, *Digitize This Book!*

7 Rak, *Boom!*

8 Berlant, "Trauma and Ineloquence," 47.

9 Berlant, 46–48.

10 I use the term "entrepreneurship" to designate a practice that is "concerned with the discovery and exploitation of profitable opportunities" (Shane and Venkataraman, "The Promise of Entrepreneurship as a Field of Research," 217). Shane and Venkataraman define entrepreneurship as consisting of two related properties: the presence of potentially lucrative opportunities, and the presence of "enterprising individuals" prepared to take action in response to the opportunities (218). In the case of confessional entrepreneurs, the opportunity occurs in the context of the rise of intimacy and affect in the construction of US citizenship outlined by Berlant, and the rise of communicative capitalism, theorized by Jodi Dean, as I explain throughout this chapter. The confessional entrepreneur combines two resources in order to respond to the opportunity: the cultural shift toward crowdsourcing, and the increasing prominence of autobiographical discourse in the cultural field. The entrepreneur creates something new to combine these resources: a textual template (secrets on postcards, short spoken word presentations such as those fostered by *The Moth*, the interview technique of *StoryCorps*) that results in freely generated products (crowdsourced) that create an intimate public which the confessional entrepreneur leads and claims authorship of. Shane and Venkataraman's model of entrepreneurship avoids accounting for the practice solely in terms of the inherent capabilities of entrepreneurs to identify and act on an opportunity (a view that sees entrepreneurs as born and inherently different from other members of the community). Rather, their account emphasizes that because entrepreneurship requires the coexistence of opportunity and an individual prepared to act, the role of the entrepreneur should be understood as a "tendency to respond to the situational cues of opportunities" rather than someone who possess "a stable characteristic that differentiates some people from others across all situations" (Shane and Venkataraman, "The Promise of Entrepreneurship as a Field of Research," 219).

11 See Jenkins et al., *Confronting the Challenges of Participatory Culture Media Education*.

12 Dean, *Blog Theory*, 3–4.

13 Berlant, *The Female Complaint*.

14 Berlant, 266.

15 Berlant, vii.

16 Berlant, 5.

17 Berlant, 5 (emphasis in original).

18 Berlant, 5.

19 Gilmore, *The Limits of Autobiography*, 19.

20 Foucault, *The Will to Knowledge*, 60–63.

21 Berlant, *The Female Complaint*, 66.

22 See Gilmore, "American Neoconfessional," 657–679; Rak, *Boom!*, 161–162.

23 Gilmore, *The Limits of Autobiography*, 14–15; Smith, "Performativity, Autobiographical Practice, Resistance," 17–33.

24 *PostSecret* is not the only project to use autobiographical fragments in this way. Another example is the practice of digital storytelling, which is used by a range of media organizations to present the experiences of marginalized communities (see Poletti, "Coaxing an Intimate Public," 73–83).

25 Rak, "The Digital Queer," 176.

26 See Morrison, "Blogs and Blogging."

27 Lejeune, "The Autobiographical Pact," 3–30.

28 In this aspect, the *PostSecret* postcards share a number of material strategies for authenticating anonymous or semianonymous autobiography with zines. See Poletti, *Intimate Ephemera.*

29 Bolter and Gruisin, *Remediation*, 53n1 (emphasis added).

30 Berlant, *The Female Complaint*, viii.

31 Stewart, *On Longing*, 139.

32 Stewart, 149.

33 Berlant, *The Female Complaint*, viii.

34 The phrase "America's most trusted stranger" is commonly used in publicity around the project. See, for example, Couillard, "Frank Warren."

35 Poletti, "Coaxing an Intimate Public."

36 Berlant, *The Female Complaint*, 212–214.

37 Religion also features heavily in the secrets; see Warren, *PostSecret.*

38 Berlant, *The Female Complaint*, 214. Optimism and ambivalence also play important roles in this formulation; see Berlant, 212–214.

39 *The International Suicide Prevention Wiki*, accessed June 21, 2014, http://suicideprevention.wikia.com/wiki/International_Suicide_Prevention_Directory.

40 My thanks to Margaretta Jolly for raising the question of melodramatic form and content in the *PostSecret* cards.

41 See "Are All 500,000 Secrets True?," accessed March 25, 2010, www.postsecret-community.com/news-faq/secrets-true.

42 Foucault, *The Will to Knowledge*, 59–63.

43 Foucault, 60.

44 See *PostSecret Community*, www.postsecretcommunity.com.

45 Affordances are design features that guide users in the intended application or utilization of an object or piece of software. For an excellent discussion of affordances and their relationship to life narration, see Morrison, "Facebook and Coaxed Affordances."

46 Rak, *Boom!*, 212.

47 Gilmore, "American Neoconfessional," 658.

48 Berlant, *The Female Complaint*, viii.

49 Baym, *Playing to the Crowd*, 1–7.

50 *StoryCorps*, "About," https://storycorps.org/about/.

51 *Six-Word Memoirs*, "Story of Six," www.sixwordmemoirs.com/about/#story-of-six-words.

52 McNeill, "Life Bytes," 145.

53 See *The Moth*, "Storytelling Tips and Tricks," https://themoth.org/share-your-story/storytelling-tips-tricks.

54 *Mortified*, "About."

55 *The Moth*, "Storytelling Tips and Tricks"; *StoryCorps*, "Great Questions," https://storycorps.org/participate/great-questions/.

56 *Mortified*, "Participate," *Get Mortified*, http://getmortified.com/participate. These instructions are subject to ongoing revision, and in the time I have been researching confessional entrepreneurship, they have evolved in two notable ways: (1) the most current (2019) version I have seen includes more media forms (videos and old blogs are a recent addition under "Unearth"), and (2) the number of steps has been refined to consolidate the role of producers in creating the content (there used to be two steps listed for production, "Excerpt" and "Frame," which are now condensed under "Collaborate").

57 See Poletti, "Coaxing an Intimate Public."

58 Berlant, "A Properly Political Concept of Love," 686.

59 *The Moth*, "About the Moth," https://themoth.org/about.

60 Isay, "Everyone around You Has a Story."

61 *Six-Word Memoirs*, "FAQ," www.sixwordmemoirs.com/faq/.

62 Rak, *Boom!*, 179–205.

63 See the infographic in Lincoln Park Strategies and Rad Campaign, "The State of Social Media and Online Privacy," regarding how many Americans read terms of service agreements.

64 *Six-Word Memoirs*, "Terms of Service," www.sixwordmemoirs.com/terms-of-service; *StoryCorps*, "StoryCorps Archive Terms of Use," https://archive.storycorps.org/terms-of-use/.

65 For the epigraph, see Valentish, "Frank Warren."

66 Friedlander, "*Mortified Nation*."

67 Friedlander.

68 Gilmore, "American Neoconfessional," 674.

69 Shane and Venkataraman, "The Promise of Entrepreneurship as a Field of Research," 217.

70 Valentish, "Frank Warren."

71 Foucault, *The Will to Knowledge*, 61–62.

72 Foucault, 58.

73 This relationship of exchange between individual and collective authority resonates with a biographical detail Warren shares during the presentation. In a personal anecdote late in the presentation, Warren tells the audience that having been raised in the Pentecostal church, he likes to "testify." The Pentecostals have a strong tradition of life narrative. Pentecostal services regularly include members testifying to fellow members, with the congregation (rather than a priest or pastor) providing witness to stories of conversion and to speaking in tongues. Pentecostalism is also partly defined, like other churches in the charismatic tradition, by a rhetoric that combines charisma and plain speak-

ing in its pastors. These elements of church culture inform the construction of Warren's persona as "America's most trusted see stranger" (see Wacker, *Heaven Below*).

74 Kristeva, *Powers of Horror*, 1–31.

75 See Coleman, "Our Weirdness Is Free," for a description of hackers as modern-day tricksters who are distinct from trolls.

76 Hernandez, "PostSecret App Discontinued Because of 'Malicious' Posts."

77 The project *has* attempted to make room for darker content. On August 31, 2013, during the weekly blog update, Warren uploaded a postcard that consisted of a printed-out Google Maps image with the handwritten commentary "I said she dumped me, but really I dumped her (body)." After uploading the postcard, Warren tweeted a request for "comments" about the latest batch of secrets that had been uploaded and inviting people to use the hashtag "postsecret" "so we can all share." He was quickly commended because "you don't censor us" and also condemned for posting "link bait" (material posted with the sole aim of getting people to visit or link to the site). A Reddit community group quickly formed to try to identify the location and investigate whether or not the postcard was reporting a crime. The police were asked to investigate, and nothing came of their assessment of the park that had been identified as the location on the card—no evidence of a body was found. Warren refused to comment. This postcard confirmed the powerful discourse of truth associated with the project. Nelson, "PostSecret Murder Confession?"

78 Hardt, "For Love or Money," 677.

79 Hardt, 678.

80 *The Moth*, "Teacher Institute," https://themoth.org/education/teacherinstitute, and "Community," https://themoth.org/community.

81 *Mortified*, "Storytelling Workshops," http://getmortified.com/workshops; *StoryCorps*, "StoryCorps DIY," https://storycorps.org/participate/storycorps-diy/; *The Moth*, "Corporate Events," https://themoth.org/share-your-story/corporate-program, and "Education," https://themoth.org/education.

82 Berlant, *The Female Complaint*, 47.

83 Dean, *Blog Theory*, 96.

84 Thrift, "But Malice Aforethought," 145–146.

85 Berlant, *Cruel Optimism*, 125.

4. COLLAGE

1 Eve Kosofsky Sedgwick, "Queer and Now," in *Tendencies*, 3.

2 See Muñoz, "Famous and Dandy," 149–152; Cvetkovich, *An Archive of Feelings*; Sedgwick, *Tendencies*; Ahmed, *The Promise of Happiness*; Muñoz, *Disidentifications*.

3 "The desire of a reparative impulse . . . is additive and accretive. Its fear, a realistic one, is that the culture surrounding it is inadequate or inimical to its nurture; it wants to assemble and confer plenitude on an object that will then have resources

to offer an inchoate self" (Sedgwick, "Paranoid Reading and Reparative Reading," 27–28).

4   Sandy, *Handpash*, n.p. (emphasis in original).

5   Poletti, *Intimate Ephemera*. For example, see my discussion of how Sandy critiques the association between zines and confessional autobiographical practice while offering and then retracting the story of a sexual encounter in *Handpash* (Poletti, *Intimate Ephemera*, 95–98) and my discussion of Sandy's use of Tweet as a means of negotiating the constant solicitation of desire that defines the consuming self in late capitalism (162–163). At the time that I wrote *Intimate Ephemera*, Sandy used male pronouns. They now use "they/their" pronouns, and the discussion in this chapter reflects that change.

6   I am echoing Sedgwick's theory of the masturbating girl, developed in "Jane Austen and the Masturbating Girl," in *Tendencies*, 109–129.

7   For some pop culture context regarding the figure of the masturbating woman in contemporary pop music, see Morrissey, "Top 10 Songs about Female Masturbation."

8   See Sedgwick, "Jane Austen and the Masturbating Girl," for an overview of the changing discourse around masturbation. See also Jacques Derrida's discussion of Rousseau, ". . . That Dangerous Supplement . . . ," in *Of Grammatology*, 141–164. Derrida's analysis gives a strong account of the interrelationship of self-representation and the presence/absence logic of logocentrism in Rousseau's work. However, in examining onanism as a supplement, Derrida's insistence that it is a means of making the absent (desired person) present (in the mind of the masturbator) enshrines onanism as an interpersonal act, at least in the fantasy of the masturbator. I am not convinced by this generalized description of masturbation, as a text like Tweet's demonstrates autoeroticism is not necessarily predicated on installing an absent lover in the mind of the masturbator. While Rousseau, as Derrida demonstrates, used onanism as a supplement for "cohabitation with women" (155–156), there are plenty of other uses for masturbation that are less direct in their supplementary relationship to sexual contact with others. See also Bersani, *Homos*, 103–105.

9   Barad, "Transmaterialities," 400.

10   Smith and Watson, *Reading Autobiography*, 36.

11   Laqueur, *Solitary Sex*; Sedgwick, "Jane Austen and the Masturbating Girl."

12   See Yagoda, "A Brief History of Memoir Bashing."

13   Smith and Watson, *Reading Autobiography*, 16. For variations on this formulation, see Miller, "The Entangled Self," 537–548; Couser, *Memoir*.

14   Butler, *Bodies That Matter*, 12–16.

15   Indeed, it is this normative component of autobiography that has been the focus of extensive criticism, most recently in the special issue of the journal *Biography* titled "(Post)Human Lives" (Whitlock and Couser). This rich vein of critical work stems from a critique of autobiography as the master genre of life narrative rooted in the autonomous self inaugurated by the Enlightenment, and extends to a con-

sideration of the role of autobiography, and life narrative studies, in the circulation and validation of that discourse (Smith and Watson, *Reading Autobiography*, 3–5; see also Whitlock, *Postcolonial Life Narratives*; Whitlock, "Post-ing Lives"). The critical focus, to date, has been on the interplay between life narrative—as a practice that incorporates a range of specific genres that share a nonfictional status—and discourses of subjectivity and identity (see, for example, Royster, "Introductory Notes," v–xii).

16 Miller, "The Entangled Self," 545.

17 See, for example, Miller.

18 Much critical activity in life writing studies examines the variety of techniques and strategies used to claim the authority to speak about the world, to convince readers of the truthfulness of their story, and the influence of these performative statements on understandings of, for example, childhood, the populations affected by the "war on terror," and experiences of trauma. See Douglas, *Contesting Childhood*; Whitlock, *Soft Weapons*; Gilmore, *The Limits of Autobiography*, respectively.

19 Couser, *Memoir*, 178.

20 Couser, 178.

21 Couldry, "Rethinking the Politics of Voice," 580. See also Couldry, "Voice as Value," in *Why Voice Matters*, 10–28.

22 See Couldry, "Rethinking the Politics of Voice," 579–582; Holmlund and Fuchs, "Introduction," in *Between the Sheets*, 1–12.

23 Miller, "The Entangled Self," 538. See also Lejeune, "The Autobiographical Pact"; Miller, "Genre as Social Action."

24 Lejeune, "The Autobiographical Pact," 3–30. See also Miller, "The Entangled Self"; Couser, *Memoir*.

25 These textual "I's" are distinct from the historical "I," the "real-life" author who remains unknowable but facts about whom are verifiable. Smith and Watson, *Reading Autobiography*, 72.

26 The recent development of graphic memoir is currently fostering similar analysis of form in order to discern how autobiographical comics produce distinct possibilities for the performative utterance of life and self. See, for example, Chute, *Graphic Women*; Chaney, *Reading Lessons in Seeing*.

27 See Poletti, "Putting Lives on the Record," for my discussion of the unacknowledged importance of the book as medium and symbol in life writing scholarship.

28 "Life Writing and Intimate Publics," Seventh International Auto/Biography Association Conference, University of Sussex, June 28–July 1, 2010.

29 Berlant with Prosser, "Life Writing and Intimate Publics," 182.

30 See Smith and Watson, "Introduction," in *Getting a Life*, 1–24.

31 See Butler, *Bodies That Matter*, 224–225.

32 Sedgwick, *Touching Feeling*, 67–91.

33 Sedgwick, 67–73.

34 Sedgwick, 69.

35 Sedgwick, 69.

36 Sedgwick was using "I do" and the conundrum of the queer subject invited to a wedding to bear witness and confirm the consensus view of marriage as a privileged site for heterosexuality prior to the introduction of marriage equality in the United States.

37 Butler, *Bodies That Matter*, 12–16.

38 Sedgwick, *Touching Feeling*, 70.

39 "Any queer who has struggled to articulate to friends or family why he or she loves them but just *does not want to be at their wedding* knows from inside the spatialized [and I would argue, material] dynamic of compulsory witness that the marriage ceremony invokes" (Sedgwick, *Touching Feeling*, 72).

40 Sedgwick, 68.

41 Sedgwick, *The Weather in Proust*, 66.

42 Sedgwick, *Touching Feeling*, 70.

43 Couser, *Memoir*, 178.

44 Couser, 178.

45 Couser, 170 (emphasis in original).

46 See Vaccaro, "Handmade," 96–97 for an indication of how the term may offer new ways of thinking about transgendered embodiment.

47 Sedgwick, *Touching Feeling*, 71.

48 Poletti, "Reading for Excess," 157–172.

49 For a close reading of such a scene, in which drag is used, see Poletti, "Reading for Excess."

50 Decades after Caouette's childhood dream, writer, musician, and blogger Steve Schalchlin would document his life with AIDS, and the process of attempting to turn his story of surviving AIDS into a musical, on his blog *Living in the Bonus Round*. Schalchlin's musical *The Last Session* and his cabaret show *Tales from the Bonus Round* indicate the potential of musical theater as an autobiographical form for a life that "cheated death" (Schalchlin's phrase) in the AIDS crisis. See Schalchlin, *Living in the Bonus Round*.

51 Dyer, "It's Being So Camp as Keeps Us Going," 113. Dyer's distinction between camp as an action ("camping about") and camp as a sensibility is being invoked here, but it is also challenged by a film like *Tarnation* where the sensibility is manifested through the production of text.

52 I am drawing here on Sedgwick's articulation of paranoia as a way of knowing and reading in "Paranoid Reading and Reparative Reading." Her summary of Melanie Klein's distinction between paranoid and depressive positions could lead us to interpret Caouette's use of popular culture as I discuss it here (and in Poletti, "Reading for Excess") as reparative. Such a reading may be consistent with Sedgwick's overall philosophy of reading as having the potential to be an active, creative, and productive process of living.

53 Gilmore, *The Limits of Autobiography*, 3.

54 Douglas, *Contesting Childhood*.

55 Sedgwick, *The Weather in Proust*, 66.

56 I am thinking here of Sedgwick's formulation of the reparative movement in the depressive position that "is an anxiety-mitigating achievement that the infant or adult only sometimes, and often only briefly, succeeds in inhabiting: this is the position from which it is possible to turn to use one's own resources to assemble or 'repair' the murderous part-objects [of the paranoid position] into something like a whole—though not, and may I emphasize this, *not necessarily a preexisting whole*. Once assembled to one's specifications, the more satisfying object is available both to be identified with and to offer one nourishment and comfort in turn" (Sedgwick, "Paranoid Reading and Reparative Reading," 8). Periperformative autobiography may be understood as an attempt to use media of inscription to give reparative practices a longer duration, and offer the resulting assembled object to others for use in their own reparative practices.

57 Christian, "Camp 2.0," 352.

58 Couser, *Memoir*, 168.

59 Berlant with Prosser, "Life Writing and Intimate Publics," 181.

60 Sedgwick, *The Weather in Proust*, 58.

61 O'Neill, "The M-m-mama of Us All," 15.

62 Muñoz, "Famous and Dandy," 149.

63 O'Neill, "The M-m-mama of Us All," 16.

64 O'Neill, 15 (emphasis added).

65 Poletti, *Intimate Ephemera*, 254–271. See also Sinor, "'Another Form of Crying,'" 240–264.

66 Halberstam, *The Queer Art of Failure*, 136.

67 Elliott's appearance in the song deserves comment in relation to the reparative practices my reading is tracing. See Anne Boyer's discussion of Elliott's music in "WTF."

68 Sandy, *Handpash*, n.p. (emphasis in original). Multiple versions of the track were released on the CD single; the version that I am drawing on for my interpretation is the official released version that was played on radio and accompanied by a video clip. This version includes the rapped interlude by Missy Elliott alluded to in note 67. Other versions released on the CD single reduce Elliott's contribution and replace her rapped performance with male rappers. In one alternate version of the track, the rapper Fabolous renarrates Tweet's performance to bring it in line with the masculine gaze and positions Tweet's actions as being for his benefit. The co-release of these multiple versions indicates the continued influence of dominant patriarchal narratives around female sexuality within popular culture, and must give pause to critical approaches that may overstate the subversive potential of performances of female sexuality in such contexts. Although there is no way to know which version Sandy draws on for their zine, I would note that were they to replace Tweet as the masturbating narrating subject of the song, this substitution would queer Fabolous's male gaze in the alternate version.

69 Poletti, *Intimate Ephemera*, 152–165.

70 Sedgwick, "Paranoid Reading and Reparative Reading," 28.

71 Ulmer, "The Object of Post-criticism," 97.

72 Cvetkovich, *An Archive of Feelings*, 261–268.

73 Gilmore, "American Neoconfessional."

74 Berlant with Prosser, "Life Writing and Intimate Publics," 182.

75 For example, the texts published in Semiotext(e)'s Native Agents series, including Chris Kraus's novels *I Love Dick*, *Torpor*, and *Aliens and Anorexia*. The rising critical interest in autofiction and autotheory, which Kraus's work is often said to typify, indicates increased scholarly attention to periperformative modes of self-life-writing, although these tend to continue to privilege the book and the literary.

76 Hayles, "Print Is Flat, Code Is Deep," 69.

77 Sedgwick, *Touching Feeling*, 90n2.

78 Hayles, "Print Is Flat, Code Is Deep," 71.

5. DOSSIERS

1 Haggerty and Ericson, "The Surveillant Assemblage," 606, 611; Poster, *The Mode of Information*, 97–98.

2 Golumbia, "Social Media Has Highjacked Our Brains."

3 Curran, "Are You Ready?"

4 See Richardson, "Pocket Technospaces," 205–215.

5 See Lupton, *The Quantified Self*, chap 1.

6 Dean, *Blog Theory*, 66.

7 Cheney-Lippold, *We Are Data*, chaps. 1 and 3.

8 Butler, *Frames of War*, 2–5.

9 Butler, "Rethinking Vulnerability and Resistance," 14.

10 Andrejevic, *Reality TV*, 35–38.

11 Haggerty and Ericson, "The Surveillant Assemblage," 614.

12 Carbone, "Artists and Records," 101. See also Pelly, "How Arnold Mesches Turned His FBI Surveillance Files into Eerily Prescient Works of Art."

13 Mesches, "The FBI Files," 287–294.

14 Barnette, *Do Not Destroy*.

15 Carbone, "Artists and Records."

16 For a recent study of the intersection of surveillance and African American literature that also demonstrates the enormous amount of material generated by FBI surveillance, see Maxwell, *F.B. Eyes*.

17 Cheney-Lippold, *We Are Data*, chap. 3.

18 Poster, *The Mode of Information*, 97–98.

19 Bauman and Lyon, *Liquid Surveillance*, 44.

20 Puar, *Terrorist Assemblages*, 205.

21 Cheney-Lippold, *We Are Data*, introduction.

22 Bauman and Lyon, *Liquid Surveillance*, 34–43. See also Cheney-Lippold, *We Are Data*, chap. 3.

23 Cheney-Lippold, *We Are Data*, chap. 1; Puar, *Terrorist Assemblages*, 155–156.

24 Butler, "Rethinking Vulnerability and Resistance," 21.

25 Chun, *Updating to Remain the Same*, 70.

26 See Foley, "Black Power in Redfern."

27 I cite this phrasing out of respect for Foley's description of these organizations; see his staff profile at Victoria University: "Professor Gary Edward Foley," www .vu.edu.au/contact-us/gary-edward-foley.

28 Keenan, "Gary Foley," 03:39.

29 Andrea Smith, "Not-Seeing: State Surveillance, Settler Colonialism, and Gender Violence," in Dubrovsky and Magnet, *Feminist Surveillance Studies*, 26.

30 Moreton-Robinson, *The White Possessive*, 146.

31 Smith, "Not-Seeing," 21–22.

32 Moreton-Robinson, *The White Possessive*, 153–172.

33 Perucci, *Paul Robeson and the Cold War Performance Complex*, 16.

34 See the overview of Robeson's career in Perucci, 8–11.

35 Steve McQueen, *Steve McQueen*.

36 Beeching, "Paul Robeson and the Black Press," 339.

37 La Planche and Pontalis, *The Language of Psycho-analysis*, 273 (emphasis added).

38 Guillory, "The Memo and Modernity," 114.

39 This is a key insight from postcolonial readings of the archive. See, for example, Anjali Arondekar's discussion of the colonial archive and the need to develop reading practices that redirect "attention from the frenzied 'finding' of new archival sources [relating to marginalized sexualities and identities] to an understanding of the process of subjectification made possible (and desirable) through the very idiom of the archive" (Arondekar, *For the Record*, 3).

40 See Ann Stoler's discussion of "the official archives of the Dutch colonial state" as "condensed sites of epistemological and political anxiety" and her discussion of "archiving-as-process rather than archives-as-things" (Stoler, *Along the Archival Grain*, 20).

41 *End Credits* is a work in progress; in a recent iteration—screened at the Holland Festival in Amsterdam in June 2018—the work is seventeen hours long. McQueen, *Steve McQueen on Paul Robeson*.

42 Guillory, "The Memo and Modernity," 116.

43 Guillory, 120.

44 Guillory, 109–110.

45 Guillory, 113.

46 McQueen, *Steve McQueen on Paul Robeson*.

47 McQueen.

48 See "Government Surveillance: Last Week Tonight with John Oliver," April 5, 2015, https://youtu.be/XEVlyP4_11M; for the introduction of the dick pic example, see 23:25–26:57.

49 Dubrofsky and Magnet, *Feminist Surveillance Studies*, 4.

50 Butler, "Rethinking Vulnerability and Resistance," 19.

51 Cheney-Lippold, *We Are Data*, chap. 1.

52 Puar, *Terrorist Assemblages*, 154–155.

53 Puar, 154.

54 Butler, "Rethinking Vulnerability and Resistance," 18–19.

55 Wheeler, *On Record*.

56 Wheeler, 5. For discussions of documents and records as life writing, see Stanley, "From 'Self-Made Women' to 'Women's Made Selves'"; Coletu, "Introduction Biographic Mediation."

57 Wheeler, 15.

58 Wheeler, 13.

59 Schwartz and Cook, "Archives, Records, and Power," 1–19; Yeo, "Concepts of the Record (I)," 315–343; Arondekar, *For the Record*; Stoler, *Along the Archival Grain*; Marshall, Murphy, and Tortorici. "Queering Archives," 1–10.

60 Beeching, "Paul Robeson and the Black Press," 339.

CONCLUSION

1 *#SafePassage*, exhibited at Foam photography gallery in Amsterdam from September 16 to December 7, 2016.

2 Of course, what Europe is (or might be) has been thrown open to debate by the recent shift in practices of migration, but the question of what "Europe" is, is a long-standing one. See Ann Rigney's discussion in "Transforming Memory and the European Project" of the contestation over and flexibility of "Europe" as a unifying concept, and "European" as an identity.

3 Sorace, "Ai Weiwei," 396–419.

4 See Maloney "Silence Surrounds Colombia's 92,000 Disappeared."

5 Ai Weiwei has long cited Andy Warhol as an important influence on his work. See, for example, Ai, "Andy Warhol," in *Ai Weiwei's Blog*, 127–131. See also Delany and Shiner, *Andy Warhol | Ai Weiwei*.

6 Obrist, *Ai Weiwei Speaks*, vii.

7 Ai, *Ai Weiwei's Blog*.

8 A recent example of this is the work *An Archive* (2015), which remediates Ai's tweets and blog writings from the period 2005 to 2013. In this work, Ai's Twitter output and blog posts are printed on sheets of rice paper and displayed in frames and boxes.

9 Ap, "Artist Ai Weiwei Discovers Hidden 'Listening Devices' in Beijing Studio."

10 Foam, "Ai Weiwei #SafePassage," accessed September 3, 2016, www.foam.org /museum/programme/ai-weiwei.

11 The structure of the exhibition could also be interpreted as an example of what Rosalind Krauss describes, following Derrida, as the "invagination" involved in the reinvention of medium that defines some of the trends in current contemporary avant-garde art that I am suggesting Ai Weiwei contributes to. See Krauss, "Two Moments from the Post-medium Condition," 55–62.

12 See the overview of controversies about the selfie in Senft and Baym, "What Does the Selfie Say?," 1588–1606.

13 Rak, "Are Memoirs Autobiography?"; Yagoda, *Memoir*.

14 Marwick, "Instafame," 137–160.

15 Lobinger and Brantner, "In the Eye of the Beholder," 1848–1860.

16 Frosh, "The Gestural Image," 1607–1628.

17 See Frosh, "The Gestural Image"; Marwick, "Instafame." See also Senft and Baym, "What Does the Selfie Say?"; Routh "The Politics of Transformation," 363–381.

18 Senft and Baym, "What Does the Selfie Say?"

19 Marwick, "Instafame."

20 Frosh, "The Gestural Image."

21 Frosh, 1621.

22 Ai Weiwei emphatically established his position on the issue of the status of the aura of the object with a series of works that took Han dynasty urns as their basis. See *Dropping a Han Dynasty Urn* (1995), a tryptic of photographs documenting Ai releasing his grip on an ancient urn and allowing it to smash at his feet; the series *Coloured Vases* (2009–2011), where ancient ceramics are painted over with contemporary, industrial paint; and *Coca-Cola Vase* (1994). See also Christian Sorace's discussion of these works as evidence of Ai Weiwei's continuation of the Chinese Communists Party's practice of "destroying traditional religious and cultural objects" during the Cultural Revolution "in order to shatter superstition" ("Ai Weiwei," 402).

23 Krauss, "Two Moments from the Post-medium Condition"; Krauss, "Reinventing the Medium," 289–305.

24 Benjamin, "The Work of Art in the Age of Mechanical Reproduction," 211–244.

25 Krauss, "Reinventing the Medium," 296.

26 Krauss, 296.

27 Krauss, 295.

28 In the photographs in *iPhone Wallpaper* that are not selfies, Ai Weiwei references the tradition of photoconceptualism, which "mobilized the unexpected formal resources in the look of 'nonart' contained in the haphazard spontaneity of the documentary photography" (Krauss, 295). See also Susan Sontag's discussion of photography, ethics, and aesthetics in which she argues, "Pictures of hellish events seem more authentic when they don't have the look that comes from being 'properly' lighted and composed. . . . By flying low, artistically speaking, such pictures are thought to be less manipulative" (Sontag, *Regarding the Pain of Others*, 23–24). The use of the vernacular form of the selfie, then, serves Ai's purpose of inserting individuals into the social field by making them visible in an aesthetically unremarkable form.

29 Frosh, "The Gestural Image."

30 In thinking about Ai's use of selfies in this way, I am drawing on Judith Butler's theory of how it is that we become subjects in the social field. Butler argues that photography plays an important role in delimiting those lives that are considered acceptable losses, and those whose loss is considered unacceptable, as I discussed in the introduction. The framing of grievable and ungrievable lives can work for

the justification of war—by bolstering a sense of outrage regarding the loss of some lives, while minimizing the grievability of those on the other side of the conflict. Or, photography can offer alternative frames that seek to expand our understanding of whose lives matter. In this sense, for Butler the photograph has two interlocking frames: the material frame—which limits the visual field—and the norms that frame the subject(s) depicted, making them legible within the social field (Butler, *Frames of War*, 51).

31 Lee, *Biography*.

32 Senft and Baym, "What Does the Selfie Say?"

33 See Marwick, "Instafame," 141.

34 See Micheline Ishay's argument that the dominant conception of human rights has its roots in European intellectual and religious traditions (Ishay, *The History of Human Rights*, 63–107).

BIBLIOGRAPHY

Agamben, Giorgio. *Homo Sacer: Sovereign Power and Bare Life*. Translated by Daniel Heller-Roazen. Palo Alto, CA: Stanford University Press, 1998.

Ahmed, Sara. *The Promise of Happiness*. Durham, NC: Duke University Press, 2010.

Ai, Weiwei. *Ai Weiwei's Blog: Writings, Interviews, and Digital Rants 2006–2009*. Edited and translated by Lee Ambrozy. Cambridge, MA: MIT Press, 2011.

Andrejevic, Mark. *Reality TV: The Work of Being Watched*. Lanham, MD: Rowman and Littlefield, 2004.

Ap, Tiffany. "Artist Ai Weiwei Discovers Hidden 'Listening Devices' in Beijing Studio." October 5, 2015. http://edition.cnn.com/2015/10/05/asia/china-ai-weiwei-finds -listening-devices/.

Arondekar, Anjoli. *For the Record: On Sexuality and the Colonial Archive in India*. Durham, NC: Duke University Press, 2009.

Barad, Karen. *Meeting the Universe Halfway: Quantum Physics and the Entanglement of Matter and Meaning*. Durham, NC: Duke University Press, 2007.

———. "Posthumanist Performativity: Toward an Understanding of How Matter Comes to Matter." *Signs* 28, no. 3 (Spring 2003): 801–831.

———. "Transmaterialities: Trans*/Matter/Realities and Queer Political Imaginings." *GLQ: A Journal of Lesbian and Gay Studies* 21, no. 2–3 (2015): 387–422.

Barnes, Susan B. "A Privacy Paradox: Social Networking in the United States." *First Monday* vol. 11, no. 9 (September 4, 2006). https://journals.uic.edu/ojs/index.php /fm/article/view/1394/1312.

Barnette, Sadie. *Do Not Destroy*. Baxter Street Camera Club of New York. January 18–February 18, 2017. www.baxterst.org/exhibitions-3/do-not-destroy/. Accessed April 9, 2017.

Barthe, Susanne, and Menno D. T. de Jong. "The Privacy Paradox: Investigating Dis-crepancies between Expressed Privacy Concerns and Actual Online Behaviour: A Systematic Literature Review." *Telematics and Informatics* 34 (2017): 1038–1058.

Baudry, Jean-Louis, and Alan Williams. "Ideological Effects of the Basic Cinemato-graphic Apparatus." *Film Quarterly* 28, no. 2 (Winter 1974–1975): 39–47.

Bauman, Zygmunt, and David Lyon. *Liquid Surveillance: A Conversation*. Cambridge: Polity Press, 2013.

Baym, Nancy. *Playing to the Crowd: Musicians, Audiences, and the Intimate Work of Connection*. New York: New York University Press, 2018.

Bechdel, Alison. "Alison Bechdel's *Fun Home*." Burlington Book Festival Presentation. September 15, 2006. www.youtube.com/watch?v=P1PV2F-mRHw.

———. *Fun Home: A Family Tragicomic*. New York: Houghton Mifflin, 2006.

Beeching, Barbara J. "Paul Robeson and the Black Press: The 1950 Passport Controversy," *Journal of African American History* 87 (Summer 2002): 339–354.

Benjamin, Walter. "The Work of Art in the Age of Mechanical Reproduction." In *Illuminations*, edited by Hannah Arendt, translated by Harry Zorn, 211–244. London: Pimlico, 1999.

Berlant, Lauren. *Cruel Optimism*. Durham, NC: Duke University Press, 2011.

———. *Desire/Love*. Brooklyn: Punctum Books, 2012.

———. *The Female Complaint: The Unfinished Business of Sentimentality in American Culture*. Durham, NC: Duke University Press, 2008.

———. "Intimacy: A Special Issue." *Critical Inquiry* 24, no. 2 (Winter 1998): 281–288.

———. "Love, a Queer Feeling." In *Homosexuality and Psychoanalysis*, edited by Tim Dean and Christopher Lane, 423–451. Chicago: University of Chicago Press, 2001.

———. "On the Case," *Critical Inquiry* 33, no. 4 (Summer 2007): 663–672.

———. "A Properly Political Concept of Love: Three Approaches in Ten Pages." *Cultural Anthropology* 26, no. 4 (2011): 683–691.

———. "Trauma and Ineloquence." *Cultural Values* 5, no. 1 (2001): 41–58.

Berlant, Lauren, with Jay Prosser. "Life Writing and Intimate Publics: A Conversation with Lauren Berlant." *Biography: An Interdisciplinary Quarterly* 34, no. 1 (Winter 2011): 180–187.

Bersani, Leo. *Homos*. Cambridge, MA: Harvard University Press, 1995.

Bockris, Victor. *Warhol: The Biography*. New York: Da Capo Press, 2003.

Bodó, Balázs. "Mediated Trust: A Theoretical Framework to Address the Trustworthiness of Technological Trust Mediators." *SSRN*, September 28, 2019. https://ssrn.com/abstract=3460903.

Bolter, Jay David, and Richard Gruisin. *Remediation: Understanding New Media*. Cambridge, MA: MIT Press, 2000.

Bourdon, David. *Warhol*. New York: Harry N. Abrams, 1989.

Boyer, Anne. "WTF." In *A Handbook of Disappointed Fate*, 67–69. Brooklyn: Ugly Duckling Presse, 2018.

Brophy, Sarah, and Janice Hladki, eds. *Embodied Politics in Visual Autobiography*. Toronto: University of Toronto Press, 2014.

Brown, Barry. *Studying the Internet Experience*. Bristol: Hewlett Packard, Publishing Systems and Solutions Laboratory HP Laboratories, HPL-2001-49. March 26, 2001.

Butler, Judith. *Bodies That Matter: On the Discursive Limits of Sex*. New York: Routledge, 1993.

———. *Frames of War: When Is Life Grievable?* London: Verso, 2009.

———. *Gender Trouble: Feminism and the Subversion of Identity*. New York: Routledge, 1990.

———. *Giving an Account of Oneself*. New York: Fordham University Press, 2005.

———. "Rethinking Vulnerability and Resistance." In *Vulnerability in Resistance*, edited by Judith Butler, Zeynep Gambetti, and Leticia Sasbay, 12–27. Durham, NC: Duke University Press, 2016.

Caouette, Jonathan, dir. *Tarnation*. New York, 2004. Distributed by Wellspring Media. DVD.

Carbone, Kathy Michelle. "Artists and Records: Moving History and Memory." *Archives and Records* 38, no. 1 (2017): 100–118.

Caswell, Michelle, Ricardo Punzalan, and T-Kay Sangwand. "Critical Archive Studies: An Introduction." *Journal of Critical Library and Information Studies* 1, no. 2 (2017): 1–8.

Chaney, Michael A. *Reading Lessons in Seeing: Mirrors, Masks, and Mazes in the Autobiographical Graphic Novel*. Jackson: University of Mississippi Press, 2016.

Cheney-Lippold, John. *We Are Data: Algorithms and the Making of Our Digital Selves*. New York: New York University Press, 2017. Ebook, accessed on an iPad using iBook edition.

Christian, Aymar Jean. "Camp 2.0: A Queer Performance of the Personal." *Communication, Culture and Critique* 3, no. 1 (September 2010): 352–376.

Chun, Wendy Hui Kyong. "Somebody Said New Media." In *New Media, Old Media: A History and Theory Reader*, edited by Wendy Hui Kyong Chun and Anna Watkins Fisher with Thomas W. Keenan, 1–16. 2nd ed. New York: Routledge, 2016.

———. *Updating to Remain the Same: Habitual New Media*. Cambridge, MA: MIT Press, 2017.

Chute, Hillary L. *Graphic Women: Life Narrative and Contemporary Comics*. New York: Columbia University Press, 2010.

———. "An Interview with Alison Bechdel." *MFS: Modern Fiction Studies* 52, no. 4 (Winter 2006): 1004–1013.

Coleman, Gabriella. "Our Weirdness Is Free, The Logic of Anonymous: Online Army, Agent of Chaos, and Seeker of Justice." *Triple Canopy* 15, no. 2 (January 2012). www .canopycanopycanopy.com/issues/15/contents/our_weirdness_is_free.

Coletu, Ebony. "Introduction Biographic Mediation: On the Uses of Personal Disclosure in Bureaucracy and Politics." *Biography: An Interdisciplinary Quarterly* 42, no. 3 (2019): 465–485.

Coole, Diane, and Samantha Frost, eds. *New Materialisms: Ontology, Agency and Politics*. Durham, NC: Duke University Press, 2010.

Couillard, Lucie. "Frank Warren: America's Most Trusted Stranger." *Daily Collegian*, November 30, 2012. www.collegian.psu.edu/archives/article_983c9cfb-7385-51e8 -a092-c290a6abce9c.html.

Couldry, Nick. "Mediatization or Mediation? Alternative Understandings of the Emergent Space of Digital Storytelling." *New Media and Society* 10 (2008): 373–391.

———. "Rethinking the Politics of Voice." *Continuum* 23, no. 4 (July 2009): 579–582.

———. *Why Voice Matters: Culture and Politics after Neoliberalism*. London: Sage, 2010.

Couser, G. Thomas. *Memoir: An Introduction*. Oxford: Oxford University Press, 2012.

Cross, Gary S., and Robert N. Proctor. *Packaged Pleasures: How Technology and Marketing Revolutionized Desire*. Chicago: University of Chicago Press, 2014.

Curran, Dylan. "Are You Ready? Here Is All the Data Facebook and Google Have on You." *Guardian*, March 30, 2018. https://www.theguardian.com /commentisfree/2018/mar/28/all-the-data-facebook-google-has-on-you-privacy.

Cvetkovich, Ann. *An Archive of Feelings: Trauma, Sexuality and Lesbian Public Culture.* Durham, NC: Duke University Press, 2003.

———. "Drawing the Archive in Alison Bechdel's *Fun Home.*" *WSQ: Women's Studies Quarterly* 36, no. 1–2 (2008): 111–128.

Danto, Arthur C. *Andy Warhol.* Princeton, NJ: Princeton University Press, 2010.

———. "The Artworld." *Journal of Philosophy* 61, no. 9 (October 1964): 571–584.

Dean, Jodi. *Blog Theory: Feedback and Capture in the Circuits of Drive.* Cambridge: Polity Press, 2010.

Delany, Max, and Eric Shiner, eds. *Andy Warhol | Ai Weiwei.* Melbourne: National Gallery of Victoria, 2015.

Derrida, Jacques. *Archive Fever: A Freudian Impression.* Translated by Eric Prenowitz. Chicago: University of Chicago Press, 1995.

———. *Of Grammatology.* Translated by Gayatri Chakravorty Spivak. Baltimore: Johns Hopkins University Press, 1976.

Deutsch, Tracey. *Building a Housewife's Parade: Gender, Politics, and American Grocery Stores in the Twentieth Century.* Chapel Hill: University of North Carolina Press, 2010.

Dinnen, Zara. *The Digital Banal: New Media in American Literature and Culture.* New York: Columbia University Press, 2018.

D'Onofrio, Robert. "2013 Year in Review." *Facebook Newsroom*, December 9, 2013. https://newsroom.fb.com/news/2013/12/2013-year-in-review/.

Douglas, Kate. *Contesting Childhood: Autobiography, Trauma, and Memory.* Piscataway, NJ: Rutgers University Press, 2010.

Doyle, Jennifer, Jonathan Flatley, and José Esteban Muñoz, eds. *Pop Out: Queer Warhol.* Durham, NC: Duke University Press, 1996.

Dubrofsky, Rachel E., and Shoshana A. Magnet, eds. *Feminist Surveillance Studies.* Durham, NC: Duke University Press, 2015.

Duggan, Lisa. "The New Homonormativity: The Sexual Politics of Neoliberalism." In *Materializing Democracy*, edited by Russ Castronovo, 175–194. Durham, NC: Duke University Press, 2002.

Dyer, Richard. "It's Being So Camp as Keeps Us Going." In *Camp: Queer Aesthetics and the Performing Subject: A Reader*, edited by Fabio Cleto, 110–117. Ann Arbor: University of Michigan Press.

Eakin, Paul John. *How Our Lives Become Stories: Making Selves.* Ithaca, NY: Cornell University Press, 1999.

Egan, Susanna. "Encounters in Camera: Autobiography as Interaction." *MFS: Modern Fiction Studies* 40, no. 3 (Fall 1994): 593–616.

Ewer, Tom. "14 Surprising Statistics about WordPress Usage." *Manage WP: Business* (blog), February 7, 2014. https://managewp.com/blog/14-surprising-statistics-about-wordpress-usage.

Fernandes, Sujatha. *The Uses and Misuses of Storytelling.* New York: Oxford University Press, 2017. Ebook, accessed on an iPad using iBook edition.

Flatley, Jonathan. *Like Andy Warhol.* Chicago: University of Chicago Press, 2017.

Foley, Gary. "Black Power in Redfern: 1968–172." *Kooriweb*, October 5, 2001.

Forrester, John. "If *p*, Then What? Thinking in Cases." *History of the Human Sciences* 9, no. 3 (1996): 1–25.

Foster, Hal. "Andy Paperbag." *London Review of Books* 24, no. 6 (March 21, 2002). www .lrb.co.uk/v24/n06/hal-foster/andy-paperbag.

———. *The First Pop Age: Painting and Subjectivity in the Art of Hamilton, Lichtenstein, Warhol, Richter, and Ruscha*. Princeton, NJ: Princeton University Press, 2014.

———. "'Made Out of the Real World: Lessons from the Fulton Street Studio." In *Robert Rauschenberg*, edited by Leah Dickerman and Achim Borchardt-Hume, 88–97. New York: Tate Publishing 2016.

———. *The Return of the Real: Art and Theory at the End of the Century*. Cambridge, MA: MIT Press, 1996.

Foucault, Michel. *The Will to Knowledge: The History of Sexuality*. Vol. 1. Translated by Robert Hurley. London: Penguin, 1998.

Frank, Benjamin. "Corrugated Box Compression: A Literature Survey." *Packaging Technology and Science: An International Journal* 27 (2014): 105–128. https://doi .org/10.1002/pts.2019.

Frei, George, and Neil Printz, eds. *The Andy Warhol Catalogue Raisonne: Paintings and Sculptures 1964–1969*. Vol. 2A. London: Phaidon Press, 2004.

Friedlander, Whitney. "*Mortified Nation*, a Movie about the Embarrassing Things We Wrote as Teenagers." *LA Weekly*, October 31, 2013. www.laweekly.com /arts/mortified-nation-a-movie-about-the-embarrassing-things-we-wrote-as -teenagers-4178876.

Frosh, Paul. "The Gestural Image: The Selfie, Photography Theory, and Kinesthetic Sociability." *International Journal of Communication* 9 (2015): 1607–1628.

Frow, John. *Genre*. Oxon: Routledge, 2005.

Genzlinger, Neil. "The Problem with Memoirs." *New York Times*, January 28, 2011. www.nytimes.com/2011/01/30/books/review/Genzlinger-t.html?pagewanted=all.

Gilbey, Ryan. "Trust Me, I'm a Film-maker: The Men behind *Catfish* Come Clean." *Guardian*, November 20, 2010. www.theguardian.com/film/2010/nov/20 /catfish-fact-or-fiction-film.

Gilmore, Leigh. "American Neoconfessional: Memoir, Self-Help, and Redemption on Oprah's Couch." *Biography: An Interdisciplinary Quarterly* 33, no. 4 (Fall 2010): 657–679.

———. *Autobiographics: A Feminist Theory of Women's Self-Representation*. Ithaca, NY: Cornell University Press, 1994.

———. *The Limits of Autobiography: Trauma and Testimony*. Ithaca, NY: Cornell University Press, 2001.

Gitelman, Lisa. *Always Already New: Media, History and the Data of Culture*. Cambridge, MA: MIT Press, 2008.

Golumbia, David. "Social Media Has Highjacked Our Brains and Threatens Our Democracy." *Motherboard*, January 5, 2018. https://motherboard.vice.com/en_us /article/bjy7ez/social-media-threatens-global-democracy.

Gopnik, Blake. "Monumental Case, but Not Much Plot: Andy Warhol's 'Empire' Shown in Its Entirety." *New York Times*, January 16, 2014. www.nytimes.com/2014/01/17 /arts/design/andy-warhols-empire-shown-in-its-entirety.html.

Greenwald, Glen. "NSA Collecting Phone Records of Millions of Verizon Customers Daily." *Guardian*, June 6, 2013. www.theguardian.com/world/2013/jun/06/ nsa-phone-records-verizon-court-order.

Guillory, John. "The Memo and Modernity." *Critical Inquiry* 31 (Autumn 2004): 108–132.

Ha, Anthony. "Edward Snowden's Privacy Tips: 'Get Rid of Dropbox,' Avoid Facebook and Google." *Tech Crunch*, October 11, 2014. https://techcrunch.com/2014/10/11/ed ward-snowden-new-yorker-festival/.

Haggerty, Kevin D., and Richard V. Ericson. "The Surveillant Assemblage." *British Journal of Sociology* 51, no. 4 (December 2000): 605–622.

Halberstam, Jack. *The Queer Art of Failure*. Durham, NC: Duke University Press, 2011.

Hall, Gary. *Digitize This Book! Or Why We Need Open Access Now*. Minneapolis: University of Minnesota Press, 2008.

Hardt, Michael. "For Love or Money." *Cultural Anthropology* 26, no. 4 (2011): 676–682.

Hayles, N. Katherine. "Print Is Flat, Code Is Deep: The Importance of Media-Specific Analysis." *Poetics Today* 25, no. 1 (2004): 67–90.

———. *Writing Machines*. Cambridge, MA: MIT Press, 2002.

Heddon, Deirdre. *Autobiography and Performance: Performing Selves*. Basingstoke: Palgrave Macmillan, 2008.

Henkin, David M. *The Postal Age: The Emergence of Modern Communications in Nineteenth-Century America*. Chicago: University of Chicago Press, 2006.

Hernandez, Brian Anthony. "PostSecret App Discontinued Because of 'Malicious' Posts." *Mashable*, January 2, 2012. https://mashable.com/2012/01/02/postsecret -app-discontinued-because-of-malicious-posts/#3uqGIR70U8q1.

Herzog, Todd. "Crime Stories: Criminal, Society, and the Modernist Case History." *Representations* 8, no. 1 (Fall 2002): 34–61.

Hesmondhalgh, David. "User-Generated Content, Free Labor and the Cultural Industries." *ephemera: theory & politics in organization* 10, no. 3–4 (2010): 267–284.

Holmlund, Chris, and Cynthia Fuchs, eds. *Between the Sheets, in the Streets: Queer, Lesbian, Gay Documentary*. Minneapolis: University of Minnesota Press, 1997.

Horton, Donald, and R. Richard Wohl. "Mass Communication and Parasocial Interaction: Observations on Intimacy at a Distance." In *Living in the Information Age: A New Media Reader*, edited by Erik P. Bucy, 41–48. Belmont, CA: Wadsworth /Thomas Learning, 2002.

Hustvedt, Siri. "A Woman in the Men's Room: When Will the Art World Recognise the Real Artist Behind Duchamp's Fountain?" *Guardian*, March 29, 2019. https:// www.theguardian.com/books/2019/mar/29/marcel-duchamp-fountain-women-art -history.

Isay, David. "Everyone around You Has a Story the World Needs to Hear." Filmed at TED2015 Conference, March 2015, video, 21:38. www.ted.com/talks /dave_isay_everyone_around_you_has_a_story_the_world_needs_to_hear.

Ishay, Micheline. *The History of Human Rights: From Ancient Times to the Globalization Era*. Berkeley: University of California Press, 2004.

Jenkins, Henry, Sam Ford, and Joshua Green. *Spreadable Media: Creating Value and Meaning in a Networked Culture*. New York: New York University Press, 2013.

Jenkins, Henry, Ravi Purushotma, Margaret Weigel, Katie Clinton, and Alice J. Robison. *Confronting the Challenges of Participatory Culture: Media Education for the 21st Century*. Cambridge, MA: MIT Press, 2009.

Johns, Adrian. *The Nature of the Book: Print and Knowledge in the Making*. Chicago: University of Chicago Press, 1998.

Joost, Henry, and Ariel Schulman, dir. *Catfish*. New York: Supermarché and Hit the Ground Running Productions, 2010. Distributed by Wild Bunch. DVD.

Kadar, Marlene. "Coming to Terms: Life Writing: From Genre to Critical Practice." In *Essays on Life Writing: From Genre to Critical Practice*, edited by Marlene Kadar, 3–16. Toronto: University of Toronto Press, 1992.

Keenan, Haydn, dir. "Gary Foley." *Persons of Interest*. Sydney: Smart Street Films, 2014. DVD.

Kember, Sarah, and Joanna Zylinska. *Life after New Media: Mediation as a Vital Process*. Cambridge, MA: MIT Press, 2015.

Koestenbaum, Wayne. *Andy Warhol*. New York: Penguin, 2001.

Kokolakis, Spyros. "Privacy Attitudes and Privacy Behaviour: A Review of Current Research on the Privacy Paradox Phenomenon," *Computers and Security* 64 (2017): 122–134.

Kozinski, Alex. "The Dead Past." *Stanford Law Review 2012 Symposium: The Privacy Paradox*, April 2012. www.stanfordlawreview.org/online/privacy-paradox-the-dead -past/.

Krauss, Rosalind. "Reinventing the Medium." *Critical Inquiry* 25, no. 2 (1999): 289–305.

———. "Two Moments from the Post-medium Condition." *October* 116 (2006): 55–62.

Kristeva, Julia. *Powers of Horror: An Essay on Abjection*. Translated by Leon S. Roudiez. New York: Columbia University Press, 1982.

La Planche, Jean, and Jean-Bertrand Pontalis. *The Language of Psycho-analysis*. Translated by Donald Nicholson-Smith. New York: W. W. Norton, 1973.

Laqueur, Thomas Walter. *Solitary Sex: A Cultural History of Masturbation*. New York: Zone Books, 2003.

Leader, Zachary, ed. *On Life-Writing*. Oxford: Oxford University Press, 2015.

Lee, Hermoine. *Biography: A Very Short Introduction*. Oxford: Oxford University Press, 2009.

Lejeune, Philippe. "The Autobiographical Pact." In *On Autobiography*, edited by Paul John Eakin, translated by Katherine Leary, 3–30. Minneapolis: University of Minnesota Press, 1989.

Leswing, Kif. "Apple Says People Send as Many as 200,000 iMessages per Second." *Business Insider*, February 12, 2016. www.businessinsider.com/eddy-cue-200k-imess ages-per-second-2016-2?international=true&r=US&IR=T.

Lincoln Park Strategies and Rad Campaign. "The State of Social Media and Online Privacy." *Online Privacy Data*. http://onlineprivacydata.com/. Accessed January 3, 2019.

Lobinger, Katharina, and Cornelia Brantner. "In the Eye of the Beholder: Subjective Views on the Authenticity of Selfies." *International Journal of Communication* 9 (2015): 1848–1860.

Lovink, Geert. *Sad by Design: On Platform Nihilism*. London: Pluto Press, 2019.

Lupton, Deborah. *The Quantified Self*. Cambridge: Polity Press, 2016.

Lussier, Germain. "Film Interview: Sarah Polley Explains Secrets of Her Brilliant Documentary 'Stories We Tell.'" *Film: Blogging the Real World*, May 17, 2013. www .slashfilm.com/film-interview-sarah-polley-explains-secrets-of-her-brilliant -documentary-stories-we-tell/.

Maloney, Anastasia. "Silence Surrounds Colombia's 92,000 Disappeared: ICRC." *Reuters World News*. August 29, 2014. www.reuters.com/article/us-foundation-colo mbia-missing-idUSKBN0GT22520140829.

Marshall, David, Kevin P. Murphy, and Zeb Tortorici. "Queering Archives: Intimate Tracings." *Radical History Review* 122 (2015): 1–10.

Marwick, Alice E. "Instafame: Luxury Selfies in the Attention Economy." *Public Culture* 27, no. 1 (2015): 137–160.

Maxwell, William J. *F.B. Eyes: How J. Edgar Hoover's Ghostreaders Framed African American Literature*. Princeton, NJ: Princeton University Press, 2015.

McNeill, Laurie. "Life Bytes: Six-Word Memoir and the Exigencies of Auto/ Tweetographies." In *Identity Technologies: Constructing the Self Online*, edited by Anna Poletti and Julie Rak, 144–164. Madison: University of Wisconsin Press, 2014.

McNeill, Laurie, and John David Zuern, eds. "Online Lives 2.0." Special issue, *Biography: An Interdisciplinary Quarterly* 38, no. 2 (Spring 2015).

McQueen, Steve. *Steve McQueen*. Art Institute of Chicago. October 21, 2012–January 6, 2013.

Mesches, Arnold. "The FBI Files." *Public Culture* 15, no. 2 (2003): 287–294.

Metz, Christian. "The Imaginary Signifier." *Screen* 16, no. 2 (July 1975): 14–76.

Miller, Carolyn R. "Genre as Social Action." *Quarterly Journal of Speech* 70 (1984): 151–167.

Miller, Daniel, ed. *Materiality*. Durham, NC: Duke University Press, 2005.

Miller, Nancy K. "The Entangled Self: Genre Bondage in the Age of Memoir." *PMLA* 132, no. 2 (2007): 537–548.

Moreton-Robinson, Aileen. *The White Possessive: Property, Power and Indigenous Sovereignty*. Minneapolis: University of Minnesota Press, 2007.

Morrison, Aimée. "Blogs and Blogging: Text and Practice." In *A Companion to Digital Literary Studies*, edited by Susan Schreibman and Ray Siemens, n.p. Oxford: Blackwell, 2008.

———. "Facebook and Coaxed Affordances." In *Identity Technologies: Constructing the Self Online*, edited by Anna Poletti and Julie Rak, 112–131. Madison: University of Wisconsin Press, 2014.

Morrissey, Tracie Egan. "Top 10 Songs about Female Masturbation." *Jezebel*, November 25, 2008. https://jezebel.com/5098965/10-pop-songs-about-female-masturbation.

Mortified. "About." *Get Mortified*. http://getmortified.com/about; "Participate." http://getmortified.com/participate; "Storytelling Workshops," http://getmortified.com/workshops.

The Moth. "About The Moth." https://themoth.org/about; "Community." https://themoth.org/community; "Corporate Events," https://themoth.org/share-your-story/corporate-program; "Education," https://themoth.org/education; "Storytelling Tips and Tricks." https://themoth.org/share-your-story/storytelling-tips-tricks; "Teacher Institute." https://themoth.org/education/teacherinstitute.

Muñoz, José Esteban. *Disidentifications: Queers of Color and the Performance of Politics*. Minneapolis: University of Minnesota Press, 1999.

———. "Famous and Dandy Like B. 'n' Andy: Race, Pop, and Basquiat." In *Pop Out: Queer Warhol*, edited by Jennifer Doyle, Jonathan Flatley, and José Esteban Muñoz, 143–179. Durham, NC: Duke University Press, 1996.

National Gallery of Victoria. *Andy Warhol's Time Capsules*. Melbourne, Australia, March 16–May 8, 2005.

Nelson, Sara C. "PostSecret Murder Confession? Anonymous Internet User Claims to Have Dumped Ex-Girlfriend's Body in Chicago Park." *Huffington Post UK*, September 9, 2013. www.huffingtonpost.co.uk/2013/09/02/postsecret-murder-confession-anonymous-internet-dumped-ex-girlfriends-body-chicago-park_n_3854836.html.

Nichols, Bill. *Representing Reality: Issues and Concepts in Documentary*. Bloomington: Indiana University Press, 1991.

Noble, Safiya Umoja. *Algorithms of Oppression: How Search Engines Reinforce Racism*. New York: New York University Press, 2018.

Obrist, Hans Ulrich. *Ai Weiwei Speaks*. London: Penguin, 2016.

Olney, James. *Metaphors of Self: The Meaning of Autobiography*. Princeton, NJ: Princeton University Press, 1972.

O'Neill, Edward. "The M-m-mama of Us All: Divas and the Cultural Logic of Late Ca(m)pitalism." *Camera Obscura* 65, no. 22 (2007): 11–37.

Oxford English Dictionary Online. "privacy (noun)"; "rummage (verb)." Oxford University Press.

———. "Word of the Year 2013." Oxford University Press. https://en.oxforddictionaries.com/word-of-the-year/word-of-the-year-2013. Accessed July 7, 2017.

Pascal, Roy. *Design and Truth in Autobiography*. London: Routledge and Kegan Paul, 1960.

"Paul Robeson, Sr." *FBI Records: The Vault*. Federal Bureau of Investigation. https://vault.fbi.gov/Paul%20Robeson%2C%20Sr.

Pelly, Liz. "How Arnold Mesches Turned His FBI Surveillance Files into Eerily Prescient Works of Art." *The Intercept*, September 30, 2017. https://theintercept

.com/2017/09/30/how-arnold-mesches-turned-his-fbi-surveillance-files-into-eerily
-prescient-works-of-art/.

Peraino, Judith A. "I'll Be Your Mixtape: Lou Reed, Andy Warhol and the Queer Inti-
macies of Cassettes." *Journal of Musicology* 36, no. 4 (2019): 401–436.

Perucci, Tony. *Paul Robeson and the Cold War Performance Complex.* Ann Arbor:
University of Michigan Press, 2012.

Plummer, Ken. *Telling Sexual Stories: Power, Change, and Social Worlds.* London:
Routledge, 1994.

Poitras, Laura, dir. *Citizenfour.* Santa Monica, CA: HBO Films, 2014. Distributed by
Netflix.

Poletti, Anna. "Coaxing an Intimate Public: Life Narrative in Digital Storytelling."
Continuum: Journal of Media and Cultural Studies 25, no. 1 (2011): 73–83.

———. *Intimate Ephemera: Reading Young Lives in Australian Zine Culture.* Melbourne:
Melbourne University Press, 2008.

———. "Putting Lives on the Record: The Book as Material and Symbol in Life
Writing." *Biography: An Interdisciplinary Quarterly* 40, no. 3 (Summer 2017):
460–484.

———. "Reading for Excess: Relational Autobiography, Affect, and Popular Culture in
Tarnation." *Life Writing* 9, no. 2 (2012): 157–172.

Poletti, Anna, and Julie Rak, eds. *Identity Technologies: Constructing the Self Online.*
Madison: University of Wisconsin Press, 2014.

Polley, Sarah, dir. *Stories We Tell.* Montreal: National Film Board of Canada, 2012.
Distributed by Madman Entertainment. DVD.

Popper, Ben. "Google Announces over 2 Billion Monthly Active Devices on Android."
The Verge, May 17, 2017. www.theverge.com/2017/5/17/15654454/android-reaches-2
-billion-monthly-active-users.

Poster, Mark. *The Mode of Information: Poststructuralism and Social Context.* Cambridge:
Polity Press, 1990.

PostSecret. Website and blog. www.postsecret.com.

Puar, Jasbir K. "'I Would Rather Be a Cyborg Than a Goddess': Becoming-
Intersectional in Assemblage Theory." *philoSOPHIA* 2, no. 1 (2012): 49–66.

———. *Terrorist Assemblages: Homonationalism in Queer Times.* Tenth anniversary
expanded edition. Durham, NC: Duke University Press, 2017.

Rak, Julie. "Are Memoirs Autobiography? A Consideration of Genre and Public Identity." *Genre* 37, no. 3–4 (2004): 483–504.

———. *Boom! Manufacturing Memoir for the Popular Market.* Waterloo, ON: Wilfrid
Laurier Press, 2013.

———. "The Digital Queer: Weblogs and Internet Identity." *Biography: An Interdisciplinary Quarterly* 28, no. 1 (Winter 2005): 166–182.

———. "Life Writing versus Automedia: The Sims 3 Game as a Life Lab." *Biography: An
Interdisciplinary Quarterly* 38, no. 2 (Spring 2015): 155–180.

Reichert, Ramón, and Annika Richterich. "Introduction: Digital Materialism." *Digital
Culture and Society* 1, no. 1 (2015): 5–17.

Renov, Michael. *The Subject of Documentary*. Minneapolis: University of Minnesota Press, 2004.

———, ed. *Theorizing Documentary*. London: Routledge, 1993.

Richardson, Ingrid. "Pocket Technospaces: The Bodily Incorporation of Mobile Media." *Continuum: Journal of Media and Cultural Studies* 21, no. 2 (2007): 205–215.

Rigney, Ann. "Transforming Memory and the European Project." *New Literary History* 43, no. 4 (2012): 607–628.

Routh, Patricia. "The Politics of Transformation: Selfie Production of the Visually Marginalised." In *The Digital Transformation of the Public Sphere: Conflict, Migration, Crisis and Culture in Digital Networks*, edited by Athina Karatzogianni, Dennis Nguyen, and Elisa Serafinelli, 363–381. London: Palgrave Macmillan, 2016.

Royster, Francesca T. "Introductory Notes: Performing Queer Lives." *Biography: An Interdisciplinary Quarterly* 34, no. 3 (2011): v–xii.

Sayre, Robert F. *The Examined Self: Benjamin Franklin, Henry Adams, Henry James*. Princeton, NJ: Princeton University Press, 1964.

Schalchlin, Steve. *Living in the Bonus Round*. http://bonusroundblog.blogspot.com.

Schwartz, Joan M., and Terry Cook. "Archives, Records, and Power: The Making of Modern Memory." *Archival Science* 2 (2002): 1–19.

Sedgwick, Eve Kosofsky. "Paranoid Reading and Reparative Reading; or, You're So Paranoid, You Probably Think This Introduction Is About You." In *Novel Gazing: Queer Readings in Fiction*, edited by Eve Kosofsky Sedgwick, 1–37. Durham, NC: Duke University Press, 1997.

———. *Tendencies*. Durham, NC: Duke University Press, 1993.

———. *Touching Feeling: Affect, Pedagogy, Performativity*. Durham, NC: Duke University Press, 2003.

———. *The Weather in Proust*. Edited by Jonathan Goldberg. Durham, NC: Duke University Press, 2011.

Senft, Therese M., and Nancy K. Baym. "What Does the Selfie Say? Investigating a Global Phenomenon," *International Journal of Communication* 9 (2015): 1588–1606.

Shane, Scott, and S. Venkataraman. "The Promise of Entrepreneurship as a Field of Research." *Academy of Management Review* 25, no. 1 (2000): 217–226.

Shanklin, Will. "2013 Smartphone Comparison Guide." *New Atlas*, November 21, 2013. https://newatlas.com/2013-smartphone-comparison-guide/29878/.

Sinor, Jennifer. "'Another Form of Crying': Girl Zines as Life Writing." *Prose Studies* 26, no. 1–2 (2003): 240–264.

Six-Word Memoirs. "FAQ." www.sixwordmemoirs.com/faq/; "Story of Six." www.sixwordmemoirs.com/about/#story-of-six-words; "Terms of Service." www.sixwordmemoirs.com/terms-of-service.

Smaill, Belinda. *The Documentary: Politics, Emotion, Culture*. Basingstoke: Palgrave Macmillan, 2010.

Smith, Sidonie. "Performativity, Autobiographical Practice, Resistance." *a/b: Auto/ Biography Studies* 10, no. 1 (1995): 17–33.

Smith, Sidonie, and Julia Watson, eds. *Getting a Life: Everyday Uses of Autobiography.* Minneapolis: University of Minnesota Press, 1996.

——. *Reading Autobiography: A Guide for Interpreting Life Narratives.* 2nd ed. Minneapolis: University of Minnesota Press, 2010.

Sontag, Susan. *Regarding the Pain of Others.* London: Penguin, 2004.

Sorace, Christian. "Ai Weiwei: China's Last Communist." *Critical Inquiry* 40, no. 2 (2014): 396–419.

Stanley, Liz. "From 'Self-Made Women' to 'Women's Made-Selves'?: Audit Selves, Simulation and Surveillance in the Rise of Public Woman." In *Feminism and Autobiography: Texts, Theories, Methods,* edited by Tess Cosslett, Celia Lury, and Penny Summerfield, 40–60. New York: Routledge, 2000.

Steedman, Carolyn. *Dust.* Manchester: Manchester University Press, 2001.

Stewart, Kathleen. *Ordinary Affects.* Durham, NC: Duke University Press, 2007.

Stewart, Susan. *On Longing: Narratives of the Miniature, the Gigantic, the Souvenir, the Collection.* Durham, NC: Duke University Press, 1993.

Stoler, Ann Laura. *Along the Archival Grain: Epistemic Anxieties and Colonial Common Sense.* Princeton, NJ: Princeton University Press, 2009.

StoryCorps. "About." https://storycorps.org/about/; "Great Questions." https://storycorps.org/participate/great-questions/; "StoryCorps Archive Terms of Use." https://archive.storycorps.org/terms-of-use/; "StoryCorps DIY." https://storycorps.org/participate/storycorps-diy/.

Strawson, Galen. "The Unstoried Life." In *On Life-Writing,* edited by Zachary Leader, 284–301. Oxford: Oxford University Press, 2015.

Thrift, Nigel. "But Malice Aforethought: Cities and the Natural History of Hatred." *Transactions of the Institute of British Geographers* 30, no. 2 (2005): 133–150.

Tilley, Christopher. "Materializing Identities: An Introduction." *Journal of Material Culture* 16, no. 2 (2011): 347–357.

Tsing, Anna Lowenhaupt. *The Mushroom at the End of the World: On the Possibility of Life in Capitalist Ruins.* Princeton, NJ: Princeton University Press, 2017.

Tumarkin, Maria. "This Narrated Life." *Griffith Review* 44 (April 2014). https://griffithreview.com/articles/this-narrated-life/?fbclid=IwAR0Zo7hkkesQjJFwGJ9_8XhGyvcElJ8qCwUYvZZWLt9FGBOelE3Q2L9hiW8.

Turkle, Sherry. *Alone Together: Why We Expect More from Technology and Less from Each Other.* New York: Basic Books, 2011.

Turner, Graeme. *Understanding Celebrity.* 2nd ed. London: Sage, 2014.

Twede, Diane. "The Birth of Modern Packaging: Cartons, Cans and Bottles." *Journal of Historical Research in Marketing* 4, no. 2 (2012): 245–272.

Ulmer, Gregory L. "The Object of Post-criticism." In *The Anti-aesthetic: Essays on Postmodern Culture,* edited by Hal Foster, 93–125. New York: New Press, [1983] 2002.

Vaccaro, Jeanne. "Handmade." *TSQ: Transgender Studies Quarterly* 1, no. 1–2 (2014): 96–97.

Valentish, Jenny. "Frank Warren: *PostSecret* Project Tour." *TimeOut Melbourne,* April 18, 2013. http://www.au.timeout.com/melbourne/aroundtown/events/5556/post-secret#picture0.

van den Hengel, Louis. "Zoegraphy: Per/forming Posthuman Lives." *Biography: An Interdisciplinary Quarterly* 35, no. 1 (Winter 2015): 1–20.

van Dijck, José. *Mediated Memories in the Digital Age.* Palo Alto, CA: Stanford University Press, 2007.

Wacker, Grant. *Heaven Below: Early Pentecostals and American Culture.* Cambridge, MA: Harvard University Press, 2001.

Waites, Sarah J. "Sarah Polley's Documemoir *Stories We Tell*: The Refracted Subject." *Biography: An Interdisciplinary Quarterly* 38, no. 4 (Fall 2015): 543–555.

Warhol, Andy. *The Diaries of Andy Warhol.* Edited by Pat Hackett. New York: Grand Central Publishing, 1989.

———. *The Philosophy of Andy Warhol: From A to B and Back Again.* New York: Harvest, 1975.

Warhol, Andy, and Pat Hackett. *POPism: The Warhol '60s.* London: Hutchinson, 1981.

Warner, Michael. "Publics and Counterpublics." *Public Culture* 14, no. 1 (2002): 49–90.

Warren, Frank. "Half a Million Secrets." Filmed at TED2012 conference. Video, 11:17. www.ted.com/talks/frank_warren_half_a_million_secrets.

———. *PostSecret: Extraordinary Confessions from Ordinary Lives.* New York: Regan Books, 2005.

Wheeler, Stanton, ed. *On Record: Files and Dossiers in American Life.* New York: Russell Sage Foundation, 1969.

Whitlock, Gillian. *Postcolonial Life Narratives: Testimonial Transactions.* Oxford: Oxford University Press, 2015.

———. "Post-ing Lives." *Biography: An Interdisciplinary Quarterly* 35, no. 1 (Winter 2012): v–xvi.

———. *Soft Weapons: Autobiography in Transit.* Chicago: University of Chicago Press, 2006.

———. "Testimony of Things." In *Challenging (the) Humanities,* edited by Tony Bennett, 17–32. Melbourne: Australian Scholarly Publishing, 2013.

Whitlock, Gillian, and G. Thomas Couser, eds. "Post(Human) Lives." Special issue, *Biography: An Interdisciplinary Quarterly* 35, no. 1 (Winter 2012).

Williams, Raymond. *Keywords: A Vocabulary of Culture and Society.* Revised and expanded edition. London: Fontana Press, 1988.

Wolf, Reva. "Introduction through the Looking-Glass." In *I'll Be Your Mirror: The Selected Andy Warhol Interviews,* edited by Kenneth Goldsmith, xi–xxxi. New York: Carrol and Graf, 2004.

Wrbican, Matt. *A Guide to the Exhibition: Andy Warhol's Time Capsules.* Melbourne: National Gallery of Victoria, Melbourne Australia, 2005.

Wurth, Kiene Brillenburg. "The Material Turn in Comparative Literature: An Introduction." *Comparative Literature* 70, vol. 3 (September 2018): 247–263.

Yagoda, Ben. "A Brief History of Memoir Bashing." *Slate,* March 30, 2007. www.slate.com/articles/news_and_politics/memoir_week/2007/03/a_brief_history_of_memoirbashing.html.

———. *Memoir: A History.* New York: Riverhead Books, 2009.

Yeo, Geoffrey. "Concepts of the Record (I): Evidence, Information, and Persistent Representations." *American Archivist* 70 (2007): 315–343.

Zuboff, Shoshanna. "Big Other: Surveillance Capitalism and the Prospect of an Information Civilization." *Journal of Information Technology* 30 (2015): 75–89.

Zuern, John David, ed. "Online Lives." Special issue, *Biography: An Interdisciplinary Quarterly* 26, no. 1 (Winter 2003).

INDEX

ABOUT THE AUTHOR

Anna Poletti is Associate Professor of English Language and Culture at Utrecht University, and coeditor of *Biography: An Interdisciplinary Quarterly*. They are a writer and scholar of contemporary life writing, youth culture, and media.

Lightning Source UK Ltd.
Milton Keynes UK
UKHW012301090820
367846UK00016B/246